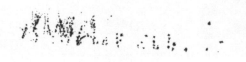

THE POLITICS OF ETHNICITY
IN EASTERN EUROPE

GEORGE KLEIN and MILAN J. REBAN, Editors

EAST EUROPEAN MONOGRAPHS, BOULDER
DISTRIBUTED BY COLUMBIA UNIVERSITY PRESS
NEW YORK

1981

EAST EUROPEAN MONOGRAPHS, NO. XCIII
ASN SERIES IN ISSUE STUDIES (USSR AND EAST EUROPE) NO. 2

ACKNOWLEDGEMENTS

The editors of this volume wish to express their appreciation to Professor Stephen M. Horak and the Association for the Study of the Nationalities (USSR and East Europe) Inc., for support in the preparation of this study. Also, we wish to thank Professor Jim Heizer for his editorial assistance.

CONTRIBUTORS

Peter John Georgeoff is Professor of Education at Purdue University, Lafayette

Trond Gilberg is Professor of Political Science at Pennsylvania State University, College Park

George Klein is Professor of Political Science at Western Michigan State University, Kalamazoo

Patricia V. Klein is an Assistant Professor of Social Science, School of General Studies, Western Michigan State University, Kalamazoo

John S. Kolsti is an Associate Professor of Slavic Languages and Literatures at the University of Texas, Austin

Z. Anthony Kruszewski is Professor of Political Science at the University of Texas, El Paso

Alfred G. Meyer is Professor of Political Science at the University of Michigan

Milan J. Reban is an Associate Professor of Political Science at North Texas State University, Denton

Ivan Volgyes is Professor of Political Science at the University of Nebraska, Lincoln

Zelime Amen Ward received her Ph.D. from and later taught in the Department of Government at the University of Texas, Austin

CONTENTS

Contributors

1. Introduction   1
   George Klein and Milan J. Reban

2. Eastern Europe: Marxism and Nationalism   7
   Alfred G. Meyer

UNITARY SYSTEMS

3. Albanianism: From the Humanists to Hoxha   15
   John Kolsti

4. Ethnic Minorities in the People's Republic of Bulgaria   49
   John Georgeoff

5. Minority Politics in the German Democratic Republic:
   Problematics of Socialist Legitimacy and National
   Autonomy   85
   Zelime Amen Ward

6. Legitimacy and Modernization: Nationality and
   Nationalism in Hungary and Transylvania   127
   Ivan Volgyes

7. Nationalism and Politics: Poland   147
   Z. Anthony Kruszewski

8. Modernization, Human Rights and Nationalism:
   The Case of Romania   185
   Trond Gilberg

FEDERAL SYSTEMS

9. Czechoslovakia: The New Federation   215
   Milan J. Reban

10. Nationalism vs. Ideology: The Pivot of Yugoslav Politics   247
    George and Patricia V. Klein

George Klein and Milan J. Reban

I

INTRODUCTION

An examination of Eastern European political systems discloses a continuing relationship between ethnicity, modernization and political development. The process commenced in the nineteenth century with the European romantic movement and was closely identified with the growth of modern nationalism which diffused across the boundaries of the Habsburg Monarchy and the Ottoman Empire, to fuel a nationalistic revival among the ethnic populations subject to German and Ottoman rule. The break-up of the Ottoman Empire in Europe and the dissolution of the Habsburg Monarchy was the culmination of this movement and resulted from the First World War. The successor states which emerged from the disintegration of the two previous structures were organized along ethnic lines by the nationalities which had rendered resistance to being absorbed into the dominant political culture of either the Habsburg Monarchy or the Ottoman Empire. In fact, some of the earliest formulations of the principle "self-determination of nations" were made with reference to Eastern Europe at the First International when self-determination was proclaimed as the new ideal.

The bewildering ethnic diversity of the region was one of the principal obstacles to self-determination. It is said that President Woodrow Wilson came to realize that the principle of self-determination was impossible to implement only when he arrived in Versailles at the Peace Conference. No map could be drawn which could separate all the nationalistic groupings by ethnicity. Multi-national states, based on ethnic self-determination, took the place of the multi-national empires. Only the defeated countries

1

could claim relative ethnic homogeneity because they were shorn of disputed borderlands, i.e., Hungary and Bulgaria. Two of the successor states, Czechoslovakia and Yugoslavia, were clearly multi-national. The others, too, were far from ethnically homogeneous. Poland had large Ukrainian, German and Jewish minorities. The Balkan states had large Turkish minorities; Bulgaria's interwar politics were dominated by the Macedonian question, which was also shared by Yugoslavia and Greece. Both Czechoslovakia and Yugoslavia experienced profound distress between the two largest nationalities in the state: the Czechs and the Slovaks and the Serbs and Croats, respectively. The very demise of the successor state of the system accentuated the fragility of the ethnic consensus on which the states of the regions rested. In World War II Czechoslovakia disintegrated under the pressure of the German occupiers in collaboration with the Hungarian and Polish states which all laid claim to Czechoslovak territory. Yugoslavia's demise at the hands of five invading armies was not dissimilar as the Axis assault led to fratricidal conflict among hostile ethnic groups.

Ethnicity figured prominently in the rise of communism in the region. During the interwar period, the appeals of communism varied from group to group as shown in Richard Burks' pioneering examination of the pattern; the ethnic factor explains much with respect to who became attracted to communism and who did not:

> We may erect almost as a principle the proposition that in eastern Europe numerically weak ethnic groups produce above-average numbers of Communists, providing these groups have a traditional or an ethnic tie to Russia. Other factors being equal, the weaker the ethnic group, the greater the proclivity. On the other hand, if there has been a strong traditional enmity toward Russia, a weak ethnic group reveals a lower than average susceptibility to the Communist appeal, and the traditional enmity can offset an ethnic bond.[1]

It was not only minorities which looked to the communist ideology for solutions. In profusely mixed national areas communism seemed to offer the only viable alternative to the pre-War virulent nationalism which had failed to integrate the area into a viable configuration. Nationalist excesses which took place under Axis occupation had the side effect of disenchanting sizeable segments of the population with the nationalist creed. The most egregious example was the German extermination of the almost entire Jewish population of the area, but there had been many manifestations of intolerance which were no less shocking such as the Croat efforts to creat a Croat Catholic State in the ethnically mixed territories of the so-called National State of Croatia (NDH) during World War II or the establishment of a similar state in Slovakia. Communist ideology offered to bridge the gap between the warring ethnic groups by promising true ethnic self-determination, whatever its specific content, and through the relegation of nationalism to a position of secondary importance. Eastern European communists stood under the influence of the Soviet claim of the 1930s that the USSR had successfully solved its ethnic problems and that East Europe could do likewise by emulating Soviet practice.

Since that era of high ideological fervor in communist circles, the history of Eastern Europe under communism has made very clear that nationalism continues to be an important factor in the East European political scene. The communist governments have viewed it with ambivalence by using and exploiting it when it suited their convenience, while condemning it in theory. The Soviets called on the Czechs and Poles to unite behind the Soviet Union for protection against German revanchism. The communist states have also viewed nationalism as a rival ideology which was capable of harnessing mass support to challenge the officially proclaimed verities of the ruling communist parties. The most prominent examples concerned the role of the Catholic Church in Poland which had claimed the role of the traditional protector of Polish national identity. In a country where such a large part of the population gives its allegiance to the church, the coexistence of the forces of communism and nationalism could lead only to an uneasy coexistence marked by occasional conflict and cooperation in the face of a foreign threat. In Yugoslavia particularistic nationalism, when it escalated beyond acceptable bounds, was at least temporarily suppressed, i.e., in Croatia in 1971. On the other hand, the Yugoslav state also claimed to give the several nationalities the maximum opportunity for free and untrammeled development. Czech and Slovak nationalism played a large part in the events of 1968, as earlier, Polish and Hungarian nationalism rose to the fore in the events of 1956 when both states faced the power of the Soviet Union in their respective efforts to maintain nationally independent socialist systems. The essentially schizophrenic attitude of the communist movements toward nationalism is demonstrated by equally ambiguous nationality policies and claims. Proletarian internationalism is associated with federalism and the relationship between the several socialist states. On the other hand, ethnic conflicts which are viewed as disruptive by the communist leadership have been labeled as bourgeois nationalism. When Tito was expelled from the Cominform in June of 1948, all of his alleged followers in the several peoples' democracies were labeled "bourgeois nationalists." In communist states conflicts of nationalities frequently assume the form of economic rivalries, because it is more legitimate to express collective economic interests. Interest representation on purely nationalistic criteria would be quickly denounced by the governments, and the principal perpetrators might face charges for incitement of hatred against constituent nationalities. The criminal codes of all communist states contain some such provisions in their constitutions or penal codes. Sometimes the conflict of economic interest spills over into overt ethnic conflict as was the case in Yugoslavia in 1971. In the instances when this has happened, internal or external interventions were swift and decisive.

Nationalism in its most vital form flows out of nineteenth century romanticism, and in many communist states it has been associated with religion. In Poland, Slovakia, and Croatia, the Catholic Church has been historically identified with the maintenance of ethnic group identity. It is no different under the circumstances of communist dominance. In all the areas mentioned, the Catholic Church competes actively for the allegiance of the ethnic constituencies. Inevitably, the coexistence of church and state in the same territory involves both cooperation and conflict and constant compromise. The communist state in which this is most manifest is Poland and to a lesser extent, Hungary. The communist governments attempt to contain the influences of the churches within what they consider acceptable limits. This fuels the tension between enforced legal norms, the politically acceptable, and the human rights provisions which are written into most codes in the constitutions of the several communist states.[2] The chapters of this book explore these dilemmas in expanded detail.

Ethnic conflicts are not uniquely communist phenomena. The Third World countries are in the process of nationalist revolutions which are displacing traditional systems similar to those which have swept Europe in the 18th and 19th centuries. These are political movements of such power that even communist states have come to accept them as given. Since the middle 1950s, Soviet foreign policy line is that leading national bourgeoisies are essentially positive forces, which will constitute a stepping stone to a socialist transformation for Third World countries. Needless to say, such forces would never be viewed as benign within the communist states. Particularistic nationalism has been on the rise in Western Europe as well. The violence of the Irish question and a Basque separatism in Spain has continued unabated for more than a decade.

Then there are the lower decibel constants of such issues as North Tyrol in Italy, the Walloon-Flemish question in Belgium, the Breton question in France or Scottish nationalism in the United Kingdom, not to mention Quebec's status within Canada. Allowing that most of the states of the world are multi-ethnic or multi-tribal, with the rising ethnic nationalistic consciousness, this factor will continue to play a major role on the world political scene.[3] To be sure, the processes of assimilation and integration cannot be neglected, though the centrifugal impetus on the whole appears stronger than the integrationist one.

The compact region of Eastern Europe has more than 130 million inhabitants separated into eight states and more than a dozen nationalities with more than a million people. The rapid transformation under communism which is now entering its fourth decade under communism, provides an unusually rich political landscape for the student of ethnic dynamics. By examining the evolving patterns the contributors to this volume hope to add not only to the better understanding of the region, but to the much belated scholarly concern with this global phenomenon.

NOTES

1. R. V. Burks, *The Dynamics of Communism in Eastern Europe*, Princeton, N.J.: Princeton University Press, 1961, p. 188.

2. For the Human Rights Approaches in Eastern Europe, see Rudolf L. Tőkés, "Human Rights and Political Change in Eastern Europe," in

his edited volume, *Opposition in Eastern Europe,* Baltimore, The Johns Hopkins University Press, 1979, Chapter 1.

3. Walker Connor, "Nation-Building or Nation Destroying?" *World Politics,* XXIV (April 1972), particularly pp. 328-30. Regarding the terms used, Connor observes that although there are different nuances in the usage of the concept of nations and ethnic groups, self-differentating ethnic groups are in reality nations, and "loyalty to the ethnic groups, therefore, should logically be called nationalism." p. 344.

Alfred G. Meyer

II

EASTERN EUROPE: MARXISM AND NATIONALISM

Socialism, as visualized, however dimly, by Engels and Marx, was going to be the reign of rationality. Capitalism was irrationality rampant. The economics and politics of individual enterprise were anarchic; the capitalist system was beset with deepest contradictions. Both founding fathers of the Marxist movement argued that capitalism was the accumulation of wealth and poverty, of power and powerlessness, of control and loss of control; and these opposites presupposed, reinforced, and reproduced each other. The more wealth, the greater the poverty; the more highly developed the productive forces, the more incapable of using them the system would be.

The root contradiction, to which all the above contradictions could be reduced, was the co-existence of collective production with individual accumulation and individual control over the means of production. The production relations had become dysfunctional to the productive forces. Private property had turned from a progressive principle of social organization to a reactionary one which made further progress impossible.

The remedy, half proposed, half predicted by Marx and Engels, would be the proletarian revolution in which the direct producers collectively would seize control of the means of production. Once private property was abolished, the productive wealth accumulated by capitalism could be administered rationally. Need rather than profitability would be the motive for all economic activity. General human concerns rather than the selfish concerns of an exploiter class would dominate all social action.

Thus summarized, Marxism appears as an offshoot of the 18th century religion of progress, enriched by radical democratic theory, the concept of the General Will, ideals of socialist communes, and Saint-Simonian notions of technocracy. Necessarily, this new, dialectical, theory of progress envisaged its ideal, rational social order—a social order transcending the contradictions of productive forces and production relations —as encompassing the entire civilized world, i.e., Western and Central Europe together with North America. At least in the beginning, this would be the space within which a transnational socialist society would be born out of the ruins of capitalist nations; so Marx and Engels seem to have believed; and then, gradually, this superior civilization would draw in, absorb, and transform the entire world.

Marx, Engels, and their followers prided themselves in the fact that they had posited their alternative society not merely as an ideal, but that they had identified the historic forces in whose class interest it would be to fight for the destruction of the old and the inauguration of the projected new society. In line with this, Marxism subsumed all social conflict into the one great conflict which really mattered—that between the vast masses of wage laborers (the proletariat) and the diminishing ruling class of capitalist property owners (the bourgeoisie).

What was the place of the nation in this vision of the future and the struggles toward it?

One cannot be totally sure about this; but the evidence suggests that in the utopia envisaged, nations would play little or no role whatever. To be sure, both Engels and Marx were typical German radical intellectuals in that they were proud to be Germans, and simultaneously were ashamed of their nation. They hoped that Germans and Germany would play a leading role in the struggle for socialism; and perhaps they also foresaw such a leading position for Germany in the socialist society once it had been achieved. At the same time, they made sure to point out many times that socialism was and should be an international movement drawing its strength from contributions made by French and English, Magyar, Polish, Irish, and many other movements. They were internationalists who believed that the coming proletarian revolution and socialist society would be the result of a trans-national proletariat.

Reconstructing their thoughts about the future society, one can take it for granted that they believed in the preservation of the great cultural heritage of all nations, Western and non-Western. The culture of socialism would preserve and cherish the art and wisdom of the ages, in many languages; it might indeed become the repository of all of Western civilization enriched by other civilizations.

In the meantime, while the struggle was still raging, they would remind the workers that existing states were executive committees of the exploiter class, and they would suggest that supporting any of these states was a betrayal of the workers' international solidarity. The workers, Marx wrote in the *Communist Manifesto,* have no fatherland.

Nonetheless, the national units existing at the time Engels and Marx were writing and active were parts of political reality to be reckoned with, and to be incorporated in the revolutionary scenario of comtemporary history as instruments of progress or of reaction. As practical political actors, the founding fathers of Marxism could not avoid taking a stand on national issues. Moreover, the ideology of nationalism, brought to life by the American and French revolutions and the Napoleonic wars, reigned in Europe and would soon spread over the entire globe. Its strength, and especially its appeal among radical political movements, should have suggested to Marx and Engels that subsuming all conflict under the class struggle was unrealistic and politically unrewarding. Indeed, in the stand they took on a variety of issues, these two men did take the strength of national ideology into account.

To be sure, they did so in contradictory or inconsistent fashion. They showed sympathy with Germans and Italians who sought to overthrow they dynastic principle of sovereignty in favor of the national principle. They also sympahized with the Poles, the Magyars, the Irish, and possibly another two or three nationalities in their struggles to liberate themselves from rule by multi-national states or empires. They voiced these sympathies not because they believed in national self-determination, but because they thought they could distinguish between progressive and reactionary nations, between viable and moribund states: The Poles were progressive compared to the barbaric Russians who ruled them; an independent Hungary would be a viable, progressive nation. A united Germany and a united Italy would become major European powers capable of sustaining and promoting modernization far more successfully than many dynastic sovereignties into which they were divided before 1870.

But why would they support the Irish against the most advanced and liberal industrial nation of the world? Why would they refuse to sympathize with the much more "advanced" Czechs in their struggle for autonomy within a relatively backward and reactionary Austrian empire? Why would they advocate a policy of propping up the tottering Ottoman Empire? And meanwhile they believed that in subduing India and in carving up Mexico, Britain and the United States were promoting the cause of progress!

The fact is that, while these and other attitudes were part of what sometimes is called the foreign policy of the First International and thus can be justified by pragmatic considerations of the moment, Marx and Engels had not considered it worth their while to pay *systematic* attention to nationalism and the problem of nationalities. The tribal, linguistic, cultural, and national divisions of human society were, from the point of view of their grand theory, an unwelcome complication, an intrusion of irrationality into their allegedly scientific model of contemporary society. Issues touching national and cultural differences therefore did not appear in their more theoretical writings. Moreover, once Marxism became the official ideology of several large working class parties, especially the German one, Marxist theory lost much of the subtlety and sophistication its founders had given it; and among the political leaders and theoreticians of the movement, the tendency to dismiss national or ethnic concerns as irrelevant to the working class became even more pronounced.

By the turn of the century, most competent observers of political and intellectual currents in Europe would have taken for granted that nationalism and revolutionary socialism were at opposite ends of the ideological spectrum, that pursuing the proletarian revolution as the goal precluded taking an active interest in national concerns, however radical or revolutionary the struggle for national liberation might appear. To be sure, there were individuals within the Marxist movement who urged that, if only for tactical reasons, the parties take national antagonisms and ambitions into consideration, in order not to alienate masses of proletariat followers. By and large, however, orthodox Marxists tended to disdain any mass following which did not join for the right reason —which national aspirations were not.

Since the Russian revolution, the relationship between Marxism and nationalism has changed drastically, in practice more than in theory. But

it nonetheless comes as a shock to read, in paragraph 3 of the introductory
essay of this book, that ethnicity figured prominently in the rise of East-
European communism. It seems to me that this sentence is the key to
this book; and the implications of the statement it makes are well worth
pondering. Ethnicity, we learn from this book, not only was a major
factor in the development of various East-European communist parties,
it also has affected and still is affecting politics in the several states of
Eastern Europe, so much so that the very nature of these regimes is
misunderstood by anyone not sufficiently aware of the ethnic issues
that are just beneath the surface. What will surprise the reader is not
only the power of ethnic concerns, but also the wide variety of ways
in which national culture, ethnic antagonisms, religious traditions, and
the like, have affected politics in Eastern Europe.

Naturam expurgas furca, tamen ipse recurret: You may rid yourself
of Nature with a pitchfork, but she will nonetheless come running back.
Since World War II, ethnicity—the tribal, racial, religious, cultural, traditional, irrational, and disruptive—has gained in strength and influence
all over the globe. Ethnicity inspires and mobilizes the nations of the
world to rebel against the universal, all-pervasive dominance of global
capitalism. National and ethnic consciousness have come to be closely
linked to movements of liberation and revolution, including those calling
themselves Marxist. New national states have been created in previously
dependent areas, who must give highest priority to the task of accumu-
lating modern means of production. Should we go so far as to assert
that, a hundred years after the death of Marx, the national state has
taken over the role and function which the property-owning entrepreneur
played within the Marxist model of capitalism?

The implication of such a statement would be that the revolutions
of our century, often carried out with the expressed aim of doing away
with the contradictions of capitalism, have, instead, reproduced them,
though in novel form; and ethnicity is revealed as a principle of social
organization (or production relations) fundamentally at odds with global
production processes. State property has replaced private property in
the means of production. The contradictions remain.

For me, this is the context within which the observations made by
the contributors to this book acquire great fascination and, despite the
great variety of treatment, acquire unity.

UNITARY SYSTEMS

John Kolsti

III

ALBANIANISM: FROM THE HUMANISTS TO HOXHA

Introductory Remarks

Albania continues to be a mystery. The origins of the Albanian language are about as obscure as the Albanian word for an Albanian. But it is the language which, through the centuries, has prevented the disappearance of the Albanians from the Balkans. It is the language which proved to be the common bond toward the end of the nineteenth century which broke down religious barriers that had divided the "nation" into four hostile religious communities. And it is the language that may be used as a weapon against the small ethnic groups which live inside Albania. The proclamation of a New Religion, "Albanianism," by the regime in 1967 may perhaps best be regarded, political ideology and technical assistance aside, as one more affirmation by Albanian-speaking people in the Balkans that they intend to preserve their national identity at any cost. Their continued isolation from both East and West, it seems, is their strategy for survival. Their path toward socialism, while it leads them closer to the splinter parties in the international communist movement, follows a fairly straight line from the Renaissance through the purges in the 1970s. A look to Albania's past is obligatory for anyone concerned about the future of Europe's newest industrial-agricultural state. But the mystery remains.

Albanian is an Indo-European language, as are Serbo-Croatian, Macedonian, Greek, and Romanian (a dialect of which is spoken by about 10,000 Vlachs in Albania). But the language of the Albanians does not belong to the subgroups of Indo-European languages spoken by Illyrian tribes who survived the mass migration of the Slavs into the Balkans in the 6th and 7th centuries. During the political upheavals in Byzantium caused by the Crusades in the 11th-13th centuries a few of these tribes, including the Arbanoi, who lived between the Mat and Black Drin rivers (in the present-day districts of Mati and Dibra northeast of Tirana), gained a degree of independence, as did the Serbs under Nemanja. In the 1200s the term "Illyria" was no longer used by foreigners to refer to non-Greek and non-Slav territory; instead the Crusaders and the Greeks called the land "Albania." The Albanian tribes referred to their land as "Arbania," or "Arberia," the terms marking the two major dialects in Albania: namely, Geg (or northern) and Tosk (or southern).

It is interesting to note that the terms "Geg" and "Tosk" may for some Albanians have a much more restricted cultural or geographic meaning. For some northern Albanians along the Montenegrin border, Gegni refers to lands traditionally occupied by tribes, or clans, farther south, in the central highland area just north of the Shkumbini River. Similarly, some southern Albanians along the Greek border consider Toskeri to lie north of the Vjosa River and extending as far as the Shkumbini, which divides the country in half.[1] The Shkumbini coincides to some extent with one of the most important isoglosses marking the two dialects: namely, rhotacism, or the consonant change $n > r$ in Tosk. Before the invasion of the Turks, then, Albanians spoke *arbanisht* or *arberisht*. Families fleeing from the Turks to Zadar in northern Dalmatia and to southern Italy and Sicily were identified as Arbanasi and Arbereshe, not Gegs or Tosks.

Several centuries of rule under the Ottoman Turks encouraged divergent political, economic and social pressures on Albanians living north and south of the Shkumbini River. Although Gegs and Tosks (that is, Northerners and Southerners) could easily communicate with each other —their language united rather than separated them—foreign influences in the north (Venetian, Montenegrin, Sunni Moslim, Vatican) and in the south (Greek, Bulgarian, Bektashi and Sunni Muslim) divided them. Since the terms Geg and Tosk denote the external and artificial barriers that for centuries retarded the political development of the Albanians, they have been discarded by the present leadership of Albania.

Albania today occupies approximately 11,100 square miles. The population, which according to the 1975 census reached 2,430,000 is about 97 percent ethnically Albanian,* over half of whom speak Geg dialects. In the early 1950s, however, Tosk was proclaimed the official, standard literary language, replacing the transitional dialect of Elbasan which had been proposed as a compromise of sorts before World War II. Enver Hoxha, in effect, extended his native dialect, which for over a century had served as a literary tool for the Albanian Orthodox and Bektashi publicists and poets who led the Tosk-dominated national awakening, into Gegni (Gegëri, in Tosk); that is, into the land of the Northern Albanians. The new literary standard did not, of course, extend across the Albanian border into Yugoslavia where approximately half of the Gegs are to be found.

In Albania itself, approximately 20 percent of the population was Orthodox on the eve of World War II. The Orthodox population was in Toskëri (Toskni, in Geg), and included the small Greek, Vlach, Slav, and Gypsy groups. About 70 percent of the population was Muslim, the overwhelming majority of which belonged to the more fanatical Sunni sect; the Bektashis made up about 25percent of the Muslim community and were concentrated in South Albania. The smallest religious group, but perhaps the most "nationalistic," was the Roman Catholic in North Albania, living in the remote mountain valleys east of the city of Shkodra.

The Peace of Death

In a Christmas address from the Vatican in 1972 the Pope reminded the world that the church in Albania had been relegated not only to "the peace of silent suffering," but to "the peace of death."[2] Earlier in the year *Kathpress* had reported the execution of a priest in Albania for

---

* Approximately 53 percent of the non-Albanian population is Greek, numbering between 35-40,000. The next largest group is Slav, approximately 15,000, comprised of Serbian and Macedonian elements. Scattered Vlach and Gypsy groups make up the rest of the non-Albanian population.

performing a religious rite in public.[3] In 1973 the Albanian press reported the execution of the priest, branding him an agent of the Vatican. Rev. Kurti and his group of believers, five years after Albania was officially proclaimed an atheist state—a step unique in the communist world—finally felt the effects of Albania's mini-cultural revolution of the late 1960s. It is important to note first that the ban on organized religion was not immediately felt in the more remote mountain districts of northern Albania where, especially among the Roman Catholic Gegs, the idea of religion was traditionally associated with the idea of nationality. To identify as a Catholic meant to identify as an Albanian in a world dominated by Muslims and Slavs. By 1972, however, it became clear that the regime felt confident enough to attack the Roman Catholic clergy without seriously damaging the loyalty of the clans which had preserved their faith through the Ottoman period. The New Religion had in effect successfully eliminated a source of potential danger to its authority. Or, as was the case centuries earlier, it forced the church underground.[4]

The Albanian Orthodox churches in the southern districts suffered a similar fate. In 1967 the Archbishop of Albania and the head of the Albanian Orthodox Church was   jailed; and by 1974, when his death was reported in *The Times* (London), the Albanian Orthodox Church had ceased to play any public role in the state it had helped to create. On the eve of the liberation of the country from the Turks the church, at least in the United States, had declared its independence from the Greek Church and had begun celebrating the mass in Albanian. In the Albanian provinces of the Ottoman Empire the language of the church continued to be Greek. The language of the Greek Orthodox Church had very nearly succeeded in determining the nationality of the Tosks along purely religious lines. It seems strange, to say the least, that the "peace of death" which reached the Tosks in the 1960s has not yet eradicated the small Greek Orthodox communities in southern Albania. The observance of Greek religious holidays is still tolerated by the regime. Possible reasons for this will be offered below.

The government has dealt less harshly with the two Muslim communities in Albania. As one Yugoslav Albanian has recently noted, the Muslims "celebrate their holidays in the customary ways, even in the towns."[5] In other words, the religious groups which most seriously *retarded* the political development of the Albanian-speaking people seem least affected by the new religion, Albanianism. But it is precisely these communities, both the Bektashi and Sunni, which most closely identified with trans-regional authority both under the Ottomans and under Ahmet Beg Zogolli, a Muslim chieftain and self-proclaimed king in the 1930s. It stands to reason, then, that the Christian groups in Albania with strong cultural ties to Italy and Greece should continue to be viewed as potential threats to the regime as long as their religious organizations were allowed to function. Turkey, in spite of the Muslim majority in Albania, had ceased to be a threat to the state which survived the Balkan Wars and World War I. But as long as Christian Albanians regarded their Muslim neighbors as "Turks," making no fine distinctions between the two sects owing to centuries of hatred and hostility, the New Religion would have no chance to succeed. The old religions, which had helped prolong Albania's backwardness, were of no use whatsoever to the post-war modernizers. But the old ways remain: the traditional loyalties of the clans, which to some extent determined their religious practices, were not eliminated by decree in 1967.

Albanianism and the Law of Lek

It is written in the Canon. The father carries a bullet with him
If the girl goes to the groom's house reluctantly then he gives
the groom's people the bullet.[6]

The impact on women of Hoxha's attack on religion and other "vestiges" from the past is treated by Ismail Kadare in his novel written during the cultural revolution of the 1960s. In the novel there are no in-laws to receive the traditional bullet: the bride had chosen her own groom outside the unwritten laws of Lek Dukagjin which for five hundred years helped preserve, or isolate, Albanian society inside the Ottoman Empire. The bride's father is viewed as a dangerous anachronism at the wedding reception. His presence is a reminder to the new generation of engineers and technicians of their own past which blocked any real progress in the country before its liberation by the partisans. The unwelcomed guest is a reminder of the blood feuds which contributed to the isolation of the Muslim and Christian clans, a fact of Albanian life which Hoxha quickly moved to eradicate in the 1940s. Just how widespread this aspect of the Law of Lek was after 1945 can only be guessed; but Yugoslav statistics show that the vendetta was still a matter of honor to Kosovars, Albanians living in Yugoslavia, long after Tito had come to power. The Yugoslavs, to be sure, had nothing to lose if the blood feuds among the Gegs continued. Kadare's novel, socialist realism aside, does offer a reflexion of the image the New Albanian Man had of himself in the late 1960s. Or, better perhaps, the New Albanian Woman, whose transformation from chattel to state minister was realized in 1976.

The first step in the long process of creating a New Albanian Man may be traced back to the seventeenth century when a new word came into use to identify an Albanian not on the basis of religion or region, but solely on the basis of language. Although Albanian humanists in the sixteenth century had begun to use the term *shqip* as a synonym for *arbërisht* "Albanian language," it wasn't until the following century that the word *shqiptar* came into use in the Balkans to designate speakers of the Albanian language. Arbëresh, or Italian-Albanian, priests expressed alarm over the fate of their language which was being bastardized not only through contact with neighboring Slavs and Greeks but also by strong cultural influences from Italy and Turkey. The efforts of the Catholic clergy to preserve the faith through works written in Albanian sharply divided the Catholic Gegs from their Sunni clansmen. For the Catholic Gegs the survival of the language meant the preservation of the *komb* ("nation"). Nowhere else in Albania were religious lines drawn as sharply as in the northern Highlands. The resistance of the Catholic districts to the authority of the Ottomans, and later to Zog's regime in Tirana, helps explain Hoxha's caution in crushing the clergy in Albania's more backward areas where, not surprisingly, the lowest percentage of highly-trained communist cadres is to be found. But Albania's humanists were forced to pursue their idea of *kombsi* ("nationality") in Italy. It was in Garibaldi's Italy, not in the culturally isolated Balkan parishes, that the Albanian literary renaissance would find its Geg voices.

The southern Albanians more than any other ethnic group in the Balkans came closest to being divided into "Greek" and "Turkish" communities. By the turn of the nineteenth century the power of the Tosk clans had been broken by Ali Pasha, an Albanian; and the spread of Greek schools into Albanian towns further increased tensions between both the Grecomans and the Bektashis, who were far less fanatic than their Sunni counterparts. The southern Albanians, then, were not culturally isolated from the world outside the Ottoman Empire, thanks primarily to the Greek schools and also the Tosk colonies in Egypt and Romania. But, unlike the Gegs, the Tosks had no literary tradition in Albanian: the hoxhas and the priests willy-nilly confused the idea of nationality with religion thereby denying the existence of a separate Albanian "nation." In the 1840s the Korcha district produced Albania's first revolutionary intellectuals. For them the preservation of the spoken language, the establishment of Albanian schools, the introduction of an Albanian Mass and the development of a national literature all had to precede the declaration of independence from the Porte. Their "turn to the West" was the first step taken by Tosks toward Hoxha's Albanianism.

Had no Muslim intellectuals decided to take that first step, there could not have been a national awakening among the Albanians. But of all the religious groups in Albania the Bektashis were perhaps most deeply rooted in their ancestral land.[7] A "point of no return" was reached when leading Bektashi families by the 1870s came to the conclusion that any hope for the survival of the *komb* would have to be placed on a policy of "self-reliance": the spoken language, not the promises of the Porte or the European powers, would be the only guarantee of any kind of freedom for all *shqiptars*. In other words, western educated Muslims had to decide whether to identify with the Christian *rayah* ("cattle") on the basis of language if not clan, or with Ottoman authority on the basis of religion. When their efforts to modernize the Turkish government from within failed, they were free to translate the ideas of the Enlightenment into their Tosk dialect, not Turkish. Their ideas and their lyric poetry were quickly published by Albanian societies outside the empire. The "Turks" had joined the Tosk-dominated national liberation movement. The alphabet of this new literary language in the Balkans was Latin: the choice of alphabet was symbolic of the turn away from the literature of the mosques and the monasteries. The alphabet would also separate them from their Orthodox Greek and Slav neighbors who, as events in the 1870s showed, would gladly partition the Albanian provinces of the Porte given the opportunity.

The Party and the Clans

Albania's religious communities, which continued to be divisive factors after 1912 and in the years between the wars, were little affected by the governments which attempted to establish central authority in the country that was carved out of former Ottoman provinces. If anything, hostility between these communities increased in the 1920s and 1930s. But the question of religious affiliation in this period continued to be "an issue that had to be subervient to other structural pressure."[8] That other pressure was the traditional social structure of the Albanians, a structure which continued to influence major political developments in Albania after World War II, as evidenced by the fact that Albania's pre-war administrative districts, which were drawn to some extent along clan lines, still exist.

The central districts gave Albania its first, and last, king. In these districts the traditional clan structure of the Gegs and the economy of the large feudal estates of the Tosk beys overlapped. While the estates provided a source of wealth for the landowners, clan assemblies afforded them opportunities to extend their political and military authority. It was the subgroups of the clans which provided the military leadership for the clans and for the "brotherhoods," or neighboring households, where patriarchal loyalties were stronger than clan ties. Clan assemblies, or *kuvend,* before which Lek supposedly debated points of law in the fifteenth century, in 1942 attempted to gain support among Mati leaders for the fascist regime then in power.[9] It was from the Mati district that Ahmet Bey Zogolli rose to power; and he knew how to use his hereditary authority to sweep away his rival, Bishop Fan Noli, Albania's revolutionary intellectual par excellence.[10] Noli, who ineffectively ruled the country for six months in 1924, failed to carry through any significant reforms because he neglected to break the power of the clans, Sunni or Catholic, a "mistake" the next generation of Tosk intellectuals would not make after coming to power during World War II. After the war an event of enormous importance was the political confrontation between hereditary military leaders and the Tosk who was sent north to disarm them. Hoxha's emissary, Mehmet Shehu, was respected, or feared, enough by the Geg clansmen that they surrendered their weapons to him. The party, in effect, established police and political control in the country's 26 districts.

Economic Developments in the Districts

Starting almost from scratch in 1945 Albania's economic development has been marked by the emergence of five major industrial-agricultural regions.[11] In Zog's Albania the major agricultural regions were located on the coastal plains adjacent to a narrow zone of dry terraced hillsides and terrain suitable for grazing and mountain agriculture. That is, where the large estates of the beys were located. The coastal plains themselves formed a second zone which reached the Adriatic in many places as malaria-infested lowlands. Extensive drainage works in the lowlands have converted the marshes into areas suitable for grain crops, an achievement that made the country self-sufficient in grains in 1976. An important economic priority for Tirana continues to be the expansion of the country's mountain agriculture into its least developed areas. Most of the country remains fragmented by its high mountain zone which extends from Lake Shkodra near the Adriatic southeast towards Lake Prespa, and which impedes the building of rail and highway links between Tirana and the Highlands. Shehu may have broken the power of the clans in the Highlands but the problem of their geographic isolation and lagging economy remains. The mountains spread across the southern part of the country, the ranges trending northwest to southeast, making land communication extremely difficult between the rapidly developing central regions and the Tosk districts along the Greek border whose schools produced Albania's first patriots and, in the 1920s, Albania's first party leaders. Should strong regional feelings emerge in the major economic regions of the country, it would seem that the Tosk districts between Lake Prespa and Gjirokastra might again show strong centrifugal tendencies, especially if and when Tosk intellectuals no longer dominate the party hierarchy.

The same may apply in the northernmost districts which are linked by river valleys to the coastal plains between Lake Shkodra and the Adriatic. The Shkodra district is rapidly going through socioeconomic changes typical for any low level of development: the polarizing tendencies in this economic region seem little different from those already observed outside the socialist, or Soviet, system.[12] The growth of the city of Shkodra, the traditional capital of the northern clans, as an industrial and agricultural center indicates the extent to which the regime has been successful in transforming the socioeconomic structure of Albania's most tradition-bound society. Novels published in Tirana at least give some insight into this transformation, a transformation that is most apparent, however, in the former market places of the beys.

The most advanced part of the country, not surprisingly, is the central region around Tirana, the heart of the manufacturing industry which was created after World War II. Tirana, at the foothills of the Dinaric Ranges, is joined by rail to Durrës, the country's second largest city and its principal port. Durrës also has rail links to the southeast with Lushnja, Albania's new breadbasket, and the cities of Elbasan and Berat situated, like Tirana, at the edge of the coastal plains. In this economic region, the largest of the five, Russian and Chinese aid went into the building of much of the country's heavy industry—and many of the regime's problems in planning industrial growth which, contrary to the economic goals of Self Reliance, indeed seem vulnerable to external economic pressures and to any serious reduction in foreign (i.e., Chinese) investments and technical assistance. But the specter of unfinished oil refineries and metallurgical combines in the 1970s has been minimized somewhat by Albania's breakthrough in the field of agriculture. It is important to emphasize the fact that Albania developed into an industrial-agricultural country in 1975, or one year before it became self-sufficient in grain crops. It is also self-sufficient in light industry which has marked the development of two Tosk economic centers: Vlora on the Adriatic and Korcha, the latter experiencing a gradual decline in its national importance, if not its political prestige, after the collapse of the Noli government.

Tosk party leaders who have risen to power since 1971 may very well raise regional issues in any internal debates dealing directly with national priorities in planning regional development. It will be interesting to see to what extent regional, if not traditional, loyalties influence the new strategic elite emerging from the Class of '71, a class followed closely by Louis Zanga in his research reports for Radio Free Europe. For Albania, ethnically the most homogeneous state in Europe, the problem of continual regional awareness remains both complex and emotional. Hoxha and Shehu, who themselves were forced to protect regional interests when the country was a subsatellite of Yugoslavia, do not have to look to the Yugoslav republics to know just how strong a foundation any movement "toward decentralization of important governmental functions and emphasis on local participation and initiatives" in fact has.[13] On the contrary, a fairly consistent attitude of the regime has been to look away from the Yugoslav experience to see that no "ideologocal infiltration" from the north penetrates Tirana. More specifically, the new Constitution (1976) is a warning to party members that developments in the Albanian-speaking region of Yugoslavia since the mid-1960s are simply not an option for the regional planners in Albania.

Kosovo: A Bridge too Close

Regional interests no doubt emerged during the discussion of the Seventh Plenum of the party in December 1968, which, as Hoffman has pointed out, initiated the first modest steps toward economic reform and decentralization of the decisionmaking process and the machinery of implementation.[14] But toward the end of 1973 it became evident that Hoxha and Shehu had come to the conclusion that the moves toward decentralization had "gone too far." In 1971 Albania had acted to restore normal dipolmatic relations with its southern NATO neighbor—after the Greek government dropped territorial claims to Toskëri, or southern Albania—and with revisionist Yugoslavia which, after the fall of Ranković in 1966, had begun de facto as well as de jure to treat Kosovars as something other than *cigani* "Gypsies" (a synonym for *shiptari* in Serbia) or *crnci* "niggers." Factors affecting the *komb*, perhaps more than Albanian-Yugoslav fear of Russian intentions in the Balkans after Prague, or Peking's "turn to the West" and its urging Tirana to do likewise, help account for "shifts" in Albania's foreign policy in the early 1970s. The resulting purges in the mid-1970s seem to have effectively atomized any opposition in the party hierarchy and the state bureaucracy to the brakes being applied to the reform movement. But the purges, as encompassing as they were, still could reach only two-thirds of the *komb:* more than a million Kosovars remained unaffected by the political terror, the "pressure of ubiquitous fear,"[15] generated by the regime. But Tirana itself proved highly vulnerable to the "ideological infiltration" reaching it from Kosovo.

Contact between Tirana and Kosovo had been established by the Germans during World War II. For the first time in modern Albanian history political boundaries were drawn around an Ethnic Albania: the former Albanian provinces of the Porte—Shkodra, Kosovo, Manastir (Bitola) and Janina—were finally joined into a single independent state. But the withdrawal of the Germans from the Balkans left the Albanians in much the same danger as after the expulsion of the Turks from these provinces. The price Hoxha had to pay for Yugoslav military assistance amounted to a rejection of the "myth" of an Ethnic Albania. Pre-war frontiers once again divided the Gegs who were caught between Tosk partisans and Tito's troops. When Shehu stripped the bajraktars of their traditional military authority over the clans he in effect forced them to accept the political dismemberment of the *komb*. But political dismemberment did not come to mean national humiliation; on the contrary, after 1947 it was interpreted as the continuing will of the race to avoid assimilation by its Slav neighbors to the east and north.

The absence of Yugoslav divisions in Albania no doubt helped prevent Tito from extending his political control across the border he had restored with Hoxha. Hoxha avoided the complete annexation of all Albanian territory by the Yugoslavs by turning to Moscow when Yugoslavia was expelled from the Cominform. As the Soviet economic system was introduced into its new satellite state in the 1950s, the Yugoslav experiments with that model scarcely touched the lives of the Kosovars with whom the local Serbian minority was continuing to "settle accounts" for acts committed during the war. Hoxha and Shehu did not have to look far to find justification for the purges that destroyed the pro-Yugoslav factions in the party. The Yugoslav government did little to alleviate the situation of the Kosovars until 1966 when Ranković was stripped of power.

The Brioni plenum which overthrew Ranković marked a turning point in the struggle of the Kosovars to gain complete equality within the Yugoslav federation.[16] Moderates fully understood that "equality" could never mean elevating the Autonomous Province of Kosovo to the status of a national republic. The Belgrade government—Christian or communist —would not seriously consider abandoning complete political as well as economic control over Old Serbia. But the Kosovars were nevertheless quick to benefit from the crackdown on the Serbian secret police: as elsewhere in Yugoslavia's multinational state, reforms of the socioeconomic structure of Kosovo were to serve political as well as economic ends.[17]

By the mid-1970s Kosovo had begun to experience dynamic development in its social, economic and cultural life; it enjoyed "complete equality" with the other nationalities.[18] At least on paper.

The regional development of Kosovo in general, and Prishtina in particular, as Tito's "bridge" to Albania posed new problems for the regime in Tirana. The "thaw" that developed in Albanian-Yugoslav relations following the events in Prague in 1968 enabled Kosovar leaders, with the help of Radio-TV Prishtina, to inform Gegs and Tosks in Albania's mountain districts about the "good life" that had been attained in Yugoslavia. Delegates from the University of Tirana to international congresses in the Balkans in the 1970s had only to look at Kosovo license plates in the parking lots and tuxedos at the evening receptions for signs of improvement in the lot of the Kosovars. The end result of the concessions granted the Kosovars was, not surprisingly, the idea that Yugoslavia's self-management society could become a sort of "Piedmont" of the Albanian population, "no matter where the population may be."[19] "Ideological infiltration" from the north, in the early 1970s, came not from Belgrade as much as from the "Second Tirana" whose regional economic problems finally began to receive serious attention from the Yugoslav government, and loans from the World Bank. Even after the step-up in economic aid to Kosovo, however, the irredentist ideas emanating from Prishtina remained as much a threat to Belgrade as to Tirana after the effects of the "thaw" had begun to wear off in the early 1970s. Modernization of the socioeconomic structure of Kosovo-Metohija would increasingly be viewed by Albanians on both sides of the border as a Serb-inspired attempt to break down the traditional structure of the *komb*. There would be little doubt about any "link" between new rounds of anti-Yugoslav polemics in Tirana and the revival of irredentist demonstrations, some of them violent, in Albanian areas of Yugoslavia.[20] Antipodal views concerning the "correct path" Albanians would have to follow in order to rationalize their Soviet economic model while at the same time safeguarding the survival of an independent Albanian state would continue to cross Tito's "bridge" in two directions.[21]

Toward the end of 1973 the regime could no longer conceal the conflict concerning the reordering of economic and political priorities that had penetrated Mao's citadel in Europe. The purges which followed Hoxha's rescinding of the modest reforms initiated just several years earlier revealed to what extent Prishtina and Belgrade had influence inside Albania's strategic elite. Between 1973-1976 the political turmoil in Tirana had affected half the ministries and approximately twenty-five percent of the middle and higher echelons of the party. The conflict of interests inside the party, Zanga suggests, seemed as much connected with the problem of succession as with the immediate impact of further reductions in economic assistance from Peking. But the purges of the mid-1970s seem also to indicate the continuing capacity of the present leadership to atomize effectively any opposition to the rigid policies of the two men who dominate the politburo and the army. In particular, any opposition to Hoxha's "easy way out" of the question on decentralizing the Soviet economic model that had been transplanted on Albanian soil in the early 1950s. To Hoxha and Shehu, and to the hand-picked technocrats who have suddenly come into prominence in the mid-1970s, any movement toward bureaucratization and rationalization in the country were by no means "inevitable."[22] The new managers selected to succeed the predominately Tosk elite in the party differ in one very important respect from the older generation of modernizers: they are not foreign trained. On the contrary, they have risen through the educational system and the lower ranks of the party to administrative positions at the local and district levels. Owing to Tirana's direct control over the entire bureaucratic structure of the country, to say nothing of Albania's small geographic size, the ideologically "correct" local leadership was able to come to the immediate attention of Hoxha and Shehu. The emerging technocrats, who first came into national view in 1971, seem to be in conflict not with the "revolutionary intellectuals" but with the very group of "managerial intellectuals" who salvaged the country's economy in the early 1960s and who, in the face of growing reluctance on the part of the Chinese to continue to subsidize Hoxha's economic plans for "self reliance," have nevertheless managed to achieve important milestones both in industry and agriculture. It would appear that managerial expertise has been sacrificed for political reliability and rigid adherence in future economic planning to the words of Enver Hoxha. Of primary interest to this study is the continuing role regional and traditional loyalties play in the political upheaval that engulfed Albania's strategic elite in the mid-1970s, and that once again severely strained relations between Tirana and Belgrade and Tirana and Prishtina.

The New Elite

The 1970s have seen the emergence of a new professional elite in the country which dramatizes the distance that now separates Europe's newest industrial state from its most backward provinces at the turn of the century. Liberation did little to lift the country out of its culturally backward existence down to its occupation by Mussolini: the Balkan Wars, World War I, the return of Zog and his clansmen to power in 1924, and Italian economic control during the 1930s severely retarded any hope early Tosk revolutionaries might have had concerning the country's educational plight. About eigthty percent of the population was illiterate in the period between the wars. The handful of persons employed who managed to earn a university-level degree—the figure given by the *Statistical Yearbook* is 380[23]—served Italian more than Albanian interests. By 1970, that is, twenty-three years after Albania ceased to be the satellite of a neighboring country, approximately 700,000 persons were enrolled in some kind of educational facility; almost 17,000 persons employed had university-level degrees.[24] But in the early 1970s, as the effects of the "thaw" were beginning to wear off, a move was made to reform the Soviet educational model, which "unnecessarily" prolonged academic programs and "alienated" students from blue collar workers and peasants. The school year was shortened to allow students more time in production or in the fields, or in military training; and more students from blue collar and rural backgrounds were encouraged to continue their schooling.

The schools and technical institutes which were producing more highly educated cadres both for professional and party organizations were at the same time carrying out perhaps one of the most significant social roles in the country: namely, raising the percentage of female graduates, some of whom were to experience almost meteoric rises up the party and administrative hierarchies. The women who have achieved professional recognition in the mid-1970s demonstrate how successful the regime has been in breaking down traditional family ties and patriarchal authority that continue to block efforts to modernize the society which, in Rusinow's words, still seems to have one foot in the heroic age.[25] The liberated woman, no less than the liberated male, trained at home, not abroad, characterizes to a great extent the new leadership that has begun to apply pressure on the older generation of revolutionaries from below. The problem of succession to power, obviously, is not limited to Hoxha and Shehu. Upward mobility of young, well-educated party candidates and members no less than the ever-present drives against bureaucratization helps account for the purges that have resulted in the dismissals of foreign-trained economic and military experts.

The Epicenter of the Purges

The first shock wave to pass through the party and administative organizations* did not reach the military establishment or the various ministries that ran the country's economy. Instead, the purges aimed squarely at the so-called "intellectualists" who perhaps had been too receptive to sights and sounds encountered on trips outside the country, or at seminars and conferences held inside the citadel itself. The end of the political "thaw" between Albania and Yugoslavia came also to signal the end of the first attempts by artists and writers to introduce "foreign influences" in their writings and broadcasts. Foreign influences were by no means limited to personal contacts inside or outside Albania: radio and television programs originating in Italy, Greece and Yugoslavia had become more easily accessible to the general public. This included the more than 20,000 members of the Albanian Party of Labor who had been admitted into the party since the V Party Congress in 1966[26] and who, in 1972, made up approximately twenty-six percent of the total membership of the party. If the mini-cultural revolution of the late 1960s failed to halt the growth of the party bureaucracy, the purges in the mid-1970s would at least control its ideological development. Experimentation with the political and economic structure of the country would suffer the same fate as experiments in the areas of education and literature. Socialist

---

* Data showing the effects of the shock waves between 1973-76 in numerical terms do not exist. One would assume, however, that the nature of the personnel changes throughout the country closely reflects the conflicting interests which emerged at the top of these organizations. Some biographical information on leading figures affected by the purges will, it is hoped, compensate for the lack of statistical data.

Realism would continue to be the rule in the Union of Writers. Limitations would be placed on artistic and literary creativity which, as in the case of economic planning, would continue to serve the political needs of the party and Hoxha's principle of Self Reliance. Socialist Realism and the Soviet economic model which had given birth to it were not yet ready—if indeed they ever would be—for the garbage bin, into which the Yugoslav writer Oscar Davičo had unceremoniously dumped his puritanical partisan hero in the mid-1950s in his novel, "The Poem." Tirana would see to it in the mid-1970s that the "intellectualists" on the Albanian side of the border would soon find themselves on the dungheap of history.

It is interesting that Hoxha and Shehu first chose to single out a Geg from Shkodra as one of the epicenters of the purges of the 1970s. Like Hoxha and Shehu, Fadil Paçrami left Zog's Albania to study abroad. He returned from Italy, where he studied medicine, and fought against Mussolini's troops; he headed the Anti-Fascist Youth League during and immediately following the war. He was fluent in Italian and French, and by 1952, when he became a member of the Central Committee of the Albanian Party of Labor, he had acquired fluency in Russian as well. Paçrami rose through party ranks to become a secretary of the Tirana party organization and the chairman of the National Assembly, the country's highest representative body. His career in journalism led to the position of editor of *Zëri i Popullit,* the party daily whose founder and first editor was Enver Hoxha in 1942. In 1973 the views expressed by Paçrami in his editorials and articles which attacked the principles of "dogmatic Socialist Realism" had begun to alarm Hoxha and Shehu. At the June meeting of the seventy-member Central Committee, Hoxha began to apply pressure on the two organizations which apparently were most vulnerable to Paçrami's leaning toward the official Kosovo, or Yugoslav, position on art and literature: namely, the Union of Writers and Artists and the Union of Working Youth. Faculty members of the University of Tirana, including the president of the Union of Writers and Artists, Dhimitër Shuteriqi, a literary historian, were singled out as the "intellectualists" whose flirtations with liberalizing "foreign influences" posed a serious threat to the survival of the party and *komb* itself. Paçrami's sudden fall from power later in the year signaled the beginning of the end of the liberalizing trends Hoxha himself had but a few years earlier initiated to reform the country's Stalinist political and economic model, and its cultural complement.

Purges in the Ministry of Defense

The fall of Fadil Pacrami was followed in 1974 by a complete turn-over in the highest ranks of the Albanian military establishment, including the Minister of Defense, Beqir Balluku, who had been elevated to his post in 1953. The turnovers were marked by the rise of relatively young officers to positions of power, and, more importantly, by the appointment of the Prime Minister, Mehmet Shehu, as the new Minister of Defense. Shehu's personal role in the dismissals of high ranking officers and his influence in hand-picking politically reliable replacements cannot be underestimated. As was the case immediately after the war, when Hoxha relied on Shehu to break the traditional military authority of the bajraktars, so also in the mid-1970s was his close personal friend asked to disarm any potential centers of opposition in the military establishment, that is, high ranking officers who were in agreement with public announcements by Balluku that sharply contradicted the official party line which stressed that the threat of the United States to the survival of the Albanian Party of Labor was no less dangerous than the threat posed by the Soviet Union. No faction within the party and the military establishment would be tolerated if it did not take seriously Hoxha's warnings against both superpowers. After all, it was the aggressive imperialistic foreign policies of the superpowers which accounted for the "European Insecurity" Conference held in Helsinki. Balluku, like Pacrami, had failed to heed the early warning shots from the citadel which announced that the brief "thaw" was officially over.

As was the case with Pacrami, Balluku had risen to power in the 1950s, after the country had become a satellite of the Soviet Union. Balluku correctly followed the political winds of the late 1950s and helped steer the country through the political and economic difficulties caused by the "revisionists" who had seized power following Stalin's death in the Soviet Union. Balluku held the Albanian military apparatus together during the purges of pro-Soviet elements in the party and state bureaucracies. He introduced innovations in the military establishment by adapting Chinese military models, creating a kind of "all people's army" and abolishing ranks fully in the spirit of the cultural revolutions in China and Albania in the late 1960s. But Chinese cultural and military influence was not to survive without criticism long into the 1970s: Nixon's visit to Peking and the general improvement of Sino-American relations soon led Hoxha and Shehu to question the course the revolution was taking in China, just as they had done a little more than a decade earlier with regard to the new leadership in the Soviet Union. One again, it seemed, a "New Class" was emerging in the party which was coming between the proletariat and the goals of the Marxist-Leninist-Stalinist path toward industrialization and modernization. Hoxha and Shehu, by carrying out an extensive purge of the country's top military leadership, have apparently prevented the military bureaucracy from assuming a new role in Albanian society vis-a-vis the other ministries and the party ideologues; the military elite would not be allowed to assume a position in society "more akin to that of the managers and engineers."[27]

The fact that Shehu was chosen to assume control of the military establishment, which in 1976 made up approximately ten percent of the membership of the Albanian Party of Labor, points out the seriousness of the purges and the "class struggle" within the party which seem to have accompanied major shifts in Albanian foreign as well as domestic policy. In 1947 and 1961 Shehu had already demonstrated his skills in executing Hoxha's policies in North as well as South Albania. He had earned his reputation by crushing dissident voices in the party and the military; his reputation, built in part on his willingness to employ terror, would prove extremely useful to Hoxha, a fellow Tosk, in 1975 and 1976, when the shock waves of the purges would engulf the center of the economic structure of the country. It is here, perhaps, that the fall and meteoric rise of Albania's technocrats provides a clearer picture of the nature and make-up of the country's strategic elite, one in which traditional and even personal loyalties continue to play a very significant role.

Turnovers in the Council of Ministers

In 1975 the purges which had just toppled from power the Minister of Defense, the Minister of Communications and the Minister of Finance (whose successor would last but two years), struck a Deputy Premier, who also served as the Chairman of the State Planning Commission, the Minister of Industry and Mines, and the Minister of Trade. In the following year two Deputy Premiers, the Minister of Agriculture and the Minister of Education and Culture were also dismissed from their posts. In the first half of 1977 the Minister of Light Industry and Food Industry lost his portfolio, and the recently promoted Chairman of the State Planning Commission was dropped as a Deputy Minister. Of the twelve ministers in the Council of Ministers only one had served since the mid-1950s, and only one other had been in office since the mid-1960s. The effect of the dismissals, then, was to remove from the highest state organ bureaucrats who had risen to power during the Soviet period and, surprisingly, during the mini-cultural revolution of the 1960s. In his Radio Free Liberty Reports Louis Zanga provides interesting information on three of the "big losers" of the purges in 1975.[28] The "losers," it turns out, were of enormous importance to the economic survival of the country following the Soviet withdrawal in the early 1960s and in the aftermath of increasingly strained relations with Peking in the mid-1970s. What made them suddenly so superfluous?

The purges of 1975 abruptly ended the career of an experienced economist, Abdyl Këllezi, who had served as Chairman of the State Planning Commission since 1968, who was elevated to the Politburo in 1971, and who in 1974 had just been appointed Deputy Premier. Like Paçrami, Këllezi had studied in Italy after Albania had been annexed by Mussolini. Këllezi came into prominence after the break with the Soviet Union, playing a major role in negotiating trade agreements with Peking and introducing the first steps toward reforming the country's Stalinist economic model in the late 1960s and early 1970s. By the mid-1970s, however, the policy of "Self Reliance together with Chinese Aid" seemed headed toward the possibility of Self Reliance without continuing large-scale economic assistance from the Chinese. Completion dates for major industrial enterprises were delayed into the next five year plan period; and in 1976 the delay in announcing the plan itself confirmed suspicions that internal struggles over the reordering of economic priorities between party ideologues and foreign-trained technocrats played a significant role in the political upheaval of the mid-1970s. If indeed the loss of Chinese support signaled a slowdown in the regime's strategy for industrialization, Këllezi's "experiments" in reforming the country's economic management system became subject to severe criticism. Like Paçrami, Këllezi had gone "too far." Published accounts of ideological exchanges between Këllezi and worker control groups, as reported by Louis Zanga, made it clear to the various state bureaucracies that the struggle against the Right—the "revisionist" and "opportunist" faction in the party and state organizations—was to be more than a popular slogan.

The dismissal of Koço Theodosi, who, like Këllezi, became a member of the Politburo in 1971 and who headed the Ministry of Industry and Mining since 1966, removed from power yet another foreign-trained manager. Theodosi, like Hoxha, had studied in France before the war; like Këllezi he was active in securing loan agreements with East European countries and was adversely affected in his sector by the apparent failure of the government to meet construction deadlines for a large oil refinery and the all-important Elbasan Metallurgical Complex which would produce the country's first steel in 1976, and which, more importantly perhaps, symbolized the regime's policy of Self Reliance. Hoxha and Shehu, in their reports to the VII Party Congress in November 1976, continued to stress the urgency of increasing overall industrial production in the country. The ultimate goal remained the processing of all the country's mineral wealth at home, and the end of exporting crude ore outside Albania. The technocrats most responsible for the significant gains Albanian industry had made in the mid-1970s seemed to become superfluous when relations with Peking seemed to go from bad to worse as the new Chinese leadership itself took a "turn to the West" and suggested to Albania's hardliners that they do likewise.

While such views were anathema inside the Maoist citadel in Europe to Hoxha and Shehu, who began in the mid-1970s to see the end of the revolution in China just as they had observed its death in the late 1950s in the Soviet Union, they doubtless made economic sense to the managerial intelligentsia which did not enthusiastically share the regime's siege mentality. Such as the case, it seems, of the third "big loser" in the political turmoil of 1975, namely, Kiço Ngjela, who had served as Minister of Trade since 1954. Ngjela, Zanga notes, did not act strongly enough to reduce the country's economic dependence on imports which, in spite of claims from the citadel to the contrary, made the country vulnerable to inflationary tendencies in the West and in the bloc countries; that is, in countries whose economy is controlled by either U.S. imperialists or Soviet social-imperialism, which is every bit as "dangerous and barbarous" as its American rival.[29] The continuation of imports of processed goods, and credit and loan agreements with any but "really non-aligned" countries should not be interpreted as anything more than warnings of future economic, ideological and political dependence on one or the other of the superpowers. For confirmation of Hoxha's rigid position the old-line technocrats need long only across the "bridge" at the political consequences of the Yugoslav "experiments." The three "big losers" in 1975 and General Balluku in 1974 chose instead, perhaps, to look at the social and economic consequences of the Yugoslav reforms which, by the mid-1970s, were finally being felt in Kosovo.

In a word, Albania simply was not to run the risk of political pluralization by going "too far" toward introducing radical reforms into its "highly centralized, rigid, authoritarian and generally primitive planning system."[30] More authority in the decisionmaking process did filter down to the district and local levels in the early 1970s; but decisions initiated from below came immediately under the scrutiny of the top echelons in the bureaucracy. That is, local managers of plants and agricultural cooperatives had direct lines to the ministries. The size of the country, no less than the continuing control over the party organizations by the hard-liners, helped facilitate the task of selecting and promoting a new, politically reliable, home-trained class of relatively young managers from the local and district levels to the Council of Ministers itself and also the Politburo, which remained firmly in the control of its predominatly Tosk partisan leadership. At the VII Party Congress, as a case in point, Hoxha with justifiable pride could boast that Albania for the first time in its history had become self-sufficient in grain crops. Gone were the malarial swamps on Zog's coastal plains. Gone, too, was Piro Dodbiba, the Minister of Agriculture who, like Kellezi and Theodosi, had been elevated to the Politburo in 1971, after rising through party ranks during the mini-cultural revolution at the height of Sino-Albanian cooperation. It is curious to note that the "winners" in the ongoing power struggle entered the national political scene in the same year, 1971, when they were elected as members or alternate members of the Central Committee. It is from the "Class of '71," Zanga points out, that Hoxha and Shehu seem to have drawn the next generation of Albania's leadership.

Piro Dodbiba's fall and the "meteoric" rise of his two successors demonstrates the clearly political nature of the purges. A close look at the new technocrats of the Class of '71 reveals attempts by the old Tosk leadership of the party to pay special attention to the regional backgrounds of the new managers as well as to their qualifications, if any, in order to maintain the existing North-South makeup of the higher echelons of the party and state organizations. The appointments of Dodbiba's successors also dramatize a major achievement in the party's campaign to give equal rights to women and to break down once and for all, the last vestiges of traditional, for the most part Muslim-inspired attitudes toward the role of women in society. Kadare's novel, "The Wedding," celebrated the first results of the regime's campaign to liberate women; Hoxha's surprise appointments in 1976 show that more than lip service was being paid the first generation of professionally-trained women in the Albanian Party of Labor.

Themije Thomaj, the first woman ever to attain ministerial rank in Albania "leapfrogged" to her new position from her local post as chairmen of a farm collective in the coastal lowlands of South Albania. In the District of Lushnja which is south and east of the port of Durrës the Këmishtaj farm cooperative had become "synonomous" with the country's new agricultural policy, which had been given high priority in the national economy during the inner-party turmoil preceding the VII Party Congress. The "great leap forward" which the operation of Këmishtaj heralded brought its young chairman into direct, personal contact with Hoxha. Curiously enough, as Zanga points out, arrangements for Hoxha's visit to Kemishtaj were handled by none other than Piro Dodbiba.[31] And it is from the district of Lushnja that Hoxha picked Dodbiba's successor as an Alternative Member of the Politburo, another woman from the Class of '71. Lenka Cuko became a candidate member of the Central Committee in 1971 and rose through party ranks to become party first secretary from the Lushnja district, Albania's new breadbasket. Thomaj and Çuko, by replacing Dodbiba in the Council of Ministers and the Politburo, demonstrated the fact that upward mobility for women through the party and state organizations was at least a reality. Hoxha stressed this fact in his report to the VII Party Congress, at the same time reminding the delegates that women now comprised twenty-seven percent of the membership of the Albanian Party of Labor, or more than double what it was in 1966.[32]

In the same year, that is three years after the fall of Fadil Pacrami and the initial attacks against the "intellectualists" at the University of Tirana and in the Union of Writers and Artists, a woman was elected to the post of Minister of Education and Culture. Tefta Cami replaced Thoma Deljana who had held the post since 1966, that is, through the mini-cultural revolution in the late 1960s and also the brief "thaw" of the early 1970s. Like Thomaj, Cami came from a rural background. After completing her training at the University of Tirana she became a schoolteacher and later a school administrator. In 1971 she was elected a candidate member of the Central Committee and went on to serve as a party secretary in the south, in Berat. In 1973 she became a deputy to the party committee first secretary in the district of Dibër. Two years later, when Hekuran Isai, the local party committee first secretary, was promoted by Hoxha and Shehu to full membership in the Politburo and the Party Secretariat, Cami in effect acquired her own direct line into the citadel. In her case, professional training and experience inside Albania together with close personal ties to a possible successor to Hoxha and Shehu combined to make her a politically reliable appointment to the Tosk-dominated party hierarchy.

The New Elite

The elevation of women to ministerial ranks in 1976 is but part of a significant process taking place in Communist societies: namely, the "massive entry into all institutional fields of new young people with relatively high technical skills and much better educations compared to those from the previous generation,"[33] provided that—at least in Albania—their education was not received in the West before World War II or in the Soviet Union after the war. The rise to prominence of the new strategic elite, drawn increasingly from blue collar and rural backgrounds, has encountered opposition from the Right, a fact emphasized by Shehu and attacked by the newest member of the Secretariat of the Albanian Party of Labor, Hekuran Isai. Hekuran Isai was elevated to full membership in the Politiburo as well as to the Secretariat in 1975, following the wave of purges in the military establishment. Isai served as party secretary in the District of Elbasan in the 1960s. In 1966 he was elected a candidate member of the Central Committee from the Elbasan district where he acquired experience in heavy industry working as a specialist in the Cerrik Oil refining center.[34] In 1971 he became a full member of the Central Committee and transferred to the Librazhe district in the mountains west of Elbasan, where he met Tefta Cami. Isai's experience in the party organization and his defense of the new role of the "blue-collar elite" in the country's bureaucratic structures seems to indicate that Hoxha and Shehu are striving to maintain a "correct" revolutionary spirit in the country in the face of growing opportunism in the international Communist movement, in China as well as in Western Europe.

If the regime must pay due attention to the upward mobility of the new cadres of managers and skilled laborers, it continues to face the traditional question of probable regional allegiences of the new leadership. Not surprisingly, fewer technically-trained party members are to be found in the more remote, backward economic regions of the country. But it is precisely from such a region that yet another candidate member elected the Central Committee in 1971 has risen to power both in the Politburo and in the Council of Ministers. In 1975 Pali Miska, a Geg from North Albania, replaced Koço Theodosi as the Minister of Industry and Mines. He joined Hekuran Isai as a full member of the Politburo in the same year. In the 1960s Pali Miska was listed as the director of the country's main lumber production enterprise in the District of Puka in the mountains west of Shkodra.[35] After his election to the Central Committee he served as the party first secretary of the Puka district, which is in the heart of the most tradition-bound territories of the Roman Catholic and Moslem clans. Pali Miska and Hekuran Isai, new party hardliners with professional skills and expertise in the industrial sector of the economy, provide a promising Geg-Tosk mixture at the very top of the Class of '71. Professional qualifications as well as political reliability had something at least to do with their rapid rise to power. The same, unfortunately, cannot be said of Kiço Ngjela's replacement.

Kiço Ngjela was replaced as Minister of Trade in 1975 by Nedin Hoxha, the mayor of the city of Gjirokastra, a district capital in the mountains approximately twenty miles from the Albanian coast at Saranda, the country's southernmost port. Why Nedin Hoxha? Although he held various administrative posts in Gjirokastra, Enver Hoxha's birthplace, this hardly seems to compensate for the fact that the new minister had no direct experience in the field of commerce.[36] His article which appeared in Zeri i Popullit in the summer of 1975, while ideologically "correct" in its attack against growing bureaucratization of the country's economic structure, scarcely qualifies him to succeed Ngjela as Minister of Trade. But Nedin Hoxha did join other Tosks in the party hierarchy whose basic strong point, on the surface, seems to be close, personal loyalty to Enver Hoxha and Mehmet Shehu. Personal loyalty, for our purposes, should be equated with traditional and regional loyalties. Appointments from the poorer administrative districts in the Geg and Tosk Highlands in effect work to balance the political as well as economic power of the more prosperous central districts along the Shkumbini River. Durrës and Tirana lie just north of the river, and Elbasan, Berat, Lushnja and Fier are to the south, where much of the country's heavy industry is located and where, as we have mentioned, Albania's breadbasket is found. Forty miles south of the District of Berat is the town of Permet, the administrative center of one of the poorest districts in the country. The District of Permet is in the mountain zone between Gjirokastër and Lake Ohrid: that is, in the heartland of the Orthodox population of Albania. It is from Permet that Hoxha picked yet another local party administrator as an Alternative Member of the Politburo where, in 1976, he joined another Tosk newcomer, Lenka Cuko. Little is known of Simon Stefani, but his name is a reminder of centuries of Greek cultural influence in South Albania.

Minority Rights in Albania

Simon Stefani is from an area of the country which not only preserved its Orthodox faith through nearly five centuries of Turkish rule but also succeeded in the last quarter of the nineteenth century to assert its national identity in the face of a policy of Hellenization being pressed by the Church of Greece.[37] A generation of Albanian patriots, when forced to identify either on the basis of language or religion, came to the conclusion that the survival of the *komb* ultimately depended on the survival of the language. The "point of no return" in this struggle for survival was reached, I believe, in 1866, when the first modern translation of the Bible was made by Konstantin Kristoforidhi, who worked as a translator for the British Bible Society.[38] An Albanian Bible meant that Orthodox Albanians had as much right to their own autocephalous church as the Serbs and Greeks. While a Moslem Albanian and Slav wall separated Orthodox Tosks from Serbs, no such religious barrier existed between Albanian and Greek Christians in the south. It is in the poorer mountain districts of South Albania that the country's only sizeable national minority lives: about thirty-five thousand Greeks, or bilingual speakers who still identify as Greek, constitute the single serious ethnic problem inside Albania.*

The problem raised by the Greeks in South Albania differs in several important respects from that of the Albanians in Kosovo, keeping in mind the fact that both minorities inhabit some of the most economically backward regions of both Albania and Yugoslavia. First, the total number of Greeks inside Albania is very small: they comprise approximately 2.4 percent of the country's population. Second, the Greeks in South Albania are by no means culturally separated from the majority of the immediate neighbors, several hundred thousand of whom once shared a common faith with them and in many cases, including that of Kristoforidhi, adopted Christian names given them by Greek teachers or simply borrowed from Greek. Nevertheless, the Greek presence in South Albania was a threat to the security of the country in the late 1940s; tensions along the Greek-Albanian border lasted long after the end of the Greek Civil War, Albania having become a Soviet satellite and Greece a member of NATO. In 1971, however, when the Greek government officially gave up all territorial claims to South Albania, it was no longer viewed as a serious threat to the internal security of the country. Normal diplomatic relations between Tirana and Athens were established in the same year. In 1971 Hoxha and Tito also restored full diplomatic relations between their countries: ethnic minorities along Albania's borders were to serve as "bridges" only insofar as they would not provide an excuse for the Soviet Union to intervene in the Balkans as it had in Czechoslovakia. Hoxha could not criticize Belgrade for its continuing social, economic and political discrimination against the Kosovars without looking over his own shoulder at the Greek communities in Albania. As the official position of the Kosovars improved in Yugoslavia in the mid-1970s, so also did that of the Greeks inside Albania, insofar as Article 43 of the new constitution recognized the rights of national minorities living in Albania. On December 28, 1976, the People's Assembly approved the new constitution which guaranteed the Greeks "the protection and

---

*	Greeks	40,000
	Vlachs	20,000
	Slavs	20,000
	Gypsies	10,000

development of their people's culture and traditions, the use of their mother tongue and the teaching of it in the schools." Article 43 does not mean, however, that the country's centuries-long problem along its southern border has been solved. In his report to the VII Party Congress Hoxha's remarks dispelled any illusions about the continuing activity of the "crazy, self-styled 'Northern Epirots' " on both sides of the Greek-Albanian border, who remain as a threat both to Tirana and to the "reasonable" politicians in Greece[39] who have correctly drawn the line separating Greek Orthodox Christians and *Shqiptars*. If the establishment of an autocephalous Albanian Orthodox Church was the first major step in dividing the Orthodox community in South Albania into two ethnic groups, the proclamation of the New Religion in 1967 made the break complete. The Simon Stefanis in the south, like the parishioners of the executed Roman Catholic priest in North Albania, have felt the ideological pressure from the regime to break the traditional religious bonds that once separated Albanians. But the administrative measures it has taken in its campaigns against religion have by no means been uniform throughout the country.

The regime's campaign against the four religious communities inside Albania has deliberately progressed from the cities and towns into the more traditional and backward mountain regions, and from the schools into the labor camps, as we read in Kadare's novel, "The Wedding." Pressure, or "persuasion," was applied more rigorously to religious groups with ties to the West than to the East: that is, Roman Catholic and Orthodox priests were viewed as greater potential threats to the regime than Sunni and Bektashi hoxhas, the latter perhaps justifiably so regarding themselves as the most tolerant, the most nationalistic, of all the religious communities in Albania.[40] It is important to note that the step-by-step campaign "took no harsh measures against older people who had been brought up in religious faiths, nor were they forbidden to practice their religious rites at home."[41] But secret pilgrimages in the Geg Highlands to sites where churches once existed contrast sharply with the continuing observances of Muslim holidays in the districts along the Greek border. The presence of a Greek minority in the south in part accounts for the lack of uniformity in the government's efforts to propagandize the New Religion.

But in the same year the new constitution was passed with its article on minority rights, the government also announced that it would act to change personal names if they were judged "inappropriate" in view of certain vaguely-defined "standards."[42] Most of the name changes, should such pressure ever be applied, would fall, it is believed, on the non-Albanian Christian minorities, the only one of any size or significance being that of the Greeks. The spread of the "peace of Death" to the Greek religious groups and changing of last names from, say, Stefanou to Stefani, in itself would not lead to the assimilation of the Greeks in South Albania by neighboring Tosk communities. A different situation would obtain, however, should the government procede to block the use and teaching of Greek in the schools. Discrimination against the Albanian minorities in Greece and Yugoslavia did not eradicate the Albanian language from groups, regardless of their religion, which refused to identify as Greek or Slav. But well over a third of Albanian-speaking people in the Balkans live outside Albania itself. The small Greek minority in Albania has survived for half a century without the protection of large numbers. It remains very vulnerable to the single most driving force behind the new Albanian constitution: Albanian nationalism.

Albanian Nationalism: Tradition and Change

In the early 1970s the Albanian Party of Labor began taking steps to prepare the nation for the coming ideological break with Peking and the more immediate struggle against increasing "ideological infiltration" from the north. The two major problems that the regime had to overcome, in Hoxha's opinion, were liberalism and bureaucracy, as well as their offspring—technocratism and intellectualism.[43] The recent purges had revealed to what extent these problems had undermined party unity and had weakened the economic and military establishment precisely at the time Albania again found itself "blockaded" by the two superpowers and abandoned by Mao's successors. Hoxha and Shehu, together with Hekuran Isai and Pali Miska and other ideologically "correct" Politburo members and ministers, proved through the purges that the country was by no means destined to follow the paths to socialism and communism taken by the Yugoslav and Soviet revisionists and opportunists in Peking and in the bourgeois communist parties of Western Europe, all of whom had betrayed the revolution by dismantling or disowning the Soviet economic model that had made Moscow under Stalin the citadel for worldwide revolution. The achievements of the Stalinist model were

repeated on a much smaller scale in Albania in both agriculture and industry in the mid-1970s, when the country for the first time in its history
became an industrial-agricultural state and self-sufficient in grain crops,
even when the Soviet Union was forced to import grain crops. Hoxha
could boast that Tirana, in effect, had emerged as the new citadel of
the "really" Marxist-Leninist revolution. If the Kremlin inspired national
communism movements in the 1930s, so now would Tirana serve as the
inspiration for "really" socialist countries, of which there are few, and
also the "splinter" parties in the West, particularly in France and Italy,
which have emerged as the enemies of Euro-Opportunism, which accepts
as "inevitable" theories of the counter-revolution already "codified"
by Stalin's successors.[44] That is, the ideas of Bernstein and Kautsky,
who are singled out by Hoxha in his report to the VII Party Congress.

Hoxha's report leads one to conclude that Albania's present leadership, in spite of its new role in the world communist movement, continues to follow at least one consistent policy that has obsessed traditionally Catholic, Orthodox, Sunni and Bektashi poets and propagandists,
patriots and revolutionaries for well over a century: namely, the survival
of the *komb*. It is not enough to write off the Albanian experience as
"Stalinist after Stalin, and Maoist after Mao." It is, in a word, Albanian.
Some answers to the "mysteries" surrounding the country's present
leadership, the "class struggle" being waged within the party, and the
policy of self reliance with or without Chinese economic assistance might
best be sought in Albania's tradition-bound past and its centuries-long
isolation from a hostile, non-Muslim world.

NOTES

1. A. V. Desnickaia, *Albanskii iazyk i ego dialekty* (Leningrad:
"Nauka," 1968), p. 47.

2. *The Times* (London), December 23, 1972, p. 3.

3. The *New York Times,* March 28, 1973, p. 21.

4. Ramadan Marmullaku, *Albania and the Albanians,* trans. by M.
and B. Milosavljevic (London: C. Hurst, 1975), p. 77. See also, Stavro
Skendi, "Crypto-Christianity Among the Balkan Peoples Under the Ottomans," *Slavic Review,* XXVI, 2 (June 1967).

5. *Ibid.*

6. Ismail Kadare, *The Wedding* (Tirana: The "Naim Frashëri Publishing House, 1968), p. 22.

7. Joseph Swire, *King Zog's Albania* (New York: Liveright Publishing Corporation, 1937), p. 7. Swire was asked to remember that "Bektashism stood between all religions—and in Albania for mediation and unity between all beliefs in the national interest."

8. Ian Whitaker, "Tribal Structure and National Politics in Albania, 1910-50," reprinted from A. S. A. Monographs (London and New York: Travistock Publications, 1968), p. 275.

9. *Ibid.,* p. 261.

10. For a summary of Albanian political activity in the early 1920s see Nicholas C. Pano, *The People's Republic of Albania: Integration and Community Building in Eastern Europe* (Baltimore: The Johns Hopkins Press, 1968), p. 20-23. For an example of what results when political propaganda enters the world of oral epic poetry see John S. Kolsti, "A Song About the Collapse of the Noli Government in Albania," *Journal of the Folklore Institute*, XII, 2/3 (1975), pp. 189-202.

11. Marmullaku, *Albania*, pp. 71-72. See also, George W. Hoffman, *Regional Development Strategy in Southeast Europe* (New York: Praeger Publishers, 1977), pp. 21-22.

12. Hoffman, *Regional Development*, pp. 208-209.

13. *Ibid.,* p. 170.

14. *Ibid.,* p. 160.

15. J. H. Kautsky, *The Political Consequences of Modernization* (New York: John Wiley, 1972), p. 173.

16. Marmullaku, *Albania*, p. 149. For a more complete analysis, see *Radio Free Europe Research (RFER)*, December 10, 1976.

17. Hoffman, *Regional Development*, p. 140.

18. *RFER*, December 10, 1976.

19. Robert R. King, *Minorities Under Communism: Minorities As a Source of Tension Among Balkan Communist States* (Cambridge: Harvard University Press, 1973), p. 138.

20. *RFER*, December 2, 1975.

21. For another view of minority groups as "bridges" see Paul Shoup, "The National Question and the Political Systems of Eastern Europe," in Sylva Sinanian et al., eds., *Eastern Europe in the 70s* (New York: Praeger Publishers, 1972).

22. See William E. Griffith's comments in Charles Gati, ed., *The Politics of Modernization in Eastern Europe* (New York: Praeger Publishers, 1974), p. 360.

23. Marmullaku, *Albania*, p. 162.

24. *Ibid.*

25. Dennison I. Rusinow, "The Other Albanians," American Universities Field Staff Reports Service, Southeast Europe Series, Vol. XII, No. 2 (Yugoslavia), p. 8.

26. Marmullaku, *Albania*, p. 66.

27. J. H. Kautsky, *The Political Consequences of Modernization* (New York: John Wiley, 1972), p. 193.

28. *RFER*, RAD Background Report (Albania), November 24, 1975.

29. Enver Hoxha, *Report Submitted to the 7th Congress of the Party of Labour of Albania* (Tirana: "8 Nëntori" Publishing House, 1977), p. 166.

30. Hoffman, *Regional Development*, p. 108.

31. *RFER*, May 18, 1976.

32. Hoxha, *Report*, pp. 89-90.

33. Zgymunt Bauman, "The Party in the System-Management Phase: Change and Continuity," in Andrew C. Janos, ed., *Authoritarian Politics in Communist Europe: Uniformity and Diversity in One-Party States* (Berkeley and Los Angeles: University of California Press, 1963), p. 96.

34. *RFER*, November 24, 1975.

35. *Ibid.*

36. *Ibid.*

37. See Stavro Skendi, *The Albanian National Awakening, 1878-1912* (Princeton: Princeton University Press, 1967). See also, George Arnakis, "The Role of Religion in the Development of Balkan Nationalism," in Charles and Barbara Jelavich, eds., *The Balkans in Transition* (Berkeley and Los Angeles: Univesity of California Press, 1963), pp. 115-144.

38. Stefanaq Pollo et al., eds., *Historia e Popullit Shqiptar*, vol. 2 (rev. ed.: Beograd: "Serbija," 1969), p. 92. See also, Dh. Shuteriqi, *Historia e Letërsisë Shiqipe* (rev. ed.: Prishtinë: "Relindja," 1970).

39. Hoxha, *Report*, pp. 205-206.

40. Tosk emigrants from Zog's Albania would find this statement hard to believe: for many, Geg and Tosk could mean only Christian Albanian. Moslem neighbors were "Turks."

41. Marmullaku, *Albania,* pp. 76-77.
42. The *New York Times,* February 27, 1976, p. 3. The Albanian Embassy in Belgrade also announced, as reported in the article, that the People's Republic of Albania henceforth would be called the People's Socialist Republic of Albania.
43. Hoxha, *Report,* pp. 119-20.
44. *Ibid.,* pp. 222ff.

BIBLIOGRAPHY

Albania. General Guideline (Tirana, 1976).

Desnickaia, A. V. *Albanskii iazyk i ego dialekty* (Leningrad: "Nauka," 1968).

Gati, Charles, ed. *The World and the Great Power Triangles* (Cambridge: The MIT Press, 1975).

Hoffmann, George W. *Regional Development Strategy in Southeast Europe* (New York: Praeger Publishers, 1972)

Hoxha, Enver. *Report Submitted to the 7th Congress of the Party of Labour of Albania* (Tirana: "8 Nëntori" Publishing House, 1977)

Janos, Andrew C., ed. *Authoritarian Politics in Communist Europe.* Uniformity and Diversity in One-Party States (Berkeley: University of California, 1976)

Jelavich, Charles and Barbara, eds. *The Balkans in Transition* (Berkeley and Los Angeles: University of California Press, 1963)

Kadare, Ismail, *The Wedding* (Tirana: The "Naim Frashëri" Publishing House, 1968)

Kautsky, J. H. *Communism and the Politics of Development* (New York: John Wiley, 1968)

_____. *The Political Consequences of Modernization* (New York: John Wiley, 1972)

King, Robert R. *Minorities Under Communism. Minorities As a Source of Tension Among Balkan States* (Cambridge: Harvard University Press, 1973)

Marmullaku, Ramadan. *Albania and the Albanians.* Trans. by M. and B. Bilosavljevic (London: C. Hurst, 1975)

Myrdal, Jan and Kessie, Gun. *Albania Defiant* (New York and London: Monthly Review Press, 1976)

Pano, Nicholas C. *The People's Republic of Albania. Integration and Community Building in Eastern Europe* (Baltimore: The Johns Hopkins Press, 1968)

Pallo, Stefanaq, et al., eds. *Historia e Popullit Shqiptar*, Volume II (rev. ed.: Beograd: "Serbija," 1969)

Shutëriqi, Dh. *Historia e Letërsisë Shqipe* (rev. ed.: Prishtinë/ "Rilindja," 1970)

Sinanian, Sylva, et al., eds. *Eastern Europe in the 70s* (New York: Praeger Publishers, 1972)

Skendi, Stavo. "Crypto-Christianity Among the Balkan Peoples Under the Ottomans," *Slavic Review*, XXVI, 2

_____ *The Albanian National Awakening, 1878-1912* (Princeton: Princeton University Press, 1967)

Swire, J. *King Zog's Albania* (New York: Liveright Publishing Corporation, 1937)

Whitaker, Ian. "Tribal Structure and National Politics in Albania, 1910-50," Reprinted from A. S. A. Monographs (London and New York: Trivistock Publications, 1968)

Newspapers and Periodicals

The *New York Times*
The *Times* London
Radio Free Europe Research: Reports on Albania (by Louis Zanga)

John Georgeoff

IV

ETHNIC MINORITIES IN
THE PEOPLE'S REPUBLIC OF BULGARIA

Any analysis of the present situation regarding minorities in Bulgaria is fraught with considerable difficulties. To the knowledge of this writer, no current data has been published by the Bulgarian government regarding this problem. Census data on the subject dates to the pre-World War II period or the immediate post-War period, at best. In 1976 *Statisticheski godishnik na narodna republika B"lgariya* (The Statistical Yearbook of the People's Republic of Bulgaria)[1] does not tabulate the population of the nationalities living in the country. However, it does provide a good summary of emigration and immigration by ethnic groups. (See Table IV.) Any analysis of Bulgaria's present ethnic situation must therefore be carried out indirectly and by projections based upon past data and what is known concerning ethnic groups subsequently and about any resultant population changes. Consequently, historical data and information must also be relied upon. This paper, therefore, is based upon the use of such techniques, limited though they might be.

Fortunately, perhaps, the situation concerning minority nationalities in Bulgaria is not now as complicated as it once was, or as it is presently in other Balkan and East European states, in Yugoslavia for example. Nevertheless, Bulgaria has her minorities and minority problems, just as do all the other states in this area of the world. According to the best available estimates, approximately 9 to 14 percent of Bulgaria's population belongs to some minority nationality group.[2] The exact percentage, and concomitantly the absolute numbers are subject to dispute, depending in part upon the definition of *minority nationality,* and whose figures are used and when.

Constitutional Provisions Regarding Minorities in Bulgaria

Historically, given the strained tenor of Balkan politics, their animosities and traditional hatreds, the Bulgarians have, perhaps, been among the more tolerant peoples in this area toward other ethnic groups within their midst. Although many cases can be cited to prove the contrary, Bulgaria has provided, and to a degree still does provide its minorities with a fair amount of freedom. Of course, such freedom is contingent upon ultimate loyalty to the Bulgarian state, and not to one's ethnic nationality—or if not loyalty, then at least passive acceptance.

The Bulgarian Constitution, adopted on May 16, 1971 is the most important legal document affecting ethnic minorities in Bulgaria. Its most pertinent points regarding minority relations follow.

Article 35

(2) No privileges or limitations of rights based on nationality, origin, creed, sex, race, education, social and material status are allowed.

(4) The propogation of hate or humiliation of man because of race, national or religious affilation is forbidden and shall be punishable.

Article 45

(7) Citizens of non-Bulgarian extraction, in addition to the compulsory study of the Bulgarian language, are entitled to study also their own language.[3]

It is usually unwarranted and scholastically dangerous to accept most constitutions at face value, for often such documents are written to serve other purposes. The case of the Bulgarian Constitution is no exception, with the stated ideals and the actual realities being quite separated, at times. The rest of this paper is devoted to an explanation of the present situation of minorities in Bulgaria, especially in terms of past events.

Minorities in Bulgaria Today

The problem of minority nationalities in Bulgaria was much more complex during the last days of Ottoman rule when Turks, Greeks, Romanians, Serbs, Hungarians, Slovaks, Czechs, and Germans were permanent residents of the area. However, of these groups, the most significant ones, extending well into the post-liberation period, were the Turks, Romanians, and Greeks. The others for the most part either emigrated to their mother countries, once the Bulgarian boundaries were stabilized, or gradually were assimilated into the overwhelming Bulgarian population. The Macedonians are a special category and may, or may not, be Bulgarians. An explanation follows later.

Bulgaria's important historic minorities include the following.

Turks. The Turkish question remains to this day a principle cause for the periods of tension between Bulgaria and Turkey. Many Turks fled Bulgaria just prior to 1878 when they saw that the end of Ottoman rule was near. After Eastern Rumelia was united to Bulgaria in 1885, additional numbers left, particularly from that region. Additional numbers continued to emigrate, particularly after World War I, between the World Wars, and later after World War II when further attempts at repatriation were made. Nevertheless, a significant number remains. Some of this group, with close relatives in Turkey, are to be repatriated to that country on a gradual basis over the span of the present decade or so, but because the Turkish economy cannot absorb all the Turks in Bulgaria who would like to leave, the number of those doing so will be limited in any event.

Pomaks. An element of the Bulgarian population sometimes closely identified with the Turks are the Pomaks.[4] However, such an identification is erroneous at worst, and seriously misleading at best. The Pomaks are Bulgarians, not Turks. They speak the Bulgarian language, not Turkish. Their origins go back to the time of the Turkish domination when groups of Bulgarians were converted to Islam under the threat of the sword or with the inducement of the proverbial carrot. Thus, as members of the Islamic faith, their conversion was rewarded by numerous favors and privileges. They can be considered a minority primarily in so far as religion is concerned and to the concomitant extent that certain of their cultural patterns are its expressions. In no way can they be labeled an "ethnic" minority, but nevertheless they are a minority of a particular kind.

Gypsies. The gypsies or *tsigani* are another minority group in Bulgaria. Although an ethnic minority, since their cultural, anthropological and social characteristics differ markedly from the larger Bulgarian group, the gypsies normally are not considered a minority nationality. The reason for this is that historically, and presently, they exhibit few of the elements normally assigned to a nationality, that is, the usual criteria by which a group is generally judged as to whether it is a nationality or not.[5] They have no contiguous territory, in the old days wandering throughout the Balkan lands under the jurisdiction of the Ottoman Empire. Their historical past has been that of the particular nation in which they found themselves when the national boundaries of Southeastern Europe were formed than one peculiar to them alone. Although possessing some commonalities in culture and customs, primary loyalties and determinants of such factors are the family in all its extended forms and the clan. They are divided in their religious adherence between Islam and Eastern Orthodoxy; and any concept of nationalism seems to have escaped them. The strongest bond between the various clans is language, although even it has been affected by the language of the particular nation in which they found themselves—in this case, Turkish and Bulgarian.

Macedonians. Possibly another important minority nationality group is the Macedonian. The term *possibly* is used here because the question of whether or not Macedonians are a distinct "nationality" may be a moot point. Presently, the Bulgarian government is hard pressed on this point. Historically, Bulgarians have regarded the Macedonians as Bulgarians (cf Table V). Their language has been considered a dialect of Bulgarian. In the past, many Macedonians held high offices in Bulgarian officialdom, including at one time the premiership. Bulgarian schools in Macedonia were considered by many to be synonomous with Macedonian schools. As late as 1912, just before the outbreak of the Balkan Wars, and independent enumeration indicated that there were 1,141 Bulgarian schools in which 1,884 teachers taught 65,474 students.[4] The influence of IMRO (Internal Macedonian Revolutionary Organization) upon the Sofia government and its politics in the latter part of the nineteenth century and the first two decades of the present century is too well known among Balkan scholars to recount again here.

Greeks. Greeks have been living in what is now Bulgaria since ancient times. Once they constituted a powerful economic, political, and educational-religious force. The Phanariots were extremely important in Bulgaria, as they were also in Romania during the eighteenth and early nineteenth centuries. Their influence extended not only politically and religiously, in that most of the higher level clerics were Greeks, but also concomitantly to education, since the schools were coordinated with the church. Instruction in these institutions was in Greek, with the result that a Grecophile Bulgarian intelligentsia was created. Likewise, Greek merchants moved into this, the Bulgarian part of the Ottoman Empire, and soon controlled much of the trade and commerce in the towns and cities. With the reaction against these Greeks which set in prior to the Liberation in the 1870s, many Greeks left Bulgaria, as did also some of the pro-Greek Bulgarians. However, a large element remained.

The Liberation saw still greater numbers leave the country, as did also the union of Bulgaria with Eastern Rumelia. Nonetheless, Greeks continued to be a significant element in the demography of Bulgaria, especially near the Greek-Bulgarian border. The Balkan Wars and World War I caused still more Greeks to be repatriated, but numbers stayed. Indeed, it was the Greeks remaining in Bulgaria along the border regions that served as a pretext for the Greek government to attempt to annex these areas after the First World War. The number of Greeks who remained in this border area following the First World War, as well as those along the Black Sea Coast, probably was not greater than 11,000.[7] Many of those who remained were repatriated during the repatriations of 1923 to 1928[8] The few who still live in Bulgaria are found along this Greco-Bulgarian border and in Dobrudja.

Jews. Bulgaria's Jewish population at one time was an important part—numerically, culturally, and economically—of Bulgarian life. Fortunately, Bulgarian Jews were spared the annihilation meted out during World War II to those in most of the rest of Europe, although they did suffer dislocation and the deprivation that subsequently accompanied such dislocation.[9] At the time there were approximately 50,000 Jews in the country.[10] After the war, though, most of them emigrated from Bulgaria, the largest number to Israel. Presently, according to Bulgarian Jewish sources, the number of Jews in Bulgaria is less than 5,000; in other words, under ten percent of the pre-World War II figure.[11]

Other Ethnic Groups. In addition to the ethnic elements in Bulgaria which go back to the time of the Turkish conquest and even beyond it, some new groups have entered Bulgaria from time to time. In 1861, Tartars from the Crimea were resettled in the country, then still a part of "European Turkey," the old Ottoman Empire.[12] After the Russian Civil War in 1917-1922, several thousand White Russians who had opposed the communists fled to Bulgaria as a kindred Slavic state with a language similar to their own. The number who finally settled there was probably never greater than 18,000.[13] When the Soviet Army entered Bulgaria during the closing days of the Second World War, a number fled the country (the exact number is debatable). Of those who remained, many were arrested and imprisoned, the Soviets in this way settling old scores with them. Again, though, the figures in this respect are unreliable. Of the original number, few probably remain in Bulgaria today. In the eleven year period from 1963 to 1974, only six Russians left Bulgaria and none immigrated into the country.[14]

At about the same time as the influx of White Russians into Bulgaria, Armenians, fleeing both Russian and Turkish oppression, also found refuge in Bulgaria. Their number in the 1934 census was close to 25,000.[15]

Bulgarian Minority Types

Hugh Seton-Watson divides the minority groups of the Danubian basin into three separate categories.[16] The first category consists of the minorities living along the border regions. Concerning this group, Andrew Gyorgy notes that ". . . their precarious situation is due to a conflict of the ethnical principle with certain historic, strategic, or economic considerations."[17] In the case of Bulgaria, minorities of this type are the Greeks along the Greco-Bulgarian border, and the few Serbs around Dragoman. If Macedonians are to be considered as a separate ethnic group, as will be discussed later, then perhaps they also need to be included in this category, for they populate much of the Macedonian part of Bulgaria; i.e., Pirin Macedonia of Southwestern Bulgaria, in juxtapostion to the Yugoslav and Greek borders.

The second category is comprised of enclaves, or isolated pockets, of ethnic minorities that are completely surrounded by the larger dominant, governing majority. Such groups are often separated by considerable distances from their national home. In the case of Bulgaria, this category is represented generally by the remaining Turks in the country who are located in the northeastern part and in the Arda basin[19] and by the Tartar minority.

The third category consists of ethnic groups that live in ethnically mixed communities. To a large extent, the Russians living in Bulgaria between World Wars, the Vlachs (about whom more will be added later), the urban Gypsies, Jews, and Armenians come under this category. An excellent example of a region in Bulgaria where such ethnic intermixture exists in Dobrudja, which was before the Second World War populated by Bulgarians, Turks, Romanians, Greeks, and even Germans (the so-called "Saxons" because many of their ancestors originally came from Saxony). Except for the Germans and perhaps the Greeks, this ethnic mixture continues to exist there. Indeed, it is to be found throughout Bulgaria's Danubian basin, but not to such an intensified degree.

Minorities Before Bulgaria's Liberation

The exact number of each ethnic group within the population of Bulgaria at the time of her liberation in 1878, is unknown. Turkish statistics for the years immediately preceeding the Liberation are essentially not reliable for several reasons, including the lack of a uniform methodology and haphazard recording procedures,[21] the reluctance of the reporting member of a household to be entirely truthful with the Turkish census taker,[22] and the bluring of ethnic consciousness among the respondents.[23]

As an English writer of the time noted regarding his travels through this part of the Ottoman Empire:

> No locality can be found where the population is exclusively of the same nationality, but a rival race crops up here and there and jostles his neighbor. We find, for instance, a quarter where the majority of the population is Bulgarian, but amongst them in considerable numbers are Turks, Greeks, Circassians, and Gypsies. In another quarter are Albanians, but they again have to bear the friction of Bulgarians, Wallachs, Greeks, and Turks; and so on all over the country. Each of these nations has its own language, religion and customs. . . ; and when it is borne in mind that in Europe alone [i.e., European Turkey] no less than eight distinct nationalities, each with a considerable population, and several others of smaller degree, can claim the rights to Turkish subjects, some idea may be formed of the obstacles in the path of good government in Turkey.[24]

The situation at the time was—and still is (communism not withstanding)—further complicated by religion. Until the Firman of 1870, the Orthodox Bulgarians owed their religious allegiance to the Greek Patriarch, and attempts were made to Hellenize them through the churches and the schools. Indeed, for a time some members of the wealthy, educated merchant class tended to consider themselves Greek, rather than Bulgarian. The same writer observed:

> The Bulgarians in Macedonia border and touch the Greek population: accordingly, we find them speaking Greek as their social, and Bulgarian as their domestic, language; but the latter is in that quarter fast disappearing. I asked some Macedonian Bulgarian peasants their nationality, and they immediately replied, "Roum," the generic name given to the Greek inhabitants of Asia Minor. They persisted that they were Greeks. "Why, then," I asked, "do you talk Bulgarian in your domestic life?" "Because our fathers did it," was the answer; and they added, "We have suffered trouble enough from being called Bulgarians, when we are Greeks." By this remark they meant that, having been

under the domination of the Greek Church, they were persecuted
if they attempted to assert their Bulgarian nationality, which is
opposed to Pan-Hellenic schemes.[25]

Further, a segment of the population spoke Bulgarian, but were Moslems in religion, having been converted to Islam upon the Turkish conquest by force or by enducements. This group of Bulgarian Slavs were
labeled Turks, although many of them, especially the women, hardly
knew a single word of Turkish. This group is still in existence in Bulgaria
today, especially in and around the area of the Rodopi mountains, but
now they are known as "Moslem Bulgarians," which is actually representative of their true condition.[26] These Pomaks, as has been noted, are
therefore not an ethnic or nationality minority group, but rather a religious one.

Complicating matters even further in any attempt to obtain an accurate
emuneration of Bulgaria's ethnic composition at the time of her Liberation
was the fact of her division into three parts resulting from the decisions
at the Congress of Berlin. Thus, North Bulgaria and the region of Sofia
became a Bulgarian principality, but nominally still a vassal of the Sultan.
South Bulgaria, known as Eastern Rumelia, continued under the military
and political control of Turkey, but with a measure of semi-autonomy.
Macedonia, also claimed by Bulgaria as Bulgarian, remained largely as
part of the Ottoman Empire. In each of these regions, therefore, a different system, or more accurately—as indicated above—systems of census
enumeration were employed. Consequently, data regarding the ethnicity
of the Bulgarian population during this period must be approached with
some care. It is for these reasons, then, that the population figures regarding the ethnicity of the Bulgarian population are quite contradictory
for the immediate pre-Liberation and initial post-Liberation period, as
is seen in Table I.

There are also cautions that need to be observed in the use of post-
Liberation data.

1. This data is from official Bulgarian sources, which may or may not
be biased. For instance, Greek statisticians often tend to present quite
a different picture regarding the Greek minority in Bulgaria during this
period than do the Bulgarians.[27]

2. Ethnicity and language sometimes differ and occasionally this difference is a notable one.

3. Ethnicity and religion likewise may not coincide. For instance, the Pomaks are members of an ethnic group whose dominant religion is Orthodox but who, for some reason of history, belong to another religious persuasion.

4. Boundary lines changed frequently during the first half century of Bulgaria's liberation, as will be discussed later. With these changes came population shifts not normally accounted for in the course of the natural increase of an ethnic group.

5. Variations in the categories employed in the various census emunerations also adds to the confusion regarding the ethnic composition of the Bulgarian populace. For instance, in the census of 1905, Romanians were listed as an individual population category.[28] In 1926, though, two categories were employed, one for Romanians who speak more or less standard Romanian and who live generally along the border areas adjacent to Romania, and another category, that of Kutso-Vlachs, whose dialect varies somewhat from standard Romanian and who live away from the border—mostly in the mountain regions.[29] Without going into particulars as to causes for such variations, it is this writer's opinion that the census of 1926 is more accurate in this respect and is probably to be preferred. Nevertheless, this variance in procedures used between the two censuses with respect to the Romanians can be confusing to the unwary or uninitiated.

6. Likewise, external migrations and exchanges of minorities have significantly changed the population data of Bulgaria.

In a large measure, then, these last four factors have had a profound effect upon the ethnic character of Bulgaria's population today.

Language and Ethnicity

Language and ethnicity sometimes differed in pre-World War II Bulgaria, and still do, because of historical and political factors. However, this difference was generally restricted to small groups within the larger ethnic minority. For instance, in 1905, the number of persons in Bulgaria for whom Greek was their mother tongue was 69,820, but of this number only 67,214 claimed Greek nationality. In 1910 this number was 50,889 versus 43,275 who said they were Greek; in 1920, the figure was 46,759 versus 42,084; and in the census of 1926, it was 12,782 versus 10,564.[28]

This apparent anomaly can be accounted for in several ways. In the Balkans, and especially near border areas, or where an ethnically hetero-geneous population exists, individuals may know several languages which they speak in varying degrees of fluency. Such cases are especially com-mon in the case of inter-ethnic marriages, where, for instance, the father might be Bulgarian, but the mother Greek. Such an individual could claim Bulgarian nationality through his father, but consider Greek his mother tongue. Moreover, before the days of careful record-keeping, it was fairly easy for persons of this type to "pass over" from one ethnic group to another, depending upon the political expediencies of the moment. "My father was a Greek, my mother was Romanian, but I am a Bulgarian" was not completely unknown—in earlier times at least.

However, the situation can be quite muddled even today. The writer knows a younger professional colleague who was born in Northern Greece, in the Macedonian part. His parents considered themselves Bulgarians and Bulgarian was the language spoken at home—albeit covertly. At the same time, all his education during this period was in Greek schools and he, of course, learned Greek fluently. All the influences outside the home were Greek. He was immersed in Greek culture, customs, literature, and thought. The Greek Civil War, at the end of World War II, brought con-siderable instability to his family; and when the partisan communist-led guerrilla movement collapsed, he and his parents fled the country. Passing through Bulgaria, they finally found refuge in Bucharest, Romania. There he learned Romanian and completed his studies, including undergraduate university work, in Romanian institutions. Except for his transit through Bulgaria from Greece to Romania, he has not lived a day of his life in Bulgaria, although in recent years he had made brief, occasional visits to the country. Yet, today, when the subject of his ethnicity is discussed, he considers himself neither Greek nor Romanian, but definitely Bulgarian.

The ethnic complexities of this region can be further illustrated by still another example. At one time, the Greek government was so anxious to incorporate the entire population along its northern frontier into its vision of "Greater Hellas" that it explained away many Slavs in this region as "bilingual Greeks."[34] Although the Bulgarians have, perhaps, never entertained such a position with regard to their ethnic minorities and have generally exhibited considerable tolerance toward them, it stands to reason that a Bulgarian in Bulgaria would stand the likelihood of having a better situation than a Greek. Hence, the tendancy for a few multilingual individuals to claim Bulgarian nationality.

Further, an individual's education sometimes was a factor. Again, in earlier times, especially, a person whose childhood language was Greek but who was educated in Bulgarian schools would most likely consider himself Bulgarian. Indeed, education and the ethnic schools were one of the most forceful means by which the various Balkan powers attempted to gain adherents to their national cause.

Religion and Ethnicity

Variants from the usual ethnic-religious patterns are generally due to other causes than those cited above. Missionaries, primarily American Protestant and French Catholic, attempted to gain adherents to their respective faiths. They established schools for the youth of the land, almost all of whom came from Orthodox homes. These schools—Western in their outlook and methodologies—were generally excellent for their times; fees were low and scholarships were available, making them especially attractive to poor Bulgarian youths. Religion accompanied secular learning in these insitutions and a significant number were converted to the theological doctrines of the schools. These converts and their descendants make up a sizeable portion of the small Protestant and Catholic bodies in Bulgaria.

Catholicism in Bulgaria also received impetus through the Act of Uniat which Dragan Tsankov, a Jesuit-educated Bulgarian, signed with the Pope in 1860.[35] This act was engineered in an attempt to break the hold of the Greek Patriarch upon the Orthodox faithful in Bulgaria. The movement briefly gained considerable momentum before it collapsed as a result of an Orthodox counterattack. Nevertheless, a remnant—which together with the subsequent converts of Catholic missionaries—formed the nucleus for Bulgarian Catholicism today, relatively insignificant though it is.

In addition, as noted earlier, there exists in Bulgaria a group of Bulgarians, known as Pomaks,[36] who are Muslims. Most are found in, or near, the Rodopi Mountains. Ethnically, this group is Bulgarian—to the degree such ethnicity can be established by historians and anthropologists. The language which this group speaks is Bulgarian, not Turkish. Nevertheless, the cultural customs, the religious practices and rituals, the familial patterns and the role of women are almost wholly Muslim, not Orthodox.

Population Migrations

The present ethnic character of the Bulgarian population has been shaped by numerous historical external migrations. In the recent years cited, the largest group to leave the country were the Turks, followed by the Armenians (cf Table VI). In this eleven year period (1965 to 1974 inclusive), 38,834 Turks left Bulgaria, emigrating almost entirely to Turkey. The relatively large number of emigrants notwithstanding, the absolute number of Turks in Bulgaria has remained relatively static—due to the natural population increase among this group. The Turkish ethnic nationality group has perhaps the highest birthrate of any in the country, rivaled only by the gypsies. The next largest emigrant group were the Armenians, 704 in number, most of whom probably went to Soviet Armenia—although the available statistical data does not document this point. A small number of Jews also left during this period—142 in all, the greater majority emigrating to Israel.

However, migrations to and from Bulgaria are nothing new. Located as it is between one of the great routes between East and West, Bulgaria has been the focal point of invasions and migrations throughout history. For the purposes of this paper, though, the most important shifts that have taken place since 1878 will be considered. Roughly, these may be divided into four: (1) the emigrations taking place from northern Bulgaria after independence in 1878 and subsequently from Eastern Rumelia in 1885 upon Bulgaria's annexation of this region; (2) the population shifts occurring after the Balkan Wars; (3) the transfer of populations taking place after World War I; and (4) the emigrations of certain minorities from Bulgaria after World War II. Each will be considered separately.

Bulgarian independence and her later annexation of Eastern Rumelia meant an end for the Moslems to their privileged position in the country. The *begs*—the rich, primarily Turkish landowners and nobles—suddenly found themselves at the losing end of a war, many of them hated by the

Bulgarian populace because of their previous cruelties and inhumanity. Deprived of land and previous privileges, most salvaged what they could and fled to Turkey. The less important Ottoman administrative officials generally also followed suit. A number of other Muslims, mainly Albanians and Tartars also left, many going to other parts of European Turkey or to Asia. The exact number of these emigrants is debatable, but as many as 100,000 may have gone.[37]

However, the larger number remained, primarily those who had been less privileged in the previous economic and political hierarchy. The fact that Bulgaria continued as a tributary principality under the suzerainty of the Sultan—albeit an autonomous one—(Bulgaria received independence officially only in 1908)[38] undoubtedly provided some feeling of security to this group.

Some Greeks also left at the same time, mainly merchants and clerics whose role had already been, or would be, displaced soon by Bulgarians. The number in this group does not appear to have been large, though, since the national economic and political rivalries between Greece and Bulgaria actually accelerated into sharper form later.

Although the border area between Yugoslavia and Bulgaria at Nish has at times been disputed with respect to the number of nationals of each country within the other's respective territory, and in 1885 was used as one of the pretexts for the launching of a war between the two nations, at present the situation has stabilized somewhat in this respect. The Serbo-Bulgarian War of 1885 did cause some Serbian nationals living in Bulgaria to leave; however, the number of Serbs there had never been large (a few thousand, at most), so that this emigration had almost an imperceptible effect upon the character of the Bulgarian population. Again, accurate statistical information in this regard is impossible to obtain.

Today, the Bulgarian minority in and around Dimitrovgrad in Yugoslavia (Dimitrovgrad is near the Yugoslav-Bulgarian frontier on the Belgrade-Nish-Sofia international highway) has been recognized, and elementary schools in their own langauge are provided for them. However, as shall be seen, Yugoslav recognition of Bulgarian nationals is restricted primarily to those Bulgarians living in this area only, since any extension to other points along the Yugoslav-Bulgarian border presents some complicated and delicate political problems.

A large number of minority groups in Bulgaria were affected in far mare significant ways by the Balkan Wars. The Treaty of Bucharest added 227,598 Bulgarians, 75,339 Pomaks, 275,498 Turks, and 58,709 Greeks to the existing Bulgarian population. At the same time, in ceding Dobruja to Romania, she lost approximately 273,000 people, making for a net gain of about 364,000.[34] Further, some of this number, mainly Turks and Greeks, left for their respective fatherlands shortly thereafter —as did also some of their co-nationals already in Bulgaria. According to official Bulgarian statistics, the number of persons in Bulgaria claiming Greek nationality dropped from 67,214 in 1905 to 42,084 in 1920.[35] During this same period, the absolute number of Turks increased from 488,010 to 520,339.[36] Since 275,498 Turks were added to the 465,641 already living in the country in 1910,[37] making a total of 741,139, this means that in the ensuing decade of the Balkan Wars and World War I about 221,000 left Bulgarian territory. This figure does not take into account those additional numbers that fled from the newly occupied territories of European Turkey. Lastly, the drop in the number of Romanians, from 78,429 in 1910 to 57,312 in 1920 can be accounted for largely by the Second Balkan War and the ceding of Dobrudja to Romania.[38]

The next great transfer of population took place after World War I as a result of the Treaty of Neuilly. According to the Greco-Bulgarian Mixed Commission created by this Treaty to regulate the exchange of minorities, almost all Greeks living in Bulgaria declared their intentions to emigrate to Greece. Between 1923 and 1928 when this population exchange took place, about 30,000 Greeks actually did so. In addition, another 16,000 left the country before the Mixed Commission had begun its work.[39] According to Bulgarian sources, themselves, the number of persons claiming Bulgarian Greek nationality dropped from 42,084 in 1920 to 10,564 in 1926.[40] By the time the exchange was ended, only a few thousand actually remained.

In the aftermath of World War II, further, significant changes took place in the composition of Bulgaria's ethnic minorities. Again, one of the groups affected were the Turks. Exact data regarding the post-war ethnic composition of Bulgaria's population is impossible to obtain. However, best estimates indicate that the number of Turks in Bulgaria dropped from a known figure of 618,268 (according to the census of 1934), to somewhere in the neighborhood of 440,000 in 1952—or from 10.2 percent of the total population to about 6 percent.[41] This was the result of the repatriation of Turks from Bulgaria to Turkey during the years 1950 to 1952. This exodus of Turks from Bulgaria has been continuing ever since, but at a much reduced rate. For instance, in the years 1970, 1971, and 1972, 11,018, 9581, and 10,465 Turks emigrated from Bulgaria to Turkey.[42] Undoubtedly, more of the Turkish population in Bulgaria would like to emigrate to Turkey, but this number has been restricted due to Turkish insistence that her economy cannot effectively absorb more newcomers. As it is now, only those with relatives living in Turkey are generally granted emigration visas. Some small emigrations have also taken place to Lebanon and Iran, but it is not clear whether these were Turks. However, it may be that some were because of the affinity of these lands in culture, history, religion, and customs to the Turks of Bulgaria.

The Jewish element of Bulgaria's population has also declined following World War II as a result of emigration almost *en masse* to the State of Israel. For many centuries Jews had formed an important part of the Bulgarian population, being involved primarily in small mercantile enterprises and increasingly in the professions. Most of Bulgaria's Jews were descendants of Spanish Jews who had fled Spain in the days of the Spanish Inquisition. Finding refuge in the Mediterranean port cities of the old Ottoman Empire, they gradually moved inland establishing thriving businesses in all of the major towns and cities. These Jews of Bulgaria did, in fact, manage to preserve much of their ancient heritage. Old Spanish was used as the language of discourse among them, the old traditions brought by their ancestors from Spain were followed, and their religious customs were generally strictly observed in their homes and synagogues.

Thanks to the intervention of King Boris, the Greek Orthodox Patriarch, and the Bulgarian people, despite the fact that Bulgaria sided with the Axis in World War II, and despite some very "close calls," not a single Bulgarian Jewish citizen lost his or her life in Hitler's gas chambers, although they were interred in concentration camps in Bulgaria. The situation, alas, was not so "fortunate" for the Jews in Macedonia under Bulgarian occupation who were turned over to the Germans almost to the last person and practically all of them were executed or lost their lives in the concentration camps of Germany and Poland.[43] Because of their precarious position in Bulgaria during the war, most decided to emigrate to the new State of Israel almost as soon as Israel came into being.

Other important minorities of Bulgaria's population affected by the events of the immediate post-World War II period were Russians, Czechs, Slovaks, Armenians, and Gypsies. Most of the Russians in Bulgaria were White Russians who had fled Russian after the Russian Revolution. Some stayed in the country awhile and then made their way West. When the Soviet Armies swept into Bulgaria at the end of World War II, some of those remaining (perhaps 3,000) were able to flee to the west, but the larger number (about 13,000) were arrested by the Soviet and many apparently were executed or forcibly returned to the Soviet Union.[44] Except for Soviet advisory, technical, and military personnel on temporary assignment in Bulgaria, few Russians live there any longer today.

Czechs and Slovaks, some of whom were Protestant Lutherans who had come to Ottoman Bulgaria in the 18th century to escape Catholic persecution were few in number, living in their own peasant villages. After the Second World War, most were forced to return to the country of their ancestral origin.

Bulgaria had a number of Armenians living in the country—as has been noted. Most fled the oppressions of the Russians during the nineteenth century, and then the Turkish atrocities and communist oppression of the early 1920s. As a result, the number of Armenians in the country increased from 11,500 in 1920 to 27,300 in 1926.[45] Many continue to live in Bulgaria. However, some emigrated to other countries, using Bulgaria as a way station, for the number dropped to about 23,500 by 1934.[46] About 1000 returned to Soviet Armenia in 1947, during the great post-War exchange of populations.

Along the boundary of Dobrudja there still live some Tartars, descendants of those who had left the Crimea in 1861, following the Crimean War. Near Varna, Gagauz are to be found, a group whose members speak Turkish but who at the same time profess the Eastern Orthodox faith. Neither of these two groups has ever been very large and each probably does not number more than a few thousand today.

Gypsies have been an element of Bulgarian life for centuries, having accompanied the Turkish conquerors as they swept over the land in the fourteen century. In 1926, 134,844 persons were of this ethnic group.[47]

About 75 percent are Moslem and the rest adhere to the Greek Orthodox faith. They have their own spoken language, Romany, with its various dialects which are spoken by most of the clans throughout Europe. Today, almost all those in Bulgaria also know Bulgarian, although this has not been true in the past. The annexation of Dobrudja to Bulgaria in 1940 added about 8,000 more gypsies to Bulgaria's population.[48]

Presently, the Bulgarian government has sought to end the nomadic ways of the gypsies and has succeeded to a large extent. Those who have acceded are to be found in the larger cities as permanent residents and are engaged in some occupation—although some of the old cultural patterns, such as begging, remain to some degree, especially among children. Families continue to be large; the level of education generally remains at the lowest level permitted by government policy; and their poverty relative to the rest of the population is still great. As a result, most today live in the slums of cities and towns.

Gypsies who insisted upon maintaining their traditional nomadic way of life, who refused to adapt a non-nomadic life style, or who opposed the policies of the Bulgarian government were foribly settled to work on agricultural enterprises in Northern Bulgaria located primarily in the Danubian plain. Although current statistical figures for this ethnic group are lacking, their birthrate still appears to be higher than that of the country as a whole. Large families, poor living conditions, and unhygenic practices possibly tend to cause a higher death rate also. Education also still appears to be given a lower priority by more members of this ethnic group than is the national average for the population as a whole. Thus, gypsy children apparently often still tend to meet only the minimum state attendance and schooling requirements, thus perpetuating the poverty cycle.

The Macedonian Question

The ethnicity of the group known as "Macedonians" has been one that has become a real issue primarily in recent years—after the Second World War. It is one on which numerous polemics have been issued by both the Bulgarian and Yugoslav goverments.

The factor that brought the whole matter to a head was the creation of a constituent Macedonian Republic within the new Yugoslav Federation toward the end of the Second World War. The foundation for the creation of the Republic was laid at the Second AVNOJ (Anti-Fascist Council for the National Liberation of Yugoslavia) late in November 1943.[49] At the meeting which was held at Jajce, AVNOJ was proclaimed the "Supreme Legislative and Executive Organ and the Supreme Representative of the sovereignty of the nations of Yugoslavia as a whole."[50] In so doing, the legal status of the Yugoslav Government-in-Exile in London, King Peter, and General Draža Mihajlović, leader of the Chetniks, was denied.

As the self-proclaimed government of Yugoslavia, the Anti-Fascist Council then declared that henceforth the new Yugoslavia would be "built up on a federal principle which would insure full equality for the nations of Serbia, Croatia, Slovenia, Macedonia, Montenegro, and Bosnia and Hercegovina."[51] Through this act, the Macedonians were promised equal status in any new post-War government led by Joseph Broz Tito and the Yugoslav Communists. The next year, on August 2, 1944, the anniversary of the Macedonian Illinden Uprising in 1903 against the Turks, an Anti-Fascist Assembly of National Liberation of Macedonia (ASNOM) was held at the monastery of Saint Prohor Pohinjski. The Assembly forthwith proclaimed the Macedonian People's Republic as an equal unit in the federal system of Democratic Federative Yugoslavia.[52]

As has been noted, Bulgarian interest and involvement in Macedonian affairs has been strong from her creation as a nation. Indeed, the Treaty of San Stefano included almost all of Macedonia within a Greater Bulgaria. The Congress of Berlin, though, forced Bulgaria to relinquish much of historic Macedonia back to the Ottoman Empire.[53] Ever since that time, Bulgarian irredentist nationalism has sought by diplomatic and military means to include Macedonia within Bulgaria. To a large extent it was this ambition that was responsible for Bulgaria's involvement in the First and Second Balkan Wars, in World War I, and in World War II.

However, at the time of the ASNOM pronouncement, Bulgaria was in a choatic state because of the war. The events in Yugoslavia regarding Macedonia passed by with hardly a Bulgarian notice. In fact, there was little concern about the matter even after the communists had established their power in Bulgaria and the situation there had stabilized.

There were several reasons for the lack of immediate Bulgarian concern. (1) Communist parties allied with the Soviet Union had assumed power in both Bulgaria and Yugoslavia. Flushed with victory, the communists in both countries also tended to view potential problems between them in a fraternal sense. (2) In any event, the Soviet [i.e., Stalin's] decision would be final on the matter. (3) This camaraderie was reflected in the fact that Dimitar Vlahov, a verteran of the Internal Macedonian Revolutionary Organization [IMRO] [54] who had become a Bulgarian communist became the first president of the fledgling Macedonian republic, a member of the Yugoslav Central Anti-Fascist Council, and a vice-president of the Federal Presidium in 1946. (4) George Dimitrov, the Bulgarian Premier, and Marshall Tito of Yugoslavia were old communist "comrades in arms," having been involved in the activities of the Cominform, and were personal friends as well. Even after Tito's break with the Kremlin, this friendship served until Dimitrov's death, as a moderating influence with regard to the Macedonian question. (5) Historically in the 1920s and 1930s the Bulgarian Communist Party officially favored a federation of Balkan states; the reasons for this policy are many, but probably had to do primarily with party strategy (to minimize dissension and maximize its base of support from all factions). Accompanying this policy was a corollary one which proclaimed separate Thracian, Macedonian, and Dobrudjian states within the proposed federation. [55] The factor of expediency which brought about the policy notwithstanding, upon their ascent to power both Tito and Dimitrov exerted considerable initial effort—albeit unsuccessfully—for the creation of such a Balkan Federation. Hence, in such a union, the "Macedonian Question" would have become passe, with Macedonia being a state or part of one of the other states within the Federation.

As a result, in 1946, the Bulgarians took a census in which individuals of Macedonian origin, particularly those living in the Pirin region of southwestern Bulgaria were encouraged to label themselves Macedonians. [56] Indeed, this procedural policy was a direct result of the decisions regarding the Macedonian question which were reached at the Tenth Plenum of the Central Committee of the Bulgarian Communist Party. [57] In such a case it was assumed by many that the Macedonians of both Bulgaria and Yugoslavia would be reunited in the form of a new Macedonian state within the Federation.

However, following Dimitrov's death in 1949 in a sanitarium near Moscow, where he had gone presumably for treatment, [58] and Tito's break with the Kremlin, the matter of a Macedonian minority in Bulgaria was soon forgotten. The results of the 1946 census on this question were subsequently never made public.[59]

After the Fifth Congress of the Bulgarian Communist Party in 1948, and especially after the April Plenum of the Central Committee in 1956, the Party began to take the position which it holds to the present that Macedonians are ethnically Bulgarians. Even so, as late as the 1956 census, Bulgaria counted a Macedonian population of 187,789 within her borders, of which 178,862 (95.3 percent) lived in the Pirin region where they constituted 63.8 percent of the population. However, by the 1965 cenus, only 8,750 individuals in all of Bulgaria listed themselves as Macedonians. In the Blagoevgrad Okrug, where the largest percentage of persons had previously declared themselves "Macedonian," the number had dwindled to approximately one-half of one percent.[60]

Concerning the "Macedonians," the *Kratka B"lgarska Entsiklopediya* (*Short Bulgarian Encyclopedia*), both in its 1966 and 1974 editions, states the following:

> . . . the Bulgarian inhabitants in the historic area, Macedonia;
> . . . the main inhabitants of the Socialist Republic of Macedonia in SFRY (Socialist Federated Republic of Yugoslavia). . .[61]

Interestingly enough, the 1963 edition also contains an article on the "Macedonian Language" (Makedonski ezik), but in the 1974 edition, the entire section was omitted.

Whether the "Macedonians" of Bulgaria are Bulgarians or a minority nationality in Bulgaria then continues to be debateable. Thus, the history of the concept "Macedonia" indeed is quite complicated and involved, and dependent more on the politics of a particular period than perhaps on the actualities. A definitive study of the problem remains to be written, and the question calls for resolution.

Bulgaria's problems regarding the rise of nationalism among minority ethnic groups in the Balkans have not been too great—certainly nothing comparable to those of her neighbor, Yugoslavia. There have been several reasons for Bulgaria's "good fortune" in this respect.

Emigration has been one of the "solutions" employed in dealing with the problem, as in the case of Jews and Turks. Repatriation has been another means, and the Greeks and Romanians who were sent to their respective countries in past population exchanges are prime examples. Lastly, integration has been still another method used, as with the Gypsies and Macedonians—assimilation and a denial of differences (rightly or wrongly) having been made a part of a rather successful official state policy.

These efforts have produced a relatively ethnically homogeneous state. Though minorities continue to live in Bulgaria, and they represent a number of different groups, in terms of the total population they are not sizeable. In this way, Bulgaria has been able to weld her people into a relatively unitary national state.

TABLE I

ESTIMATED POPULATION OF BULGARIA BY NATIONALITY
BEFORE THE LIBERATION
(c. 1870)[a]

Bulgarians		1,500,000	
Osmanli Turks		500,000	
Tartars		80,000 to	100,000
Circassians		70,000 to	90,000
Albanians		60,000 to	70,000
Romanians		35,000 to	40,000
Gypsies		20,000 to	25,000
Jews	about	10,000	
Armenians	about	10,000	
Russians	about	10,000	
Greeks		7,000 to	8,000
Serbians		4,000 to	5,000
Germans, Italians, Arabs, etc.	about	1,000	

a. After data in *The Encyclopedia Britannica*, Vol. IV, Ninth edition. (Chicago: R. S. Peale Company, 1891), p. 516. This data is for the vilayet of Tusa or the province of the Danube (although the two do not absolutely coincide), a political division of European Turkey, which became more or less Bulgaria proper after her liberation in 1878. It does not include Eastern Rumelia which later was annexed by Bulgaria. The data thus is limited and suspect to some extent but is perhaps the best estimate available.

TABLE II

ESTIMATED POPULATION OF BULGARIA
Record of the Census of January 1, 1893 [a]

Bulgarians	2,505,326
Turks	569,728
Romanians	62,628
Greeks	58,518
Gypsies	52,132
Spanish-speaking Jews	27,531
Tartars	16,290
Armenians	6,445
Germans and Austrians	3,620
Albanians	1,221
Russians	928
Czechs	905
Servians	818
Italians	803
Not specific	3,820

a.   John Scott Keltie, ed., *The Statesman's Year-Book; Statistical and Historical Annual of the States of the World for the Year 1901.* (London: Macmillan and Company, 1901), p. 1143.

TABLE III

POPULATION OF BULGARIA IN 1910[a]

Bulgarians	3,518,756
Turks	465,641
Romanians	79,429
Greeks	43,275
Gypsies	122,296
Jews	40,133
Germans	3,402
Russians	2,505
Other nationalities	62,076

a. John Scott Keltie and M. Epstein, ed., *The Statesman's Year-Book: Statistical and Historical Annual of the States of the World for the Year 1921.* (London: Macmillan and Co., Limited, 1921), p. 728. This data is from the census of December 31, 1910.

Of the new population added after the Balkan Wars (i.e., as a result of the Treaty of Bukarest), 227,598 were Bulgarians, 75,337 were Pomaks (Bulgarian Moslems), 275,498 Turks, and 58,709 Greeks, making a total of 637,142. Since about 273,000 of the inhabitants of Dobruja were passed to Romania, the total gain to Bulgaria was about 364,000. Ibid., p. 727.

TABLE IV

THE POPULATION OF BULGARIA
by Religious Adherence[a]

Religious Group	1934 Census		1952 Estimate	
	Absolute Number	Percentage of Total Population	Absolute Number	Percentage of Total Population
Eastern Orthodox	5,130,000	84.4	6,538,000	89.07
Moslems	821,000	13.5	700,000	9.54
Catholics	46,000	0.8	57,000	0.78
Protestants	8,000	0.1	10,000	0.13
Jews	48,000	0.8	3,000	0.04
Others	25,000	0.4	32,000	0.44

a.   After L. A. D. Dellin, *Bulgaria* (New York: Frederick A. Praeger, 1957), p. 77.

TABLE V

STATISTICAL DATA CONCERNING THE POPULATION OF MACEDONIAa

Statistics and Publications	Nationality of Statistician	Year	Total Number of Population	Bulgarians	Greeks	Serbs	Vlachs	Turks	Albanians	Gypsies	Jews	Miscellaneous
V. Teploff-Statistical data concerning Bulgaria, Thrace and Macedonia (in Russian), Petersburg, 1877.	Russian	1877	1,479,417	1,172,136	190,047	(1) 41,284	63,895		12,055			
St. Verkovitch-The Ethnography and Topography of Macedonia (in Russian). Petersburg, 1889.	Serbian	1889	1,949,043	(2) 1,317,211	222,740		74,375	240,264	78,790	10,568	(3) 1,612	3,483
Prof. G. Weigand-The National Struggle of the Balkan People. Leipzig, 1898.	German	1898	2,194,000	1,200,000	220,000		70,000	695,000			9,000	
Dr. Cleantis Nickolaidis-Macedonia. Berlin, 1899.	Greek	1899	1,820,500	454,700	656,300		41,200	576,600				91,700
Professor Vasil Kantchew	Bulgarian	1900	2,258,225	1,181,336	228,703	700	80,767	499,204	128,711	54,557	67,840	16,407
Nue Constantine-The Rumanians-Koutzovlachs (Arumanians), Bucharest, 1913.	Rumanian	1913	2,200,527	512,000	153,000	21,700	(4) 350,000	1,030,420	12,000	25,000	65,600	2,807
Robert Pelletier-The Truth of Bulgaria. Paris, 1913	French	1913	1,437,000	1,172,000	190,000		63,000		12,000			
Richard von Mach-Der Macht-bereich der Bulgarischen Exarchat in der Turkei. Leipzig, 1906	German	1906	1,334,827	(5) 1,166,070	95,005		56,118		6,036	8,550		3,048
Vladimir Sis-Macedonia. Zurich, 1918.	Czech	1918	2,173,849	1,047,012	204,367		67,865	520,845	184,300	43,100		106,360
Official Turkish Statistics-Published in the Salonica Newspaper "ASR," No. 2, January, 1905.	Turkish	1905	2,903,920	(6) 1,203,696			(7) 199,717	1,500,507				
Prof. Yordan Ivanoff-The Macedonian Question, Historically, ethnographically, and statistically. Paris 1920.	Bulgarian	1912	2,342,524	1,103,111	267,862		79,401	548,225	194,195	43,370		106,360
Leon Dominian-The Frontiers of Language and Nationality of Europe (Published by the American Geographical Soc. of New York), 1917.	American	1917	(8) 1,438,084	1,172,136	190,047		63,895		12,006			

Remarks to Table V.

(1) These Serbs are of the Vilayet of Kossovo, north of Shar Mountain.
(2) In this number are included also the Bulgarian Pomaks (Bulgarian Mohammedans).
(3) The author has omitted to mention in this number the Jews of Salonica, Kavala, Veria, Bitolia and Kostour.
(4) In this number are included also the Bulgarian Pomaks.
(5) In this number are included also the Bulgarian Patriarchists.
(6) The Serbs included in this number are of the Kossovo Province which is north of Shar Mountain.
(7) L. Dominian gives statistical data only about the Christian population of Macedonia.

a. After Christ Anastasoff, "The Case for an Autonomous Macedonia" (Indianapolis: Published by the Central Committee of the Macedonian Political Organization of the United States and Canada, 1945), pp. 1 and 2.

For a criticism of these statistics, as well as of the Greek position in this controversy, see George E. Mylonas, *The Balkan States* (St. Louis, Missouri, the author, 1946); and Char. K. Soteropoilou, *Apantesis pros Vorran* (Athens: publisher not stated, 1962). The latter volume is especially critical of present Yugoslav claims regarding the population of Macedonia. Since this study reviews the problem of minorities here as Bulgarian policy perceives it, the Bulgarian data has been cited herein.

TABLE VI

EMIGRANTS FROM BULGARIA
1948 to 1961
by Ethnic Group[a]

Year	Bulgarians	Turks	Gypsies	Armenians	Jews	Russians	Others	Totals
1948	366	35	—	1	15401	1	35	15839
1949	132	1525	—	8	19118	3	779	21565
1950	105	55746	15	19	1038	4	466	57393
1951	27	98252	—	13	1088	—	97	99477
1952	36	—	—	2	463	—	14	515
1953	28	—	—	10	346	—	16	400
1954	6	6	—	5	199	—	26	242
1955	433	—	—	52	147	133	55	820
1956	19	4	—	139	109	47	52	370
1957	54	1	—	58	38	2	122	275
1958	1	1	—	27	56	4	19	108
1959	5	2	—	27	49	10	36	129
1960	14	1	—	32	102	13	19	181
1961	3	1	1	15	57	2	5	84

a. After data in the article "B"lagariya," in B"lgarska akademiya na naukite, *Kratka b"lgarska enstiklopediya*, vol. I (Sofia: Izdatelstva na b"lgarskata akademiya na naukite, 1963), p. 342.

TABLE VII

EMIGRANTS FROM BULGARIA
1964 to 1974[a]

Countries to Which Emigrants Went	1965	1966	1967	1968	1969	1970	1971	1972	1973	1974
Austria					1					
German Democratic Republic	1									
German Federal Republic	1	1	1							
Greece		3	2							
Romania			1							
USSR				1						
Turkey				1	2529	11018	9581	10465	5259	1348
France		4	1							
Czechoslovakia	1	1		1						
Sweden								2		
Yugoslavia				1		1				
Israel	7	89	7		1	6				
Lebanon	32	34	70	317	161	6				
Iraq		4								
Canada				1						
United States of America		5		5						
Brasil			2							
Australia				4	1					
Other Countries							11	90	1	
Totals	42	141	85	330	2693	11031	9594	10555	5260	1348

Grand Total for the Ten Year Period, 1964 to 1974 is 41,115. With a total population of 8,227,866 as of December 31, 1965, this makes roughly 5 percent. Of this number, the largest, by far, are the immigrants to Turkey and Lebanon—presumably Turks—or in the case of Lebanon also Armenians.

Countries specifically mentioned as being the recipients of no emigrants from Bulgaria during this period are: Belgium, Great Britain, Italy, Poland, Hungary, Switzerland, or any other country of Europe not mentioned above, Argentina and Paraguay.

a. After Narodna Republika B"lgariya, Ministerstvo na informatsiyata i s"obsheniyata, *Statisticheski godishnik na Narodna Republika B"lgariya* (Sofia: the author, 1975), p. 66.

NOTES

1. Narodna Republika B"lgariya. Ministerstovo na informatsiyata i s"obshteniyata, *Statisticheski godishnik na Narodna Republika B"lgariya, 1975 [Statistical Yearbook of the People's Republic of Bulgaria, 1975]* (Sofia: D"rzavno izdatelstvo, Nauka i izkustvo, 1975), p. 66.

2. L. A. D. Dellin, editor. *Bulgaria.* (Mid-European Studies Center of the Free Europe Committee, Inc., Frederick A. Praeger, 1957), pp. 75-77. A more recent estimate puts the figure of national minorities in Bulgaria at 1,200,000 out of a total population of 8,706,000 (census of December 31, 1974), or 13.8 percent. See John Paxton, ed., *The Statesman's Year-Book: Statistical and Historical Annual of the States of the World for the Year 1976-1977* (New York: St. Martin's Press, 1976), p. 797. The true figure probably is somewhere between these two estimates. Although no hard statistical data is available on the subject, it is commonly accepted knowledge that certain minorities, such as the gypsies, Turks, and Pomaks, have a higher birth rate and larger families than do the Bulgarians. It would stand to reason, therefore, that their numbers are likely to be increasing in proportion of the total population. Hence, this may account —in part, at least—for the difference between the older and more recent estimates.

3. People's Republic of Bulgaria. *Constitution.* Article 35, paragraphs 2 and 4, and Article 45, paragraph 7.

4. For a detailed historical study of this group, see Kiril Vasilev, *Rod opskite b"lgari mokhamedani [The Moslem Bulgarians of the Rhodopi Mountains]* (Plovdiv: D"rzhavno izdatelstvo, Khristo G. Danov," 1961).

5. The exact characteristics which constitute a nation have been subject to considerable debate among political scientists, historians, and kindred scholars of the problem. According to Ernest Renan,

A nation is a soul, a spiritual principle. Two things which are really only one go to make up this soul or common principle . . . . The one is the possession in common of a rich heritage of memories. And the other is actual agreement, desire to live together, and the will to continue to make the most of the

joint inheritance. The existence of a nation is a daily plebis-
cite . . . ."

(Quoted in George E. Mylonas, *The Balkan States: An Introduction to
Their History* [St. Louis, Missouri: Eden Publishing House, 1946], p.
194).

Wolfgang Friedmann states the matter in a slightly different way by
providing a series of characteristics more or less in common to all nations.
He writes as follows:

> . . . Unity of race, of language, of territory, of religion, of gov-
> ernment, of economic interests. . . [and] the possession of a
> common tradition, a memory of sufferings endured and victories
> won in common, expressed in song and legend, in the dear names
> of great personalities. . . , in some combination make a nation.

(Wolfgang Friedmann, *The Crisis of the National State* [London: Macmillan, 1943], pp. 5-6).

Professor Carl Becker also has noted:

> A common language does not by itself make a nation, because
> the people of England and the United States speak one language
> but form two nations, and the people of Switzerland speak three
> languages and form one nation. All we can say is that a nation is
> a group of people who feel that they are enough like each other
> and enough unlike other groups so that they wish to live under
> their own law and government.

(Carl Becker, *Modern History* [New York: Silver Burdett Company, 1946],
p. 9). Given all these factors, presented in so conflicting and ambiguous a
manner, it becomes obvious that a concise, absolute definition of the word
nation, and concomitantly *nationality* is impossible. In part, this explains
the conflicting loyalties, the rival attempts by the Balkan powers to
"nationalize"—especially in the past—those elements of the indigeneous
population possessing little or no national awareness. Perhaps, then, the
best summary definition of nation is a group that possesses most of the following attributes—and especially the last one enumerated: a continguous

territory, a common historical past; a culture and tradition; a religion (or lack of it); a language; and a near universal belief that the particular group constitutes a nation.

6. Institut za istoriya pri BAN, *Makedonskiyat v"pros [The Macedonian Question]* (Sofia: the author, 1968), p. 30.

7. G. P. Genov, *Bulgaria and the Treaty of Neuilly* (Sofia: Hristo G. Danov, 1935), p. 130.

8. See Stephen P. Ladas, *The Exchange of Minorities: Bulgaria, Greece, and Turkey* (New York: Macmillan, 1932), p. 120ff.

9. See Frederick B. Chary, *The Bulgarian Jews and the Final Solution, 1940-1944* (Pittsburgh: University of Pittsburgh Press, 1972).

10. Eugene K. Kecfe, et al., *Area Handbook for Bulgaria* (Washington: U.S. Government Printing Office, 1974), p. 58.

11. Based upon informal conversations with Bulgarian Jews which the writer has had. See also Keefe, *Area Handbook,* p. 58 and L. A. D. Dellin, *Bulgaria,* p. 76.

12. Dellin, *Bulgaria,* p. 77.

13. *Ibid.*

14. *Statisticheski godishnik,* 1975, p. 66.

15. M. Epstein, ed., *The Statesman's Year-Book: Statistical and Historical Annual of the States of the World for the Year 1939* (London: Macmillan, 1939), p. 755 indicates 23,976 Armenias-Georgians. See also, Bernard Newman, *Bulgarian Background* (London: Robert Hale, 1961), pp. 187-188; and—for a historical review—Sir Charles Eliot, "The Armenians," in *Turkey in Europe* (London: Frank Case, 1965), pp. 382-414. Eliot's work concludes with the year 1907 and does not include subsequent developments regarding the Armenians as an ethnic group.

16. Hugh Seton-Watson, *Eastern Europe Between the Wars, 1918-1941* (Cambridge: Cambridge University Press, 1942), pp. 269-272.

17. Andrew Gyorgy, *Governments of Danubian Europe* (New York: Rinehart, 1949), p. 28.

18. R. H. Osborne, *East-Central Europe* (New York: Frederick A. Praeger, 1967), p. 92.

19. For instance, in some areas, only men were counted; in others both men and women; and in still others, the entire population.

20. It was common practice in certain areas to omit certain male members of the family, since a special tax was levied upon them in lieu of military obligations from which they were exempted as Christians.

21. It was common at the time for certain of the Orthodox inhabitants of the Ottoman Empire to change nationalities with the changing material inducements, as the Balkan States rivaled each other for advantage in the Empire.

22. James Baker, *Turkey* (New York: Henry Holt, 1877), pp. 11-12.

23. *Ibid.*, p. 20.

24. Vasilev, *Rodopskite b"lgari mokhamedoni.*

25. See for instance Mylonas, *Balkan States,* pp. 183-193.

26. J. Scott Keltie, ed., *The Statesman's Year-Book: Statistical and Historical Annual of the States of the World for the Year 1911* (London: Macmillan, 1911), p. 672.

27. Genov, *op. cit.,* pp. 144-147; and George Clenton Logio, *Bulgaria Past and Present* (Manchester: Sherratt and Hughes, 1936), p. 269.

28. Genov, *Bulgaria,* pp. 129-130.

29. Mylonas, *Balkan States,* pp. 188, 227.

30. Mercia Macdermott, *A History of Bulgaria: 1393-1885* (New York: Frederick A. Praeger, 1962), pp. 141, 157-158, 282-332.

31. Osborne, *East-Central Europe,* p. 92; and Vasilev, *Rodopskite.*

32. See Dellin, *Bulgaria,* p. 76; Keefe, *Area Handbook,* pp. 57-58; and Ladas, *Exchange of Minorities,* p. 706.

33. *Great Soviet Encyclopedia* (A translation of the third edition), Vol. III (New York: Macmillan, Inc., 1973), p. 556.

34. J. Scott Keltie, ed., *The Statesman's Year-Book: Statistical and Historical Annual of the States of the World for the Year 1921.*

35. Genov, *Bulgaria,* p. 130.

36. *Loc. cit.*

37. *Statesman's Year-Book, 1921,* pp. 727, 728. Apparently, in the five years between the census, 1905 and 1910, about 22,500 Turks had left the country, for their absolute numbers had dropped from 488,010 to 465,641.

38. *Ibid.,* p. 727 and Genov, *Bulgaria,* p. 130.

39. Ladas, *Exchange of Minorities,* pp. 121-122 and James Barros, *The League of Nations and the Great Powers* (Oxford: Clarendon Press, 1970). The latter volume describes the Greek-Bulgarian border incident of 1925, which added fuel to the already smoldering resentments, and its resolution.

40. Genov, *Bulgaria,* p. 130.

41. Dellin, *Bulgaria*, p. 76.
42. Narodna Republika B"lgaria. Ministerstvo na informatsiyata i s"obshteniyata, *Statisticheski godishnik na Narodna Republika B"lgariya, 1975*, p. 66.
43. Chary, *Bulgarian Jews.*
44. Dellin, *Bulgaria*, p. 77.
45. Genov, *Bulgaria*, p. 130.
46. *The Statesman's Year-Book, 1939*, p. 755. The Armenians in Bulgaria almost all follow the Armenian-Gregorian church rite. Catholicism and much of traditional Protestantism holds that Christ had two natures, divine and human, both independent, and both in his person. Thus he could choose to do wrong, but did not. The Bulgarian Armenians, along with their co-nationals and co-religionists in other countries are Mono-physites—that is, the Christ's human nature is merged in his Divine nature in such a way as the two become one, so that his human nature chooses good automatically. In this belief, they distinguish themselves both from the Eastern Orthodox Church as well.

Prior to World War I, most Armenians in Bulgaria and the Ottoman Empire were under their Patriarch at Constantinople. Since that time, the Bulgarian Armenians formed their own, independent archbishopric which was given autonomus status by the council of Echmizdzin in 1928. For further information see "The Armenian Rite" in the *New Catholic Encyclopedia*, vol. I (New York: McGraw Hill, 1967), p. 835, as well as other related articles cross-referenced in it.

47. Logio, *Bulgaria Past and Present*, p. 269.
48. Dellin, *Bulgaria*, p. 76.
49. Stephen E. Palmer, Jr. and Robert R. King, *Yugoslav Communism and the Macedonian Question* (Hamden, Connecticut: Archon Books, 1971), pp. 100-101.
50. *Ibid.*, p. 100.
51. *Ibid.*
52. *Ibid.*, p. 111.
53. D. Kossev, et al., *A Short History of Bulgaria* (Sofia: Foreign Languages Press, 1963), pp. 220-221.
54. Palmer and King, *Yugoslav Communism*, pp. 101-103; 107.
55. *Ibid.*, pp. 19-46.
56. *Ibid.*, p. 15.

57. Institut za istoriya pri BAN, *Makedonskiyat v"pros*, pp. 36-37.

58. J. F. Brown, *Bulgaria Under Communist Rule* (New York: Praeger Publishers, 1970), p. 22. The situation under which Dimitrov died has led to speculation in some quarters.

59. Palmer and King, *Yugoslav Communism*, pp. 15 and 229.

60. *Ibid.*, pp. 191 and 240.

61. B"lgarska akademiya na naukite, *Kratka b"lgarska entsiklopediya*, Vol. III (Sofia: the author, 1966), p. 325; and B"lgarska akademiya na naukite, *Entsiklopediya: A-YA* (Sofia: the author, 1974), p. 465.

Zelime Amen Ward

V

MINORITY POLITICS IN THE
GERMAN DEMOCRATIC REPUBLIC:
PROBLEMATICS OF SOCIALIST LEGITIMACY
AND NATIONAL AUTONOMY

Entangled between two diverse as well as fundamentally antithetical goals, the self-image of the German Democratic Republic today is in a state of flux.* At one end of the political spectrum, socialist legitimacy, i.e., public recognition and confirmation that the former Soviet zone of occupation has been transformed since 1949 into an orthodox member of the communist community, must be pursued. At the other end of the spectrum, the central concern is national autonomy, that is, the prerogative to look toward and act in favor of specific national interests and to have the validity of the pursuit of those exclusive interests acknowledged by other states. including those of the communist community.

Where the balance will fall between the two goals, which in their extremes are mutually negating, is undetermined, for the ideological dilemma is a recent one. During the early decades of the GDR, the obeisance of the state to schoolbook socialism and to the Soviet model preempted any possibility of confusion about long-range national goals. The Soviet prototype was closely followed, an endeavor at which the

* The author gratefully acknowledges the invaluable commentary of M. Donald Hancock, Vanderbilt University, during the preparation of this chapter.

GDR became so adept that by the 1960s, it was recognized as the arch-typical socialist state in Eastern Europe.

By 1967, however, the Stalinist "system-building" phase of commun-ism and post-Stalinist (revisionist) "system-management" phase[1] were completed in East Germany. At the Seventh Party Congress of the Social-ist Unity Party (SED), the arrival of the GDR at the plateau of an ad-vanced socialist society was proclaimed, and in the wake of that accomp-lishment, the GDR began to navigate toward a future that had no detailed dimensions or structural prerequisites. "New theoretical questions"[2] emerged in the GDR, and as the challenges to theoretically unilinearity began to multiply, especially in Eastern Europe, it became apparent that there was no single prototype of mature communism.

The present trek of the GDR beyond the advance proclaimed in 1967, and toward a developed socialist state[3] appears to be neither desultory nor determined. The GDR is politically, socially, economically and inter-nationally a "work in progress." A new self-image is being fashioned, but the contours of its ultimate facade are blurred.

Can any recent change be discerned in the ideological direction of the GDR? The immediate and most politically astute response to the question of future direction reverts back to the nation itself, to the need for a transition from the restrictive Soviet mold to an East German social-ist variant that incorporates the concept of national autonomy. As in the cases of other Eastern European nations, the existence of the GDR as a unique embodiment of advanced socialism, rather than as merely another homogeneous spin-off of the Soviet model, can no longer be denied.

This newly recognized "nationalist" orientation pays homage not so much to a farsighted leadership as to a national populace (penetrated in part by the Western emphasis on nationhood) that will not quiescently accept historical oblivion in the name of Soviet socialism. For their part, however, East German political leaders have acknowledged the imminence of change. As a method of both shoring up the wizened political system and guaranteeing a measure of control over future options, they have begun to construct an ideology that merges the concept of national autonomy with that of socialist legitimacy.[4] The new ideological pattern, although not clearly outlined, is primarily an extrapolation of germinal historical trends and of present conditions in the East German polity.

Nationalism

In its sense of national awareness and historical self-consciousness, Germany always has stood in a uniquely strong position.[5] The spirit of nationalism has fostered public vigilance in Germany toward the comparative standing of the nation among its neighbors as well as internationally. This same spirit at times has produced an exaggerated pride in national accomplishments as well as an obdurate refusal to recognize national failings. The history of German development since the formal unification of the nation in 1871, particularly as that history emanates from the shadow of the late but aggressive process of German industrialization during the successive four decades, has included intense public commitment on the part of a large segment of the German populace to regimes as ideologically-focused and as disparate as the Empire under Bismarck's chancellorship, the Weimar Republic, Nazi totalitarianism, and the two postwar German showcases of socialism and capitalism.

After the formal division of Germany in 1949 into an eastern and a western segment, the intensity of the ideological burden, imposed through political engineering by the U. S. and the U. S. S. R. to garner national attachment to yet another ideology, continued. In both German states, albeit more thoroughly and expansively in the GDR, any abiding sense of nationalism was to be replaced *in toto* through reeducation programs in schools, at the work place, at home and in the media. As West Germany strove to become the premier example of capitalist democracy in Europe, the GDR pursued an ardent course toward a Marxist-Leninist democracy.

By the mid-1960s, each of the two Germanies was heralded as the most prominent embodiment in Europe of their respective ideological orientations, and as the two nations heightened their standing in terms of ideological exactness, they also were becoming recognized as twentieth-century symbols of advanced industrial polities.[6] In spite of contrasting ideologies, both German societies were becoming meccas of technology. (Nor was the German public insensitive to these developments.)

Concurrently, fissures began to erupt in the monolith images of both the capitalist West and the communist East, eroding the fraternal harmony of the two ideological camps. Fervor for a capitalist or Marxist-Leninist ideology became subjected to national competition within each bloc, an event which further helped to rekindle the latent sense of national pride.

For the East German citizen specifically, who had been summoned during the immediate postwar period not only to subjugate his or her empathy toward German tradition and culture with an international ideology but in fact to deny that tradition, sublimation rather than denial had ensued. During the 1950s, East Germans did indeed officially proclaim their socialist citizenship to the exclusion of their German heritage. But the shift during the 1960s toard retrieving that heritage, and the continual seeking of a self-identity thereafter, attest to the impossibility of engineering, for intellectual and emotional attachments to the past, a *tabula rosa* similar to the structural effacement that epitomized a defeated Germany.

Alternative Future Ideologies

Within the ambit of the recoursing of nationalism in the GDR, there appear to be three major alternative routes toward which the public sense of nationalism may be directed. First, the emergence of national pride could produce a form of xenophobia reminiscent of earlier periods in German history, in particular the racial prejudice of the Nazi period.

Second, national self-esteem could connect an additional element to the extant communist ideology without noticeably changing the basic ideological components. The end product would resemble that of any other mixture, whether physical or abstract. The components, nationalism and Marxism-Leninism, would intermingle and complement one another yet remain substantially unaltered, in that no singular new element was produced. The characteristics of ideological development in the GDR, in this case, would comprise merely a summation of the characteristics of the two component ideologies.

Third, nationalism could play a more active role in ideology and policy. Rather than merely attaching itself to the Marxist-Leninist framework, nationalism would interact with Marxism-Leninism so as to effect a basic transformation. A singular new ideological foundation would be created, a foundation that constitutes more than just the sum of the parts ensuing from a mixture. The transformed foundation would extend beyond the traits of the two component ideologies, became a new and inseparable ideological unit, and provide a patently changed and enhanced direction for ideological development in the GDR.

Which of these courses toward nationalism will be pursued in the GDR as it moves toward a new stage of socialism that incorporates socialist legitimacy with national autonomy is an enigmatic issue. It is doubtful that any long-term decision of future balance has yet been made by the communist leadership of the GDR.

There are, however, several significant indicators of the ideological future. These include:

(1)   the configuration of the political culture, with the historically-rooted values, beliefs and attitudes that it reveals;

(2)   the process of political socialization, i.e., the teaching and instilling of political norms, through which the contents and lessons of the political culture are both reinforced and revised, for present use and for the future; and

(3)   the status of minority politics in the GDR.

This last indicator is particularly relevant, as it provides an objective gauge of the strength of the bifurcated goals of nationalism and socialism.

Three groups are central to minority politics in the GDR today: Sorbs (who constitute the only sizeable ethnic minority), foreign workers, and political dissidents. An analysis of the latitude that is made available to these minorities in both gaining recognition and advancing their specific group interests reveals, in broad strokes, the present course of ideology as well as the ideological future that is projected by the political elite. On one hand, the prohibitions and allowances that circumscribe the status of ethnic minorities, i.e., the Sorbs and foreign workers, signal the intensity of nationalism as a dominant ideology. On the other hand, variations in the treatment of political dissidents suggest the degree to which Marxism-Leninism remains the paramount ideological source.[7]

The Reemergence of Germanic Culture

For the communist leadership of the GDR, the pitfalls of exposing sterile socialist doctrine to multicolored historical traditions appear to be outweighted by the advantages. Especially during its first decade, the East German public had regarded the new nation as only a truncated section of the homeland of the Germanic peoples; there was a popular reluctance, in not unwillingness, to identify with the GDR rather than with prewar "Germany" as a unified whole.

During the 1960s, a striking transfer of public allegiance to the new East German state, which incorporates a population of 17,000,000 on 42,000 square miles, occurred. Problems of popular loyalty, however, were not wholly eliminated, and today during the late 1970s, they again are mounting. In particular, history and nationalism, as a source of allegiance, are being reexamined, despite the official position that:

> The nation has. . .no special meaning that lies beyond that of the capitalist or socialist society; [the nation] is not the embodiment and unfolding of a national spirit, a *Volk* spirit, or similar idealistic constructions. Moreover it is the definitive processes of the given economic social-unit that have come to have the most significant meaning for national life and the nation.[8]

The reawakening of popular interest in ethnic and national cultural backgrounds, a phenomenon that began simultaneously in a number of western nations during the societal relapses of the 1970s, has had mutual spillover effects across most industrial nations. Perhaps as a response to the monolithic sameness of industrial technology, or perhaps as a tributary of the wellspring of anomie and alienation produced by lost battles of the 1960s, political retrenchment and right-wing recidivism, the populations of most industrial societies now are embarking on a new search for their origins and traditions.

The East German response to this search has been a cautious reopening of history, including programs of public education on Prussian history, the Bismarckian era and the Nazi period. Although these programs will inhibit the promulgation to the public of a doctrinaire approach toward socialist history, they may be a strong asset to the political elite as it attempts to court and maintain public allegiance and to allay feelings of unrest about the past.[9]

The decision by the communist leadership to revise history and explore cultural traditions is a gamble, but one in which the bets are hedged. Only selected periods of history will be reawakened for the public, and in no case will strongly conflicting interpretations and perspectives be presented. Public education still will involve basically a singular orientation toward history, with flexibility of interpretation only on minor points. East German citizens will not have the opportunity to evaluate a variety of fundamentally differing perspectives.

Since the process of political socialization continues to be rigidly delimited and controlled by the political leadership, allowing no latitude for public assessment, the new orientation toward doctrine and history appears less pertentous. It represents at best a type of *controlled change,* in which there is a marked movement of public attitudes without intellectual ferment.

A significant part of recent changes is oriented toward Prussia, which once was the largest and most prominent of the German states. During late 1978, a television series, consisting of five one-hour segments focused on Prussia, was aired on five consecutive Friday evenings. The heroic period from 1806 to 1815 covering the uprising of Prussia and its alliance with Czarist Russia against Napoleon was portrayed with verve and adulation. Prussian generals such as Gerhard von Scharnhorst, the army reformer (for whom the series was named), and Carl von Clausewitz, the military philosopher, were depicted as heroes, reformers and concerned leaders.

East German history texts probably will follow suit. In *Forum,* the SED publication for university students, communist historian Ingrid Mittenzwei contends that Prussia constitutes a significant part of German history and should not be casually dismissed as "reactionary." She argues for a less uniform historical perspective, i.e., that German history includes "the good with the bad, revolt and innovation together with submission and acquiesence" and that "in the history of a nation there are not just great hours of success." More pointedly, as an indication of change in the official historical outlook, Mittenzwei maintains that "even the ruling classes contributed to social development" and that "confusion in people's minds must be dispelled."[10]

A further indication of the new focus on German (vs. socialist) history was the official East German response to placing GDR cosmonaut Siegmund Jaehn on a Soviet space mission during the fall of 1978. The mission was hailed with the slogan: "the first German in space is a citizen of the German Democratic Republic."

Political Socialization

During the past century, with the brief exception of the Weimar period, the population of East Germany continually has had to adapt to the rigors of an authoritarian state or dictatorship. In addition, the postwar era, with its hardships and political subservience, endured much longer for the East Germans than for West Germans.[11] Consequently, East Germans, to a greater extent than their brothers and sisters to the West, have found some of the traditional German values continually reinforced. These include order, discipline (especially in the interest of the community), and hard work.

> The society of the GDR is to be understood largely through that aggregation of life styles, behavior patterns and value judgments that have been perceived as German by Germans throughout their history and that characterizes them as Germans in the eyes of their neighbors . . . It [East German society] values order, hard work and conscientiousness; it has a weakness for *Gemuetlichkeit* . . . and is ready to adapt and to submit to discipline for the sake of some highly esteemed virture.[12]

These values fit socialist ideology, yet in the East German case are not derived from that ideology but rather from early German traditions. For the population of the GDR, socialist ideology is affirmed and maintained by the activation of traditional German values and attitudes. Although not officially promulgated, nationalism, as an elemental part of the traditional values, also plays a role, albeit a rather ambivalent one, in the support of Marxism-Leninism.

Throughout the 1950s, the public had a very limited sense of pride in, or belongingness to, a distinct society and culture. For the average citizen of the GDR, there was a gulf between the pervasive socialist ideology and reality. A socialist consciousness had not developed. At best the Marxist-Leninist ideology was externally accepted; it was not an integral part of life.

During the 1960s, the East German gradually began to identify himself or herself with a unique state and social system; there was a growth of self-awareness and of a sense of national individuality. There also were other, more significant factors which helped make the GDR appear, to its citizens, to be lawful and just and to guarantee personal security and prosperity. These included:

(1)   the transition away from the devastating conditions of the immediate postwar period;

(2)   the demise of Stalinist cohesion and repression;

(3)   the building of the Berlin Wall in 1961, which eliminated hopes for a rapprochement with western capitalism and allowed the GDR to concentrate on internal societal development;

(4)   the exposure of the Golden West, during the 1960s, as largely a myth; and

(5)   the outstanding economic and social achievements of the GDR, including the rise to the top as the most industrially progressive nation of the eastern bloc and as the most prosperous in terms of standard of living.[13]

This last factor is perhaps the most critical. East Germans, for example, are justifiably proud of their education system, which they believe to be more equitable and more effective than that of the FRG.[14] In fact, East German achievements in education and in sports have garnered for the fledgling socialist nation considerable international renown. East Germans also show high esteem for their system of health services, guaranteed employment, and social security and believe that their political system ensures greater social equality and justice than does the capitalist West German system.

The growth of a positive orientation toward what appear to be the realities of East German society has activited and reinforced the socialist ideology, as have the traditional German values that are coterminus with socialist values (e.g., order, hard work, discipline, and a sense of community). The citizen of the GDR is finding it less difficult to identify with the state and its ideological underpinning, not because of the content of the ideology, but primarily because the socialist ideology overlaps in part with early German tradition, as well as due to political developments that have given East Germans a sense of pride in their "new" nation.

The significance of tradition and political realities in promoting public acceptance of Marxism-Leninism is underscored by the diminution by the populace of socialist values that are not related to the Germanic tradition.

It is questionable, in particular, that the industrial or agricultural worker is more positively oriented toward the political system because it follows the ideological contours of a "workers' state." For the East German worker, rather than being aware of an abstract commitment to a "workers' state," it is of greater importance to receive a fair wage, to have good working conditions, to have a voice in decisions at the work place, and to have both the means and the time for individual leisure activities. For citizens of the GDR, there has not been a "social failure of economic success."[15]

Today socialism in the GDR is no longer simply a sterile combination of institutions and ideology. In a specifically German variant, Marxism-Leninism has been internalized by East Germans. The economic system is regarded as the cornerstone of the social system, which itself is based on the work ethic as a central category not only in Marxist anthropology but also in the Germanic cultural heritage. In sum, the social structure of the GDR is an amalgam of early Germanic traditions and the new sense of Marxist-Leninist ideology which has been gradually merged into the public consciousness.[16]

Linkages to the Process of Minority Politics

In many respects, German history is a compendium of conflict between divergent ethnic minority groups and the German majority. The first-century Germanic tribes described by Tacitus were scattered; other groups were interspersed among the *Germanii*. The "First Reich," which endured for more than a millenium, from 800 to 1806 under Charlemagne and his successors, was continually beset by problems of ethnic diversity. Alsace-Lorraine, for example, still constitutes a source of antagonism between France and Germany. After the defeat of Napoleon and the restoration to Prussia of some of its former territories, the Congress of Vienna in 1815 created the German Confederation. This comprised a weak amalgamation of states with differing customs and linguistic proclivities. The Confederation was subjected to further internal division by the ongoing competition between Austrians and Prussians for supremacy.

The more recent history of Germany, since its establishment as a nation in 1871 until the postwar era, has included ethnic rivalries and internal dissension between Prussians and non-Prussians, as well as among the various regional groups, from Bavarians to Rhinelanders. In addition, the infamy of Aryan persecution of the Jews under Hitler has added a gnarled and perverted dimension to the history of German ethnic and racial strife.

Yet the contemporary facade of German society, particuarly for the German Democratic Republic, is not tied to pressures from minority ethnic groups. After World War II, Germany was segmented into zones of occupation according to plans developed at Yalta and later was divided formally into two distinct political systems. However, it was at the Potsdam Conference during July and August 1945, when the eastern section of prewar Germany was truncated with finality, that the major question concerning the representation of ethnic minorities was resolved. With the transfer to Poland of the Oder-Neisse territories, which during the 1940s had included a five percent Polish minority (a decline from 15 percent in 1910), and the ensuing migration westward from those territories of approximately four million ethnic Germans, the question of large ethnic minorities in Germany became a moot issue. This was true particularly of the Soviet-occupied sector, which in 1949 was granted partial sovereignty and established as the German Democratic Republic.[17]

In the GDR today, popular attitudes toward ethnic minorities, as well as toward political dissidents, have been determined by three broad sets of experiences:

(1) By the German historical experience, including the traditional values of order, disciplined work, subservience of the individual to the community, and German nationalism. In both Germanies during the past decade there has been a resurgence of nationalism and, although more muted, of arrogance toward other peoples and cultures.

(2) By popular indoctrination to the political system and Marxist-Leninist ideology. This has been accomplished through comprehensive and interwoven government policies of political socialization in educational institutions, at the work place, in the home, and even in state-supported programs for leisure activities.

(3) By political developments, including the problems of adaptation to an advanced industrial society. Technological growth has placed strong emphasis on the traditional German values, such as the work ethic and personal sacrifices for the sake of the community, thereby denigrating the

worth of the divergent historical experiences and cultural views of other
ethnic groups. The ideological battle that has been waged between the
two Germanies and the East German focus on competition with other
eastern-bloc nations also have reinforced Germanic values. The lesson
learned by citizens of the GDR through their tandem growth in the
economy and rise in status has not been lost. For a large part of the
populace, the maintenance of what is perhaps a vaunted sense of superiority appears to be tied to the continual strengthening of the early German
cultural traditions. Other political developments that influenced popular
attitudes toward minorities and dissidents include the elimination of
economic and emotional poverty that dominated the postwar years,
the demise of Stalinism, the building of the Berlin Wall, the exposure
of the myth of the Golden West, and, together with rising economic
prosperity, the social achievements of the GDR in education, sports,
employment, health and social security.

The Sorbs

Today the Sorbs, a Slavic people, constitute the only significant ethnic
minority claiming East German citizenship.[18] The term "Sorb" frequently
is used synonomously with "Wend" or "Lusatian," as the Wends of
Lusatia, in the southeastern region of the GDR, represent the only contemporary descendants of the Sorbs. In ethnicity, the Sorbs are related
most closely to the West Slavs and the Serbs. Ethnically, linguistically
and culturally, the Sorbs also are related to their neighbors, the Poles
and the Czechs. Yet the Sorbs constitute a separate ethnic entity, with
their own language, history, culture and traditions.

Population estimates for the Sorbs, most of whom reside around
Bautzen, Hoyerswerda and in the Spree Forest, vary. According to a
West German source, there are between 35,000 and 70,000 Sorbs in
the GDR.[19] An East German source states, however, that in the bilingual
areas of the GDR, approximately 100,000 Sorbs reside among 500,000
Germans.[20] In any case, the Sorbs are declining in number.

In German, the terms *lausitzer* and *lausitzisch* have never been applied
specifically to the Sorbs. Prior to 1945, the popular and widespread
reference to the Sorbian population was that of *Wende* or *wendisch;* the
words *Sorbe* and *sorbisch* were rarely used. In the GDR today, however,

the use of *Sorbe* and *sorbisch* is replacing *Wende* and *wendisch*. This is required by the GDR for all official publications and encouraged by the government for use in the vernacular.

A major thrust behind the government emphasis on *Sorbe* and *sorbisch* was the disparaging identification of the *Wende* as someone who was inept and awkward. Ethnic puns and slurs about the *Wende* were derived from the verb *wenden* ("to turn") and the plural of *die Wand* ("the wall"), *die Wände*. Derogatory linguistic usage is part of the process of socialization to community norms, and it is to the credit of the GDR that it has attempted (with considerable success) to eradicate the slurs and the prejudice they represented.

It is unclear whether Germans or Slavs first occupied the territory between the Oder and Elbe, but the peoples who inhabited the lands east and west of the Oder until about 400 B.C. probably were not Slavs. Beginning at the end of the third century (when Germans did inhabit Lusatia), with the emerging fissures in the Roman Empire, the Germanic peoples moved westward, gradually deserting the territory between the Elbe and Oder. Thereafter, during the sixth and seventh centuries, the Slavonic peoples, who were previously located east of the Oder, migrated to, and settled, the territory vacated by the Germans. The Sorbs of Lusatia are now the only remaining descendants of these early Slavonic tribes.

Beginning in the eighth century, however, and continuing through the twelfth, the balance began to shift as successive waves of German invaders and colonists swept eastward across the Elbe into Slavonic lands, those of the Sorbs as well as of other Slavonic peoples. As a consequence, even a century ago, the Sorbs were characterized as a little Slavonic island in a German sea.[21]

Today the Sorbs not only are isolated, as the analogy infers, but also beset with inner fissures. Lusatia has no political or recognizable natural boundaries, and not all of Lusatia is inhabited by Sorbs. Running from south to north, stretching lengthwise across Lusatia, is the Spree River. Its upper reaches contain Upper Lusatia; the lower reaches, where the river divides into multitudes of separate streams, cover Lower Lusatia and include the Spree Forest, denoted by Sorbs as the Marshes (Błota). To the south of Lusatia, the Sorbs are separated from the Czechs by a broad strip of territory whose inhabitants for centuries have been exclusively German-speaking. To the east, Sorbian territory previously had included regions on the right bank of the Neisse, but these were germanized early in this century and later came under Polish hegemony when the new boundaries were established after World War II. Today the most easterly Sorbian dialect, that of Mužakow (Muskau) is extinct, and pressures for assimilation bode the further decline of the cultural and linguistic heritage.

Although most of the towns in Lusatia have always been predominantly German, there were, prior to 1945, many villages that were exclusively Sorbian (albeit with Germans as political administrators and police). However, many of the Germans who were expelled in 1945 from territories to the east of the Oder-Neisse and from the Sudentenland were resettled in Lusatia. Thereby the villages began to lose their Sorbian exclusivity, as the towns became even more heavily German. Today there is no single village with an exclusively Sorbian population. The highest proportion of Sorbs is in the Kamenz area, northwest of Bautzen, where Sorbian is the accepted vernacular language and German is the exception. The population is predominantly rural and Catholic. There is a somewhat similar predominance of Sorbs and Sorbian customs in two other area (near Hoyerswerda and in the northern Bautzen area), but the remaining bilingual areas are mixed, with both German and Sorbian in use. Indeed many previously Sorbian areas have been almost completely germanized. Younger generations are being quickly assimilated by the surrounding German culture and language. Beyond the rural Catholic villages, the sound of a child speaking Sorbian is a rarity.

Today Bautzen, the traditional capital of Upper Lusatia, has a population of 44,000, of whom about 1000 are Sorbs.[22] Cottbus, which lies on the Spree, has a population twice that of Bautzen (i.e., 80,000) and is the major town of Lower Lusatia. Yet the population of Cottbus today is almost exclusively German.[23]

The official stance of the SED toward ethnic minorities follows the broad policy guidelines of the Soviet Union (guidelines, moreover, that were adopted at an earlier point in time by Czechoslovakia and Yugoslavia). Extensive cultural autonomy is guaranteed to minorities, whereas special privileges are denied. Yet the reality of minority politics in the GDR does not always fit the theoretical mandates. East German policy toward the Sorbs is ambiguous; it is in some respects supportive of the Sorbian culture and in other respects antagonistic to it. This is typical of the pattern for most of Eastern Europe:

> Since the Party regimes in Europe could not avoid inheriting the ethnic diversity of previous governments, there remains a nervous sensitivity to the divisive potential of ethnic/national identity. The lack of consistency in minority politics is symptomatic of nagging suspicions about the power of language and culture to unite large ethnic groups against the central regime.[24]

On March 23, 1948, the Landtag of Saxony passed the Act for the Protection of the Rights of the Sorbian People, which authorized the founding of Sorbian-language schools, the use of Sorbian in official proceedings and the appointment of Sorbian officials. (The right to use Sorbian in official proceedings, however, is rarely exercised beyond the local level.) The Act was strengthened on September 9, 1950, by a law providing more explicit support for the Sorbian population and its traditional culture.

Article 11 of the Constitution of October 7, 1949, made explicit that:

> Through legislation and administrative action, the foreign-speaking parts of the population of the republic are to be encouraged in their free ethnic development; in particular, they may not be obstructed in the use of their mother-tongue in matters of education, internal administration and legal processess.[25]

This guarantee was similar to that provided in Article 113 of the Weimar Constitution, a proviso which remains, however, largely unrealized. The 1968 Constitution of the GDR, as well as the constitutional revisions of 1974, in Article 40 provide guarantees to the Sorbian population of the GDR that are less explicit than those set forth in the original Constitution:

> Citizens of the German Democratic Republic of Sorbian nationality have the right to cultivate their mother-tongue and culture. The exercise of this right is to be guaranteed by the state.[26]

According to a noted analyst, "the precise wording of such legislation may be relatively unimportant."[27] Yet the fact remains that in 1968, when the GDR was beginning to pursue "new theoretical questions," a basic change was made in the official government stance toward the Sorbian population. The change removed explicitness and thereby part of the strength of the guarantees contained in the original document. Such a major change in phrasing cannot but portend the intent, at least on the part of the communist leadership, to weaken the future thrust of programs designed to promote Sorbian cultural autonomy.

The Sorbian areas of Lusatia are located within the administrative districts (*Bezirke*) of Dresden and Cottbus. Within these two *Bezirke*, a number of administrative regions (*Kreise*) have been officially designated as "bilingual."[28] Government documents and publications in these *Kreise* are printed in both Sorbian and German. Local government meetings as well as judicial proceedings may be conducted in Sorbian. In general, German is to be used throughout the judicial system in the GDR unless an involved individual cannot speak German. A Sorb, however, always is guaranteed the right of using his or her native language in the courts of law, even if he or she is fluent in German. Other concessions to the special rights of Sorbian citizens also are made in the educational system, the communications media, the arts and academic research.

At the national level, there is at least token symbolic political representation for the Sorbs. Within the Ministry of Culture of the GDR, there is an Advisory Commission for Sorbian Questions. Among the 500 members of the People's Chamber (*Volkskammer*) are four Sorbian deputies, of whom three are women, and previously one member of the State Council (*Staatsrat*) of the GDR, Marja Krawcec, was Sorbian. This latter position, however, is of marginal significance, as the State Council, which originally "occupied a supreme and unchallengeable position in the areas of domestic and external affairs" has been shorn of its most important functions and "has experienced a loss of symbolic and real authority over the past several years."[29] This change was made evident particularly by the 1974 revision of the 1968 Constitution. Sorbs also have representation on the *Bezirk* councils of Dresden (with nine Sorbian deputies and Cottbus (with 18 Sorbian deputies), as well as within local governments of the twelve bilingual *Kreise* (i.e., approximately 2000 local Sorbian office-holders).

Yet the interest and commitment of the present national political leadership to the Sorbian people is lukewarm at best. Among national leaders, only Wilhelm Pieck, the first president of the GDR, demonstrated any genuine concern for the status of the Sorbs.

Sorbs have an SED-regulated ethnic movement, the Domowina, which was founded in 1912 and, after being banned by the Nazi regime in 1937, was reestablished in 1945. The major function of the Domowina is to nurture the development of a Sorbian ethnic consciousness. The Domowina is strongest in rural villages, where it has active local branches, although there are also branches in major Lusatian towns. In university and student towns beyond Lusatia, i.e., Leipzig, Berlin, Dresden, Magdeburg and Freiberg, there are special local student branches of the Domowina.

The most obvious effect of Domowina influence is in the educational system at the local level, where there is frequent and close contact between the local Domowina branches and the Sorbian schools. In addition, parents' committees at the schools include Domowina representation.

In 1966 and 1968, the Domowina organized a Festival of Sorbian Culture, comprising a series of concerts, films, plays, folk music and sports activities. The festivals were covered by the various media and further publicized by exhibits at the local level. Whether these festivals, however, helped to promulgate the Sorbian culture is questionable. Especially to the younger generation, much of Sorbian culture, as encapsulated through a time-constrained "festival" period, may appear to be a strange although fascinating rural anomaly within the development of a bustling urban East German technocracy.

Since 1951, the Domowina has held intermittent national meetings, i.e., the Union Congresses, several of which have been attended by delegations from the Central Committee of the SED. In general, however, the Domowina appears to be gradually losing members as well as public support. There was a pronounced waning of strength during the 1950s, when the Domowina, under SED pressure, endorsed the industrialization of Central Lusatia and agricultural collectivization (measures which were highly unpopular among Sorbs and in rural Lusatia).[30] Since that time, there has been a slow tapering of grass-roots membership.

A variety of educational facilities provides opportunities for preserving the Sorbian language and culture. In bilingual areas, parents may send their children either to a school where Sorbian is the primary language

SORBIAN REPRESENTATION ON GOVERNING BODIES*

BILINGUAL ADMINISTRATIVE REGIONS	Volkskammer November 14, 1974	Bezirkstag[1] November 14, 1974		Kreistag[2] Election Date			Town/Community Council May 19, 1974		
	D+ SC	D+ SC	Mem: StCm	D+ SC	Cncl Mem	Mem: StCm	D+ SC	Bgm	Mem: StCm
Cottbus Bezirk									
1. Calau	—	2	2	3	—	3	38	4	60
2. Cottbus-Land	—	2	2	17	1	21	329	15	491
3. Cottbus-Stadt	1	3	3	5	—	5	—	—	—
4. Forst	—	—	—	2	—	2	20	1	52
5. Guben	—	—	—	5	1	4	43	2	84
6. Hoyerswerda	—	7	6	32	4	32	449	19	624
7. Luebben	—	—	—	1	1	—	14	—	9
8. Spremberg	—	1	1	6	1	6	22	1	11
9. Weisswasser	—	3	2	13	1	11	197	11	315
Senftenberg[3]	—	2	1	—	—	—	—	—	—
TOTAL	1	20	17	84	9	84	1112	53	1646
Dresden Bezirk									
1. Bautzen	3	11	11	31	1	35	390	33	424
2. Kamenz	—	1	1	15	—	14	160	8	286
3. Niesky	—	—	—	6	1	5	33	2	51
Dresden-Stadt[3]	1	1	—	—	—	—	—	—	—
TOTAL	3	13	12	52	2	54	583	43	761

Dresden and Cottbus *Bezirke*

TOTAL	4	33	29	136	11	138	1695	96	2407

Wissenwertes ueber die Sorben. Nach Stichworten geordnete Information zu den wichtigsten Fragen ueber das Leben der sorbischen Bevoelkerung. 2nd rev. ed. (Bautzen: VEB Domowina-Verlag, 1976), p. 3.

1. Between 160 and 200 delegates are selected by the voters in each *Bezirk* on "District Day" (*Bezirkstag*). These delegates, in turn, determine the composition of the District Council.

2. Between 45 and 120 delegates are selected by the voters in each *Kreis* on "Region Day" (*Kreistag*). These delegates, in turn, determine the composition of the Regional Council. The data on this table for the *Kreistag* include the City Delegate Assembly of Cottbus.

3. Senftenberg and Dresden-Stadt are not official bilingual administrative regions.

Abbreviations: D+SC: Delegates and Successor candidates; Mem:StCm: Membership on Standing Committee; Cncl Mem: Council Member; Bgm: *Buergermeister*.

of instruction (an "A" school) or to a school where Sorbian is taught as a language while all other instruction is in German (a "B" school). In many cases, the children of German parents attend Sorbian classes in the "B" schools; indeed in some areas, the proportion of children attending Sorbian classes in the "B" schools is increasing. This may be due to the recognition that bilingual children have an expanded potential for learning other languages, or to the ease with which a Sorbian-speaking student can learn Russian (which is a required language in all East German schools). In any event, the positive attitude toward Sorbian demonstrated by many Lusatian German parents has helped to erode past prejudices and enhance the standing of Sorbian traditions in the respective Lusatian communities.

The Sorbian language also is employed in other educational institutions, including kindergardens, vocational schools, business academies (*Betriebsakademien*), and people's high schools (*Volkshochschulen*). In Bautzen and Cottbus, there are Sorbian high schools (*Oberschulen*); in Drosta (in the Bautzen district), a Sorbian home-people's high school (*Heimvolkshochschule*); and in Bautzen, a bilingual German-Sorbian people's theater. For adults and seniorschool graduates, further instruction in Sorbian is available at the two Central Sorbian Language Schools in Disschen and Milkel.

In Lusatia, there are over 500 bilingual school instructors. Those who teach in kindergarden and in the lower school grades obtain the Sorbian language qualifications that are required in Sorbian areas at the Sorbian Institute for Teacher Training in Bautzen. Instructors of Sorbian at the senior-school level are trained in Sorbian language and literature at the Sorbian Institute at Karl-Marx University in Leipzig, which is the only Sorbian-oriented institute of higher education in the GDR. The advanced study of Sorbian language and culture is further supplemented by research at the Slavonic Institutes of the Academy of Sciences of the GDR in Berlin, as well as at the Sorbian Ethnological Institute in Bautzen. Despite these provisions, younger generations are becoming increasingly divorced from their cultural heritage, and opportunities for education in the Sorbian language and culture already are beginning to exceed the demand.

The Domowina People's Press, which was founded in 1947 and came under state control in 1958, is overwhelmingly the major publisher of Sorbian literature, including books, periodicals and newspapers. Its services to the Sorbian literary community have been immeasurable. In addition, the Writers Union of the GDR includes a Study Circle or Sorbian Authors, and the periodical *Neue Deutsche Literatur* occasionally publishes a selection of Sorbian writings in German translation.

The Sorbian daily newspaper, *Nowa Doba* (New Era), published in Bautzen, is written in the Upper Sorbian dialect and includes international and national news. *Nowy Casnik* (The New Newspaper) is a weekly written in Lower Sorbian and containing only reports of local events.

The first radio transmissions in Sorbian originated in Dresden in 1949. Four years later, *Radio DDR,* a state radio network, established a separate Sorbian section, which has been located in Cottbus since 1957. During the past two decades, the weekly Sorbian transmitting time on the network has been extended from one and one-half hours to five hours. Yet even this extension is far from adequate, and the East German television network, *Deutscher Fernsehfunk,* provides no regular programming in Sorbian.

Although there are some counter-trends, such as the increased tendency of German parents to enroll their children in Sorbian language courses, the growing vitality of the Domowina Press, and the mildly expanded Sorbian allotment of Sorbian radio transmissions, the broad spectrum of present conditions augurs an uncertain future. The state is seeking a new direction for East German socialism, one in which Sorbian interests are marginal, if even extant. Concomitantly, for the average Sorb, immersed in an expanding "German sea," the incentives for maintaining an interest in one's ethnic identity are slowly evaporating. The general waning of the Sorbian/Wendish culture and the integration and assimilation of its people within the German mainstream may be attributed primarily to four factors:

(1)   The shift of national theoretical focus to a new stage of socialist transformation. As manifested by the new constitution of 1968 and its 1974 revisions, the GDR is moving toward a new plateau of development based on heightened economic coordination and advanced technological growth, with decreased latitude for the diversity represented by Sorbian cultural interests.

(2)   The renewed recognition of, and expanded emphasis on, the Germanic culture and heritage of East Germans. As the ideological shift

is made from socialism to germanic socialism, further strains are placed on the already beleaguered Sorbian culture.

(3)   The political and economic (and also social) disadvantages that accrue to an individual who maintains a Sorbian identity. Although the state supports Sorbian educational and cultural institutions, it does not provide more than political tokenism. Significant and even minor political decisions and changes are made exclusively by the Germany majority. Economic issues also are decided by the overriding German majority at all levels of state and party government. These developments cannot be disregarded in particular by the younger generations of Sorbs who now are planning their future careers and lifestyles.

(4)   The increasing migration of ethnic Germans into previously homogeneous Sorbian areas. This includes the post-1945 resettlement of expelled Germans as well as migrations due to the fast-paced growth of industrial concerns in Lusatia. The GDR has vast supplies of brown coal. The Black Pump Combine, which is the largest brown coal processing plant in the world for producing electricity and gas, is located in the middle of Lusatia, between Spremberg and Hoyerswerda, on what is probably the largest brown coal deposit in Europe. Economic planning in the GDR calls for intensified exploitation of the brown coal deposits. In consequence, employment opportunities in Lusatia have surged and so also has its German population. The town of New-Hoyerswerda, for example, was built exclusively to house the industrial workers and their families, who are overwhelmingly German.[31]

Foreign Workers

Beyond the question of a divergent ethnic group among its citizenry, the GDR faces another issue of minority politics: the expanding body of foreign workers. During the mid-1960s, when between 30,000 and 40,000 persons, primarily Poles and Hungarians, joined the work force in East German industry, foreign workers became a recognizable minority. By the end of 1972, there were 13,000 Hungarian and 12,000 Polish workers in the GDR. The Polish workers include border-crossers as well as approximately 6,000 assembly line workers who are sent to the GDR through contracts with Polish firms. The Hungarian workers are employed on the basis of a 1967 Agreement, which was extended in 1970, between Hungary and the GDR. They are largely young skilled workers, drawn by the opportunity for career development or by the higher wages, and they usually remain in the GDR for three years. However, an increase in the number of Hungarian workers, as provided in the Agreement, will be difficult to attain. In fact, Hungary, due to its own labor-market problems, has barely been able to arrange the present trasition of workers.[32]

Only 0.5 percent of all those who are employed in the GDR are foreign workers. Consequently, they have not had a significant impact on the East German labor market, which has a severe shortage of skilled and semi-skilled workers. According to official statements, however, there are no plans to increase the number of foreign workers in the near future.

Between East German citizens and the foreign workers, there is a sense of tension which is manifested primarily in social discrimination. In spite of mutual membership in the socialist community of nations, relations between East Germans and the ethnically different foreign workers are worsening. The situation has been exacerbated, in particular, by the growing focus on Germanic nationalism (albeit within a socialist framework).

In addition, there is the dilemma of differing policies among Marxist-Leninist states toward "liberalization" of their political systems. Young foreign workers from "liberal" Hungary, for example, encounter difficulties in adapting to the more rigidly authoritarian structure of the GDR, thereby provoking a negative reaction from the German communities in which they reside.

Political Dissidents.

The advent of a third minority issue, the question of political dissidents, was signaled by the 1953 workers' revolt, but there was a waning of popular dissent during the 1960s, in conjunction with the gradual accretion of legitimacy to the new German socialist state. Today, however, political dissent is again on the rise. For a small but vocal minority, dissent involves an open public pronouncement; for a larger group of East Germans, it is voiced privately and manifested more subtly through political apathy and alienation.

Among dissenting intellectuals, there are, at one end of the political spectrum, those who critique the present social order, yet maintain the delicate balance between perfunctory loyalty and open heresy. At the other end of the spectrum are those who have become a strong and recognized voice of nonconformity and change.

Within the first group,[33] are the revisionists of the early to mid-1950s, constituted primarily of academics who, within a Marxist-Leninist framework, explored new political alternatives to the prevailing orthodoxy. These included philosopher Ernst Bloch and followers of the Hungarian philosopher and literary critic György Lukács. Lukács' writings, such as *History and Class Consciousness*,[34] were the first to move systematically from Marx back to Hegel, substituting Marx's proletariat for Hegel's *Geist* as a carrier of historical consciousness. Physicist Robert Havemann (who later emerged in a position of strong open dissent) and other natural scientists, who, during the "physicists' strife" from 1953 to 1956 attempted to reconcile Marxism-Leninism with the principles of experimental science, also numbered among the revisionists. Others included members of the "Harich-Gruppe" within the SED, who advocate "humanistic renewal."[35] Critics of the 1960s and early 1970s whose work received public recognition and government neutrality if not acclaim included cyberneticists Georg Klaus and Uwe-Jens Heuer, whose writings advocate reduced central party and state power in favor of decentralization and expanded individual decisions ("self-regulation"),[36] as well as authors Ulrich Plenzdorf and Volker Braun, who explore the distress of those unable to conform to the prevailing ideological and social norms.

A major and abrasive source of dissent are the intellectuals who openly have declared their disaffection. The 1975 Helsinki Accords, with their "third basket" pledging adherence to human rights (to which the GDR was a signatory), quickly became a flagship for the renewal of open political dissent.

Although the GDR prides itself (despite the recent intrusion of Germanic ideology into socialist doctrine) as the most orthodox of the Eastern European systems, and despite the oppressive presence of a score of Soviet divisions on East German soil, the GDR had in the past maintained a middle-range profile toward political dissent. On the scale of political liberalization, the GDR fell between comparative liberals, i.e., Hungary and Poland, and the retrenchment states, i.e., Czechoslovakia,

Bulgaria and Romania. In particular, East Germany during the early 1970s, had displayed an image of relative leniency toward dissident writers and artists.[37]

Beginning in late 1976, the regime began to respond to the defiant intellectuals with harassment, repression, exile and imprisonment.[38] Stefan Heym, a well-known and respected author, was denied travel rights to West Germany. Moreover, during the summer and fall of 1977, almost two dozen artists and intellectuals were exiled. The first notable incident was that of Wolf Biermann, a singer and poet, whose ballads focused on the ironies and inconsistencies of East German socialism. In November 1976, during a concert tour in the BRD, he was charged with "defamation" of the GDR abroad, stripped of his citizenship and barred from returning home. There was an immediate and unprecedented storm of popular protest, led by twelve authors who petitioned the government to rescind the decision. The request was denied; many of those who signed the petition were either coerced into withdrawing their names or fired from their jobs. The remaining signatories were denounced. Physicist Robert Havemann, an outspoken critic of the government and close friend of Biermann, was placed under house arrest despite his failing health. (During World War II, Havemann was imprisoned by the Nazis with Erich Honecker and later became an SED member. These strong background credentials have made Havemann's open expressions of dissent particulary incisive as well as embarrassing to the government.)[39]

Rudolf Bahro, formerly an inconspicuous middle-aged executive in an East Berlin rubber factory, joined the chorus of public dissent with the publication of his book, *The Alternative,* which was banned in the GDR but became a bestseller in the FRG. According to Bahro, "the political superstructure [of the GDR] has bogged down in the devil's circle of the old division of labor, of which [the political system mow] is a concentrated expression."[40] In addition, "particularly within the dimension of the total political economy, bureaucratic-interest formulas easily sail unrecognized under the flag of the common good."[41] Bahro draws parallels to Orwell's *Animal Farm* and converts the major precept that "all are equal but some are more equal than others" into a phraseology that is current among Marxist-Leninist systems: "All individuals must adapt themselves to the society, but some are more societally worthy than others."[42] In September 1977, Bahro took a further step of open defiance and agreed to be interviewed on West German television. During the interview, he denounced the despotic socialism of Eastern Europe and, in particular, the party and state leaders of the GDR as exploiters of the working class. Bahro proposed that a new League of Communists be formed, harking back to the original group of supporters of Marx in London during the 1840s. On the day following the interview, Bahro was arrested by agents of the State Security Service (*Staatssicherheitsdienst*) on charges of espionage.

Sarah Krisch,[43] a poet who was a signatory to the Biermann petition, was subjected to anti-semitic taunts, probably by government security agents. "Get out, Jewish pig," was painted over the entrance to her East Berlin apartment. In September 1977, she was forced to agree to leave the GDR.

Reiner Kunze, also a well-known poet, whose book of verse and prose, caustically entitled *The Wonderful Years*, presents vignettes of life in the GDR, was similarly coerced into leaving. His daughter was branded as the child of "an enemy of the state" and was forced to leave school before her final examinations; his wife, who worked at a hospital, was refused a generally perfunctory promotion. The most frequent references in Kunze's book were to the omnipresence of security forces in the GDR and the socialization of the young to militarism:

> He holds a pistol in each hand, he has a toy tommy gun hanging on his chest.
> "How does your mother feel about these weapons?"
> "*She* bought them for me."
> "And why?"
> "Because of the bad people."
> "And who is good?"
> "Lenin."
> "Lenin? Who is he?"
> He thinks hard, but does not know what to answer.
> "You don't know who Lenin is?"
> "The captain."[44]

Other dissenters who have joined the exodus include two popular rock musicians, Gerulf Pannach and Christian Kunert, and composer Tilo

Medek. Writer Juergen Fuchs, after a period of imprisonment for publishing in the West an account of his interrogation by the secret police, was deported to West Berlin.[45]

The dissent among intellectuals is compounded by disaffection at all levels of society, and by an oppressive government response which serves only to heighten the disaffection. The workers in the "workers' state" are discontented with turbid demands to produce more for fewer rewards. The youth are growing more restive in the face of heightened regimentation.

Ironically perhaps, it was not only the Helsinki Agreement, which was in part externally imposed on the GDR, but more importantly the earlier progressive reforms, which were internally imposed under Henecker, that initiated the expansion of dissent beyond the small core of intellectuals to the general public. The GDR was caught, in effect, as were other Eastern European states,

> in the dilemma of having to innovate in order to strengthen their own internal legitimacy, efficiency, and stability, but at the same time having to satisfy their external audience as well. The partial autonomy gained by the East European states in the last fifteen years has made their political task more difficult, for they are now expected to achieve domestic successes on their own and without the weapons of coercion, while at the same time the ways in which they can move toward such successes are severely circumscribed by the USSR.[46]

In an attempt to raise the standard of living, Honecker and the East German leadership strengthened economic ties with West Germany.[47] Consumer items became more readily available, including Western goods that could be purchased only with Western currencies in the Intershops of the GDR. However, the Soviet Union, fearful of the closer cooperation between the two Germanies, pressured the SED to revise its policies. One facet of the SED response to Soviet demands was the restricting of Intershop merchandise to only those with official passes for such purchases.

The changing Intershop policy symptomized an abrupt seesawing of policies at broader levels. Concurrently, the expectations of the public were raised and then shattered. During the early 1970s, a network of economic agreements between the GDR and the West began to bear fruit. These were buttressed by an already established and growing barrage of western influences (e.g., the influx of millions of visitors from the FRG and daily television broadcasts from the West).[48]

By the mid-1970s, however, not only was the leadership of the GDR unable to satisfy rising public expectations but also found its decision-making options hemmed by Soviet pressures for a return to more doctrinaire approaches. The claim that "Honecker's relations with the Soviet leadership are undoubtedly better than those of Ulbricht"[49] no longer was valid. Honecker's political fortunes, both internally and internationally, were declining.

The consequence was a return to oppression, beginning about 1976. Western journalists were expelled and any indication of even mild dissent was vehemently attacked. The flood of East German citizens, for example, who, in the wake of internal liberalization measures during the early 1970s as well as of the Helsinki Agreement, had requested permission to emigrate found themselves subjected to various forms of intimidation, in particular the threat of job dismissal. (By late 1976, 100,000 persons, and by late 1977, 200,000 persons had requested permission to emigrate. Yet fewer than 10 percent were granted exit permits, and many of those who were not allowed to emigrate lost their jobs as a result of their applications.)

A further source of dissent, the Catholic church, remains somewhat insulated from political harassment. As only 10 percent of the population of the GDR is Catholic, the political strength of the church is derived largely from its financial condition rather than from a sizeable numerical following such as exists in Poland. During 1977, for example, a contribution of fifteen million dollars was received by the church in the GDR from the Catholic hierarchy in West Berlin.[50] The East German government is unwilling to refuse this type of largesse and thereby allows the church a degree of political latitude that is unusual for a socialist state.

For its part, the Catholic church occasionally takes stands against government mandates. A prime example is the unpopular program of compulsory military education in high schools. Open criticism of the program not only demonstrated the strength of the church but also added to its following. In the GDR, disillusioned youth are directing themselves toward the Catholic church in greater numbers than in any other Eastern European nation except Poland. In addition, not only the church spokesmen but also the East German Catholic laity is beginning to make demands for social, political and economic progress which the government is unwilling (if not also unable) to satisfy. Relations between the Catholic church and the state/party leadership appear gradually to be shifting toward the advantage of the church, while also becoming more stressful.

Perhaps the most sordid aspect of attempts by the political leadership to quell dissent is the East German trade in human lives. The silence that has been observed since 1963 by the West German press as well as by the government sources about the trade in humans (*Menschenhandel*) between East and West Germany was broken recently by a French television correspondent, Michel Meyer, in his book, *Ransom: Human Trade in Germany.*[51] During the past decade and a half, under the rationale of inner-German reconciliation, West Germany has purchased the freedom of 14,000 political prisoners of the GDR, ranging from bored youths to men and women caught trying to escape to Western Europe, to political dissidents. During 1977, a record 1500 East German political prisoners were ransomed. The ransom fee has been based on the skill and reputation of the individual, from unskilled laborers to scholars and medical doctors. Since 1975, the price paid per individual has ranged up to 70,000 marks ($35,000).

In any case, the large numbers of applicants for emigration reveal that dissent in the GDR encompasses a significant proportion of the population—a proportion that indeed may be expanding. However, there is a wide variance in the intensity of manifestations of dissent, ranging from a small group of outspoken intellectuals to the large, more subdued group of those who apply for exit permits. It also might be hypothesized that there is another, perhaps even larger, group of dissenters among the general public who have taken no actions that would allow them to be identified as such.

The Regional and International Dimensions

Until the 1970s, the frontiers of the GDR with Poland and Czechoslovakia were almost as tightly sealed as those between the GDR and the West. In 1971, when there was a focus on more active participation by the GDR in the regional community, visas were no longer required for crossing the Polish or Czech frontiers to the GDR. As East German relations with Comecon neighbors became more relaxed and the influx of foreign workers, visitors and tourists increased, there was a growing awareness of the diversity represented by different minorities, an awareness that stimulated, in some cases, greater tolerance, and in other cases, prejudice. In general, during the 1970s, minority groups in East Germany, including political dissenters, were more carefully scrutinized by both the public and the government than during the preceding decades.

International political and economic transformations further encouraged greater awareness of minorities, especially dissenters. The strong Soviet presence, both physically and ideologically, in East Germany[52] inhibits even subtle expressions of dissent and provides a rationale for government retribution against dissenters.[53] Similarly, the need to maintain an active economy provides added pressures for the restraint of dissent as well as for a policy toward ethnic minorities that is designed to encourage a growth in productivity.

The economic status of the GDR, due primarily to a variety of trading links with the West, is not faltering so severely as in some other Eastern European states, such as Poland and Bulgaria, where debt service has already passed the 50 percent mark.[54] Yet the need for economic growth is used to encourage a policy of tolerance toward dissenters and of acceptance toward ethnic minorities (both foreign workers and Sorbs) *insofar as* they adhere to the Germanic ideology with its focus on "hard work" and "community above individual."

The GDR also is beginning to exhibit in its international policy the recalcitrance that began to dominate its internal policy during the late 1970s. In 1979, the GDR made provisions for the direct election of delegates from East Berlin to the *Volkskammer,* in violation of the Four Power Agreement on Berlin, which provides for only appointed delegates from East or West Berlin to the *Volkskammer* or the West German *Bundestag.* Pressure from the Soviet Union as well as from old-line party officials and bureaucrats who feel threatened by even a minimally open polity may lead to further restrictive actions toward détente and to widespread incursions against the normalization of East German relations with the West.

Creative Retrenchment: The Perimeter for Future Choices

The German political culture as well as the agents of socialization which support, extend and dictate variances in that culture in the GDR today, are attuned with a resurgence of German nationalism. An indication of the ultimate configuration of this new sense of nationalism within the Marxist-Leninist ideological framework is provided by the status of minority politics in the GDR today. Government policies and public attitudes toward ethnic minorities, i.e., Sorbs and foreign workers, indicate the degree to which German nationalism has been allowed to become an inspissate element within the East German political ideology. In complementary fashion, government policies toward dissidents, as well as their proportions among the populace, provide an estimate of the latitude allowed for variations in the official Marxist-Leninist dogma.

An overreaching perspective is that of recent changes in the future models and plans that have been promulgated by the communist leadership of the GDR. From a progressive orientation toward "new theoretical questions" in the early 1970s, the GDR appears to have changed course in mid-stream during the late 1970s and reverted back to the old model of "system management."

Of the three alternative courses toward nationalism that were set forth at the outset of this chapter, it appears that East Germany today is following the middle-range course of merely attaching nationalism to the extant communist ideology. Although this course yields some inner conflicts, such as the question of whether, on specific issues, national autonomy or socialist legitimacy takes precedence, it allows a greater diversity of future options than does the "active" (third) course. Yet the middle-range course also excludes a very significant option, that of a policy and society that are qualitatively different from those of the past (a policy option, moreover, which was on the threshold of acceptance during the early 1970s).

Today the increasingly obdurate government stance toward dissent precludes any implementation of the third option, i.e., that of a harmonious transformation of the questions of national autonomy and socialist legitimacy into a singular concerted ideological course. There appears rather to be a retrenchment toward ideological rigidity.

Government policies toward ethnic minorities also indicate the choice of an unqualified mixture of nationalism and socialism, i.e., the middle-range (second) ideological option. Some government policies, notably the official use of Sorbian language in bilingual areas and the structuring of the educational system in Lusatia, have enhanced the status of the Sorbian minority. Yet other policies, such as the granting of only token political representation to Sorbs and the lack of programs to assist foreign workers in their transition to a new living environment, prevent the effective participation of all but ethnic Germans in the political or social life of the nation. The broad policy orientation is one of placing a benign cordon around ethnic minorities. Officially, the status of the Sorbs has not been threatened, but in fact, through the industrialization and germanization of Sorbian areas, their status is being eroded from year to year. Although it is patently false to classify Bautzen as "the make-believe capital of a Red wonderland of symbolism,"[55] implying the total lack of Sorbian autonomy, there has been no government effort to revitalize rather than merely maintain the waning Sorbian culture. Indeed it appears that the crucial, albeit unspoken, government policy is to dictate that the Sorbian culture be allowed to "run its course."

For the future, ideology in the GDR appears to contain an element of heightened nationalism joined to an increasingly doctrinaire form of socialism. The new theoretical direction that appeared to be so promising earlier in this decade already has met its demise. Honecker, who introduced that promise, now is "more a man adrift than the helmsman who seemed so sure of his course in 1971."[56] Conjointly, the era of "new theoretical questions," in which the ideologies of nationalism and socialism interact to foster the transition to a new stage of socialist development, no longer remains a viable option. For at least the near future, the GDR will continue as a nation of retrenchment, in which the rekindled sense of nationalism becomes the appendage of a traditional Marxist-Leninist ideology.

Retrenchment, however, is not an inexorably meritless policy move, especially in view of the multifaceted problems that assailed the political leadership when it embarked on a course of active change during the early 1970s. Retrenchment has two facets. One the one hand, it sanctions ideological rigidity, including the oppression and defamation of those who allow their nonconformity (in behavior or attitudes) to the social order to become visible. Yet even here there is a hedge. The hegemony of the officially promulgated Marxist-Leninist ideology has become so ridden with fissures, due to the expansiveness of opinion differences within the general public, that a restoration of pre-1971 conditions is virtually impossible. On the other hand, retrenchment can provide a positive opportunity for regrouping the intellectual and spiritual forces of the nation and for revitalizing the East German polity. On that basis, a set of alternative futures can be perhaps more realistically projected and appraised. Rather than an uncharted and thereby somewhat aimless foray into the future, retrenchment can provide a more surefooted range of policy choices that will help avoid the pitfalls of the past.

Retrenchment, in its full meaning as a form of system change that is not a mere reversion to the past but rather a creative yet circumspect move into the future, provides one very tangible model for socialist development. Across Eastern Europe, the contours of mature socialism are only now beginning to unfold. The GDR, as it moves into the 1980s with a view toward both the failed experiments of the past and the needs of a more diversified polity of the future, may serve as a very useful model for social, political and economic development in advanced socialist societies.

In addition, there remains, for the GDR specifically, the fact of a German national consciousness that is becoming more expansive as well as more intense. Within the perimeter of the course it chooses, the GDR must assume the responsibility of transforming the fundamentally antithetical and tension-laden questions of national autonomy and socialist legitimacy into a viable statement of Marxism-Leninism. It is this meld of socialism and nationalism within a framework of productive retrenchment that makes the East German model a unique future alternative for the evolution of mature communism.

NOTES

1. The terms are from Alfred Meyer, "Authority in Communist Political Systems," *Political leadership in Industrialized Societies: Studies in Comparative Analysis,* Lewis J. Edinger, ed. (New York: Wiley, 1967).

2. Commentary in *Pravda* on the "transition to the stage of developed socialist society" pointed to "a general problem of the socialist countries,

at least within Europe, posing new theoretical questions." Quoted in
Guenter Heyden, ed., *Gesellschaftsprognostik. Probleme einer neuen
Wissenschaft* (Berlin: VEB Deutscher Verlag der Wissenschaften, 1968),
p. 47. Also cited in M. Donald Hancock, "Intellectuals and System
Change," *The German Democratic Republic: A Developed Socialist
Society,* Lyman H. Legters, ed. (Boulder, Colorado: Westview, 1978),
p. 133.

3. In his speech to the *Volkskammer* on September 27, 1974, Honecker, for example, supported the constitutional revisions on the basis that
"the Constitution must give expression to the new qualitative advances
during the establishment of the developed socialist society in our country,"
See *Die neue Verfassung der DDR* (Cologne: Verlag Wissenschaft und
Politik, 1974), p. 9.

4. Yet even during the early 1970s, at the same point in time when
Honecker was propounding liberalizing reforms of the political system,
official economic analyses were rife with references to the need to follow
the details of the Soviet model. See, for example, Akademie der Wissenschaften der DDR, *Zu theoretischen und praktischen Problemen der
weiteren Vervollkommnung der Planung der Volkswirtschaft entsprechend
den Beschluessen des VIII. Parteitages der SED,* Sitzungsberichte des
Plenums und der Klassen der Akademie der Wissenschaften der DDR,
Jg. 1973, Nr. 4 (Berlin: Akademie Verlag, 1973). But were such publications merely image-building ploys designed to preempt Soviet criticism?

5. Some of the more celebrated studies of German nationalism include
Fritz R. Stern, *The Politics of Cultural Despair: A Study in the Rise of
the Germanic Ideology* (Berkeley: University of California Press, 1961);
Hans Kohn, *The Mind of Germany: The Education of a Nation* (New
York: Scribner, 1960), as well as works with a focus on the Germanic
ideological heritage, e.g., Werner Conze, *Die deutsche Nation. Ergebnis
der Geschichte* (Goettingen: Vendenhoech and Ruprecht, 1963); George
L. Mosse, *The Crisis of German Ideology: Intellectual Origins of the
Third Reich* (New York: Grosset and Dunlap, 1964); and Kurt Sontheimer,
*Antidemokratisches Denken in der Weimarer Republik. Die politischen
Ideen des deutschen Nationalismus zwischen 1918 und 1933* (Munich:
Nymphenburger Verlagshandlung, 1962). Most discussions of the current
status of German nationalism, however, focus on West Germany rather than
on the GDR. See, for example, Ralf Dahrendorf, *Society and Democracy*

in Germany (Garden City, New York: Doubleday, 1967); Karl W. Deutsch and Lewis J. Edinger, *Germany Rejoins the Powers: Mass Opinion, Interest Groups, and Elites in Contemporary German Foreign Policy* (Stanford: Stanford University Press, 1959); and Abraham Ashkenasi, *Modern German Nationalism* (New York: Wiley, 1976).

6. For analyses of the comparative political, economic and social status of, and relations between, the two Germanies, see Anne Hartmann, et al., *BRD-DDR. Vergleich der Gesellschaftssysteme* (Cologne: Pahl-Rugenstein, 1971); Wilhelm Bruns, *Deutsch-deutsche Beziehungen. Praemissen, Probleme, Perspektiven* (Opladen: Leske Verlag and Budrich GmbH, 1978); and Martin Schnitzer, *East and West Germany: A Comparative Economic Analysis* (New York: Praeger, 1974). Also useful is a concise lecture by Alfred Kantorowicz, *Deutschland-Ost und Deutschland-West. Kulturpolitische Einigungsversuche und geistige Spaltung in Deutschland seit 1945* (Muensterdorf: Verlag Hansen and Hansen, 1971).

7. More expansively, the study of minority politics is a component of the reawakened analytical focus on the nature and bases of political participation. The direction of Eastern European political studies has shifted during the past decade from mobilization and patterns of control to inclusion and the activity of plural groups. For theoretical analyses of these concepts, as well as applications to specific Eastern European systems, see Jan F. Triska and Paul M. Cocks, eds., *Political Development in Eastern Europe* (New York: Praeger, 1977); Ivan Volgyes, ed., *Political Socialization in Eastern Europe: A Comparative Framework* (New York: Praeger, 1975); Archie Brown and Jack Gray, eds., *Political Culture and Political Change in Communist States* (New York: Holmes and Meier, 1977); as well as the debate on the meaning and validity of participation as a focus in the analysis of communist systems between Donald Barry and Jerry Hough in "Notes and Views," *Problems of Communism*, Vol. XXV, No. 5 (Sept./Oct. 1976), pp. 93-95.

8. Alfred Kosing, *Theoretische Probleme der Entwicklung der sozialistischen Nation in der DDR*, Sitzungsberichte der Akademie der Wissenschaften der DDR, Gesellschaftswissenschaften, Jg. 1975, Nr. 2/G (Berlin: Adakemie Verlag, 1975). See also the analysis of nationalism as defined by the military press of the GDR—a definition which largely constitutes an argument against any form of national reunification that is based exclusively on the mutuality of ethnic and cultural backgrounds

in the two Germanies: Dietmar Kreusel, *Nation und Vaterland in der Militaerpresse der DDR* (Stuttgart; Seewald Verlag, 1971).

9. Archie Brown notes that "the failure thus far of the long-term effort to create a 'new man' with distinctively socialist values does mean . . . that the party leaderships within the Soviet Union and Eastern Europe have had to respond to political and social pressures with more than slogans and talk of 'moral incentives.' One form the response can take (and has taken) is to seek legitimacy in national terms and to lay an increased stress on national symbols." For the GDR specifically, its communist leaders must be "cautious, and more highly selective, in the use they make of appeal to national sentiment." See Archie Brown, "Eastern Europe: 1968, 1978, 1998," *Daedalus*, "Looking for Europe," Vol. 108, No. 1 (Winter 1979), pp. 158 and 161. For an incisive analysis of similar shifts in three major multinational socialist states from an ideological position that excludes ethno-national concerns to a government strategy that reflects greater sensitivity to national cultures, see Gary K. Bertsch, *Value Change and Political Community: The Multinational Czechoslovak, Soviet, and Yugoslav Cases,* "Sage Professional Papers in Comparative Politics," No. 01-050 (Beverly Hills: Sage, 1974).

10. Ellen Lentz, "Interest in Prussia Reviving," *New York Times,* December 18, 1978, p. A5. An expanded exploration of Prussian history also is being conducted in the FRG. A recent example of this new emphasis on Prussia was the four day conference on "Prussia and Its Image in History" held during late 1978 in West Berlin and attended by more than one hundred scholars from major industrial nations. Otto Buesch, who presided, defined the Prussian state as "an artificial product" based on a "curious mixture of authoritarianism and rigid military discipline on the one hand, coupled with religious tolerance, a strong sense of justice, duty and honor, and dynamic attempts at reform and innovation." For the near future, a major exhibition of life in Prussia is planned for West Berlin during 1981.

11. For a more expansive study of the political, social and economic development of the GDR as a singular socialist system, numerous texts are available. The more recent and/or celebrated works include Legters, *The German Democratic Republic;* Hermann Weber, *DDR. Grundiß der Geschichte 1945-1976* (Hannover: Fackeltraeger Verlag, 1976), which includes biographical sketches of 112 postwar personalities in the GDR

as well as a chronology of significant events between 1945 and 1976; Kurt Sontheimer and Wilhelm Bleek, *The Government and Politics of East Germany* (New York: St. Martin's 1975); John M. Starrels and Anita M. Mallinckrodt, *Politics in the German Democratic Republic* (New York: Praeger, 1975); Peter C. Ludz, *Die DDR zwischen Ost und West. Politische Analysen 1961 bis 1976* (Munich: Beck, 1977); Heinz Rausch and Theo Stammen, eds., *DDR. Das politische, wirtschaftliche und soziale System*, 2nd rev. ed. (Munich: Beck, 1974); Werner Broell, Wolfgang Heisenberg and Winfried Suehlo, *Der andere Teil Deutschlands* (Munich: Guenter Olzog 1971); and Karl-Heinz Eckhardt, *Die DDR im Systemvergleich. Didattisches Sachbuch zum Verstaendnis von Plan- und Marktwirtschaft* (Hamburg: Rowohlt, 1978).

12. Hermann Rudolph, *Die Gesellschaft der DDR—eine deutsche Moeglichkeit? Anmerkungen zum Leben im anderen Deutschland* (Munich: R. Piper, 1973), pp. 40-41.

13. In his analysis of shifting priorities in the relationship between the technical/economic elites and the political elite, Thomas A. Baylis explores in depth the East German response to the dilemma of technological development within a Marxist-Leninist framework. Ultimately with Honecker, there emerged an ideological mix between values of productivity and efficiency and those of the class struggle. See Baylis, *The Technical Intelligentsia and the East German Elite: Legitimacy and Social Change in Mature Communism* (Berkeley: University of California Press 1974). An earlier elite analysis is that of Peter C. Ludz, *The Changing Party Elite in East Germany* (Cambridge: MIT Press, 1972).

14. One of the most recent developments is the complex of music schools, which have grown from their inception in the 1960s to the point at which there is one school in every sizeable community. Children in their first year of school, at age six, are selected for special musical training oriented toward developing performers of international stature. At age twelve, a talented child may transfer to special schools for more intensive training or to a boarding school with a special music program. Before the transfer, however, the child already will have played in bands and orchestras and participated in competitions organized at the national level—similar to the already renowned East German sports program. See "East German Children Receive Special Early Training in Music," *New York Times*, November 26, 1978, p. 88.

15. Although his polemics stress the superiority of Western capitalism over Marxism as a state ideology, Raymond Aron also criticizes what he

considers to be the debilitating illness of the West, i.e. "the social failure of economic success." See Aron, *In Defense of Decadent Europe,* Stephen Cox, trans. (South Bend, Indiana: Regnery/Gateway, 1979).

16.   For trenchant analyses of popular attitudes and behavior in East Germany, as well as the underlying processes of socialization and rein-forcement, see Rudolph, *Die Geselleschaft . . . ,* and the summary of Rudolph in Sontheimer and Bleek, pp. 44-49. Note also Arthur M. Han-hardt, Jr., "Political Socialization in the German Democratic Republic," *Societas* (Spring 1971); Richard Davy, "East Germany: View from Both Sides of the Wall," *The Times* (London), September 20, 1977, p. 12; and Archie Brown, *Daedalus,* pp. 151-174. Brown's conclusions, which support those of Rudolph, expand the perspective beyond the GDR: "It would appear that in a number of Eastern European Communist states the most that has been won is the acceptance of some of the policies (especi-ally social) that have been pursued, while the Marxist-Leninist ideological foundation on which these policies are supposed to rest has still to win any comparable degree of acceptance." (Brown, p. 156.).

17.   For detailed exploratory documentation of the numerous changes in prewar and postwar ethnic composition of the Oder-Neisse territories, including migrations, wartime military and civilian deaths, and expulsion policies, see W. W. Kulski, *Germany and Poland: From War to Peaceful Relations* (Syracuse: Syracuse University Press, 1976), pp. 73-82.

18.   The comprehensive and incisive volume by Gerald Stone, which contains data on which much of the author's analysis is based, is the only detailed study of the Sorbs available in a language other than Sorbian. See Gerald Stone, *The Smallest Slavonic Nation: The Sorbs of Lusatia* (London: Athlone Press of the University of London, 1972). Useful commentary on the Sorbs also is available in *Wissenswertes ueber die Sorben. Nach Stichworten geordnete Information zur den wichtigsten Fragen ueber das Leben der sorbischen Bevoelkerung,* 2nd rev. ed. (Bau-tzen: VEB Domowina-Verlag, 1976); as well as Bundesministerium fuer innerdeutsche Beziehungen, *DDR Handbuch,* Peter C. Ludz, ed. dir. (Cologne: Verlag Wissenschaft und Politik, 1975), pp. 233-234 and 770-771. Detailed linguistic maps, as well as intermittent textual references to the Sorbs may be found in Guenter Bellmann, *Slavoteutonica. Lexika-lische Untersuchungen zum slawisch-deutschen Sprachkontakt im Ost-mitteldeutschen,* "Studia Linguistica Germanica," Ludwig Erich Schmitt and Stefan Sonderegger, eds. (New York: Walter de Gruyter, 1971).

19.   Bundesministerium fuer innerdeutsche Beziehungen, p. 771.

20.   *Wissenwertes*. . . , p. 43.

21.   William Richard Morfill, *Slavonic Literature* (London, 1883), p. 240.

22.   For a detailed examination of the Upper Lusatian territory, its towns and villages, see Jan Meschgang (Jan Meškank), *Die Ortsnamen der Oberlausitz* (Bautzen: VEB Domowina-Verlag, n.d.).

23.   Note also the process of germanization even among Sorbs who migrated to the United States. See Reinhold Olesch, "The West Slavic Languages in Texas with Special Regard to Sorbian in Serbin, Lee County," *Texas Studies in Bilingualism,* Glenn G. Gilbert, ed., "Studia Linguistica Germanica," Ludwig Erich Schmitt and Stefan Sonderegger, eds. (Berlin: Walter de Gruyter and Co., 1970); and Jan L. Perkowski, "A Survey of the West Slavic Immigrant Languages in Texas," *Texas Studies*. . .

24.   Daniel N. Nelson, "Dilemmas of Local Politics in Communist States," *The Journal of Politics,* Vol. 41, No. 1 (February 1979), p. 36.

25.   *Die Verfassung der Deutschen Demokratischen Republik* (Berlin: Amt fuer Information der Regierung der Deutschen Demokratischen Republik, 1949), p. 16.

26.   *Die neue Verfassung der DDR* (Cologne: Verlag Wissenschaft und Politik, 1974), p. 93.

27.   Stone, p. 162.

28.   The bilingual *Kreise* are Bautzen, Kamenz and Niesky (in the Dresden *Bezirk*), and Calau, Cottbus-Stadt, Cottbus-Land, Forst, Guben, Hoyerswerda, Luebben, Spremberg and Weisswasser (in the Cottbus *Bezirk*).

29.   Starrels and Mallinckrodt, *Politics in the GDR*, p. 190.

30.   For a comprehensive study of tension between the industrializing sectors and the rural agricultural economies, see Konrad Mueller, *Die mitteldeutsche Landwirtschaft 1945-1974. Ein agrarsoziologisch-sozial-geographischer Beitrag zu ihrem Strukturwandel* (Berlin: Dietrich Mueller Verlagsbuchhandlung, 1975).

31.   For a detailed study of the geographic and economic repercussions of the development of the brown coal industry in the Cottbus area, see Hermann Schubert, "Einfluesse der Braunkohlen-industrie auf die territorialen Teilstrukturen. Dargestellet am Beispiel des Bezirkes Cottbus," *Beitraege zur territorialen Produktionsstruktur,* Geographische Gesellschaft der Deutschen Demokratischen Republik, ed., Vol. 13 of

"Wissenschaftliche Abhandlungen" (Gotha/Leipzig: VEB Hermann Haack, Geographisch-Kartographische Anstalt, 1976), pp. 105-118.

32. Data on foreign workers in the GDR are given in Bundesministerium fuer innerdeutsche Beziehungen, p. 39.

33. For an extended analysis of the role of intellectuals in fostering the development of mature socialism in the GDR, exclusive of those who stand in open defiance to the political system, see Hancock, "Intellectuals"

34. György Lukács, *History and Class Consciousness: Studies in Marxist Dialectics,* Rodney Livingston, trans. (Cambridge: Massachusetts: MIT Press, 1971).

35. For an analysis of the Harich-Gruppe, see Wolfgang Goerlich, *Geist und Macht in der DDR* (Freiburg im Breisgau: Walter-Verlag, 1968), pp. 53-56.

36. On the cyberneticists, see Ludz, *The Changing Party Elite,* pp. 367-407.

37. When Erich Honecker replaced Walter Ulbricht in 1971 as First Secretary of the SED (and in spite of the fact that Ulbricht continued to exercise considerable control as Chair of the Council of State), Honecker, over Ulbricht's opposition, became a trailblazer for liberation in the arts. Beginning in 1976, however, it appears Honecker promoted an atavistic government approach. For a quasi-official biography, i.e. one written by a close friend and confidant, of formative influences on Honecker prior to 1971, see Heinz Lippmann, *Honecker and the New Politics of Europe,* Helen Sebba, trans. (New York: Macmillan, 1972).

38. Government repression of political dissidents is not unique to the GDR. For a sharp literary satire of antidemocratic tendencies in West Germany, in particular the state security agencies, see Heinrich Boell, *Berichte zur Gesinnungslage der Nation* (Cologne: Kiepenheuer and Witsch, 1975). The numerous nonfictional critiques of West German democracy include the classic work of Karl Jaspers, *Wohin treibt die Bundesrepublik? Tatsachen, Gefahren, Chancen* (Munich: R. Piper, 1967); and Hans Dichgans, *Das Unbehagen in der Bundesrepublik: Ist die Demokratie am Ende?* (Duesseldorf: Econ-Verlag, 1968). In addition, the recent spate of terrorist activities has provoked a wide range of restrictions on personal liberties. Note, for example, commentaries by John Dornberg, "West Germany's Embattled Democracy: The Antiterrorist Menace from the Right," *Saturday Review,* June 10, 1978, pp. 18-21; and David Zane

Mairowitz, "Scissors in the Head: West Germany's Extreme Reaction to Extremism," *Harper's*, May 1978, pp. 28-31.

39. See, for example, his "Meinungsstreit foerdert die Wissenschaften," *Neues Deutschland*, March 4, 1958, p. 5; *Dialektik ohne Dogma? Naturwissenschaft und Weltanschauung* (Hamburg: Rowohlt, 1964); *Berliner Schriften*, Andreas W. Mytze, ed. (Berlin: Europaeische Ideen, 1976); and *Robert Havemann, ein deutscher Kommunist. Rueckblicke und Perspektiven aus der Isolation* (Hamburg: Rowohlt, 1978).

40. Rudolf Bahro, *Die Alternative. Zur Kritik des real existierenden Sozialismus* (Cologne: Europaeische Verlagsanstalt, 1977), p. 179.

41. *Ibid.*, p. 184.

42. *Ibid.*, p. 208.

43. Her early writings, with Rainer Kirsch, include *Berlin-Sonnenseite* (1964) and *Gespraech mit dem Saurier* (1965).

44. Reiner Kunze, *The Wonderful Years*, Joachim Neugroschel, trans. (New York: George Braziller, 1977), p. 14.

45. For recent commentary and data on the growing dissent among intellectuals, consult "Exile for Heretics: A Crackdown on Nonconformity," *Time*, October 3, 1977, p. 48; and Peter Pragal, "Twilight for Honecker? Renewed Oppression Signals Change in East Germany," *Atlas World Press Review*, July 1979, p. 42.

46. Zvi Y. Gitelman, *The Diffusion of Political Innovation: From Eastern Europe to the Soviet Union* (Beverly Hills: Sage, 1972), p. 53.

47. For data on the expansion of trade between East and West Germany from 1970 to 1974 (Table 55, p. 169), as well as for cogent analyses of major economic changes in the GDR between 1950 and 1974, see Raimund Dietz, *Die Wirtschaft der DDR 1950-1974*, "Forschungsberichte," Nr. 37 (Vienna: Wiener Institut fuer Internationale Wirtschaftsvergleiche beim Oesterreichischen Institut fuer Wirtschaftsforschung, 1976).

48. Commentary on Intershop policies, as well as on current living conditions in the GDR is provided in Hartmut Zimmerman, "The GDR in the 70's," *Problems of Communism*, Vol. XXVII, No. 2 (March/April 1978), pp. 1-40. For a perspicacious and optimistic analysis of *Kulturpolitik* in the GDR during the early 1970s, see Volker Gransow, *Kulturpolitik in the DDR* (Berlin: Verlag Volker Spiess, 1975). An example of the greater latitude allowed to authors during the early 1970s is the

publication of Rainer Kirsch's collection of four free-form biographies which, although essentially orthodox, contain subtle criticisms and questions. See Rainer Kirsch, *Kopien nach Originalen. Portraits aus der DDR* (Berlin: Verlag Klaus Wagenbach, 1974).

49. Jonathan Steele, *Inside East Germany: The State that Came in from the Cold* (New York: Urizen Books, 1977), p. 224.

50. David A. Andelman, "East Bloc Catholics Gain in New Power Shift," *New York Times,* December 31, 1978, p. 2E.

51. Michel Meyer, *Des hommes contre des marks* (Paris: Éditions Stock, 1977). Also see "Trade in Humans Divulged," *Christian Science Monitor,* April 26, 1978, p. 6.

52. For a broad analysis of the position of the GDR within the Warsaw Alliance and of the present relationship of East Germany to the Soviet Union, see N. Edwina Moreton, *East Germany and the Warsaw Alliance: The Politics of Détente* (Boulder, Colorado: Westview, 1978).

53. Indeed for most Marxist-Leninist political systems, "the notion of an individually centered political order, of the freedom and autonomy of group organization and association, of competing allegiances that may be manifested in organized political opposition, is anathema." See Joseph LaPalombara, "Monoliths or Plural Systems: Through Conceptual Lenses Darkly," *Studies in Comparative Communism,* Vol. VIII, No. 3 (Autumn 1975), pp. 305-332.

54. David A. Andelman, "Eastern Europe's Dilemma: It's in the Red," *New York Times,* February 4, 1979, Sec. 12, "International Economic Survey," pp. 52-53.

55. Franz von Nesselrode, *Germany's Other Half* (New York: Abelard Schuman, 1963), p. 137.

56. Pragal, "Twilight for Honecker?"

Ivan Volgyes

VI

LEGITIMACY AND MODERNIZATION:
NATIONALITY AND NATIONALISM IN
HUNGARY AND TRANSYLVANIA

Introduction

It is a tautology to say that everything is interconnected in Eastern Europe and neat boundaries cannot be drawn. Social scientists trying to study one problem inevitably discover the impossibility of understanding that particular issue without reference to other topics. The ease with which in Western literature one deals with "integration" or "assimilation," "nation-building" or "state-building" is absent from discussing these same topics in Eastern Europe for, in the latter case, processes that occurred more or less simultaneously in the West occurred in a dichotomous manner in the East. In some cases the state developed after the nation, while the nation developed after the state in others. An "integrated citizenry" has existed in cases where the minorities were not assimilated in some instances, while in others the minorities were assimilated but the citizenry was simply not "integrated" into the national polity. Consequently, generalizations regarding the topic of minorities and legitimacy are of limited use when applied to Eastern Europe and the following case study of nationality, minorities, and legitimacy,

An earlier version of this paper was published in *Crossroads* (Israel), Vol. 2, No. 6.

concentrates on the example of Hungary; it will, hence, avoid the tempting though not very profitable task of creating models that are only applicable to one state at one time during the historical process.

What is a Nation?

No acceptable, agreed-upon, scientific definition of the "nation" exists for social scientists. In the earliest definition, the French Academy of Sciences defined the nation in 1694 as the community of a state, living under common laws and using a common language. This definition proved to be too vague. Disraeli and Renan, a great theoretician of nationhood, added more concrete *characteristics* to their definitions of nationhood. To Renan, in addition to such delineatable attributes as race, language, geography, religion, and common interests, the nation was also a spiritual idea, the end-product of a common past and a trust and desire to share in a common future.[1]

No definition, however, has proved equally applicable to all cases— not Renan's not Stalin's, not the *Encyclopaedia of Social Sciences.* And especially confusing have been situations such as Eastern Europe, where the concept of the nation has not always been coupled with the attributes of the state. For instance, no one doubted the existence of a Polish nation throughout history, but a Polish state did not re-appear after the Partitions until 1918. No one doubted the existence of a Hungarian nation, but the Hungarian state likewise disappeared from the map of Europe for nearly 400 years.

To further confuse the reader, one more *caveat* should be entered here; social scientists and historians alike lack the precision to define what elements of the definition of the nation are *attributes, consequences,* or *pre-conditions* of becoming a nation. Thus, for example, we cannot generalize that the attributes of common language, common economy or structure of the state are the consequences of having been a nation or pre-conditions for the creation of a nation. One could convincingly argue either way, using different examples from the development of nations in Eastern Europe.

How then can one define the "nation" in Eastern Europe if not by attributes of the nation-state? We can only project it as a conscious entity of identification of people with one another either within the boundaries of a state or outside. The Magyar nation includes 2.5 million Magyars living in Romania, the Yugoslav nation includes Serbs and Slovaks, Croats or Macedons and even the *Gastarbeitern* from all these groups living in Western Europe. But does the Yugoslav nation include some Albanians who wish to belong to Albania, some Croats who want to secede, or does the Czechoslovak nation include Hungarians who live on the territory of Czechoslovakia but who wish to belong to the Hungarian nation? Questions like these cannot be answered by glib generalizations, only by a painstaking explanation of each case on very special and separate bases, taking each example as a *sui generis* problem. Using such a tack, will not create generally applicable social science models, but given our scant knowledge of international realities, I believe, it is the only honest way of approaching this problem.

The Development of Nationalism

In addition to a mode of behavior, nationalism is a feeling, an attachment, an emotion, an attitude exhibited or possessed. As such it is subjective, not open to quantifiable measurement that can be applied to the observance of behavior. Hence, while one may be able to measure the intensity of attachments, one cannot measure or analyze the extent of its possession among the population.

Although Marxist theoreticians claim that nationalism has only developed along with the establishment of a bourgeois mode of production, we need not accept this rather ridiculous claim. In fact, as Huizinga has pointed out in *The Waning of the Middle Ages,* one can find numerous examples of national hatred during the medieval period in trade centers where large numbers of foreigners lived side-by-side, in the courts where foreign kings were brought in or imposed upon unwilling nobles, and among the supposedly universal Christian clergy. It is quite clear that ethnic separatism and hence nationalism first developed among the members of feudal nobility, especially in Eastern Europe, where they were the first to challenge the universalism of the Church, its language, and practices. Centers of learning and knowledge, the medieval universities, exhibited nationalism; incredible fights have been reported at nearly all institutions of higher learning among students who desired to be taught in their specific native languages. Whether in Paris or in Prague, nationalism during the Middle Ages belittled others and projected images of national stereotypes of character that have prevailed throughout the centuries. Nationalism was evident as a guiding force in the conflict between Germans and Czechs during the Hussite Wars. And even if there were multinational efforts during the Crusades against the "infidels," even if the peasant of the Middle Ages seemed to have professed to be first of all a Christian, secondly a member of his family and village community, and only thirdly a member of a national group, one cannot escape the conclusion that there were already indisputable ties that bound him and the rest of his *conféres* to a concept of national attachment.

The sense of nationalism, of course, was further encouraged by the natural tendency that kings often sought to enhance their legitimacy by claiming to have been descended from' ancient lines or famous and frequently mythical figures. Their peculiarism and the rise of humanism drove additional nails into the coffin of Catholic universalism. The Reformation further reinforced the nationalist trend. The 1703-1711 Rakoczi rebellion against Habsburg rule, for example, carried the banner of "Pro patria et libertate," and combined nationalism, anti-Catholicism and a drive for the re-creation of the nation-state within definable boundaries.

But the great impulse to nationalism was given not by spiritual, but by secular events: the French Revolution and the subsequent entry of the masses into political activity. Organized political activity here must be differentiated from previous *coups* or *jaqueries.* It was a direct result of the need of leaders to rely on masses and also of the spreading Enlightenment that gave rise to attempts to "forge" a nation. From the close of the 18th century, however, nationalism began to be wedded to another phenomenon, the desire to possess an independent state. Whether seeking the root of national identity among the peasantry as romantic nationalists were wont to do, or among the aristocracy and nobility as the "realist *status quo*" politicians attempted, national aspirations sought to fulfill these desires through the possession of an independent state. And that, of course, has been the crux of the problem in Eastern Europe.

Nationalism is Temporary

Compounding this problem, we need additional *caveat.* The concept of nationalism in Eastern Europe was always dependent upon the definer.

To use just a few examples, the *natio Hungarica* expression in the Middle Ages in Hungary referred only to the nobility; hence a *nobilis Hungarus* was a member of this aristocracy. As society developed in the eigthteenth and nineteenth centuries, however, that definition began to include members of the developing bourgeois and the commercial classes as well; as the Age of Reform merged with the Age of Nationalism, the term "Hungarian nation" expanded to include all members of society, peasants and the budding working class as well. But what is important to realize is that the enemies of or opposition to the various sentiments of "nation" also played an important role in defining the progressive or regressive character of the term itself. The Hungarian "nation" and the nationalism associated with it in the Middle Ages stood for an independence, a guaranteed social order, an opposition to being ruled by others. The reform-nationalism of the eighteenth and nineteenth centuries stood for opposition to monarchial absolutism, for reform, and revolution against the occupying Habsburg power. After the Compromise of 1867, however, the nationalism exhibited stood for exercising an independent rule in opposition to attempted autonomy and self-rule by nationalities.[2]

The conflict between Magyars and non-Magyars living in the territory of Hungary, of course, was not new. As indicated above, national feelings had always existed among *some* members of the nation, national conflicts between Magyar and non-Magyar groups were evident during the Middle Ages as much as nationality conflicts were evidenced elsewhere in Europe. What was interesting, however, from the perspectives of the non-Magyars was that they could hardly be called "nationalities" in the sense that the term has been used in modern times. Indeed, it is clear that the policy of the Magyars from the eleventh century throughout the thirteenth century had been one of allowing the free settlement of any non-Magyar group on the territories of the Hungarian Kingdom and encouraging Czechs, Germans, and Croatians as well as some Hungarian groups, such as the Szeklers, to settle in order areas and exist as they wished. Especially during the Middle Ages there have been no forced assimilation attempts made by any Hungarian ruler toward these groups and an autonomy that was unparalleled during the age was extended to them.[3] We cannot talk of purposive oppression of the minorities during the feudal age either, for the feudal oppression weighed equally upon the Romanian, the Slovak or upon the Hungarian peasant. The *natio Hungarica* included only a small number of non-Magyar nobles; hence the oppressing classes was largely Magyar and it oppressed all peasants, regardless of their nationality or group affiliation.

The Turkish occupation of Hungary further confused the ethnic picture. Literally hundreds of thousands of people fled from the South to the Northern periphery where Croatians, Hungarians and Slovenes mingled, intermarried or coexisted with Slovaks, Czechs, Poles and Russians. As a consequence, ethnic identity began to be confused; people possessing ethnically Hungarian names claimed to be Slovaks and vice-versa. During these years, especially during the fifteenth century, the term *Hungarus* appeared, but this was a territorial term only; it did not refer to the possession of a claimed or accepted mother-tongue, nor did it refer to ethnic identification. It is extremely interesting for researchers to peruse the registries of students at the major universities of the region, whether at Krakow or in Prague, and to witness the frequency of students' claim to be *Hungarus,* in spite of the possession of such names as Jedliček or Vitorsky. Only during the latter part of the fifteenth century can one find such notes as a student claiming to be *quidam de Ungeris, Slavus tamen natione!*

The Turkish occupation of Hungary was thus responsible for the intermingling of ethnic groups to a great extent. Indirectly, it was also responsible for the advance of civilization in the Northern Uplands. Here Slovak and Magyar languages were equally taught, publications were printed in Russian, Croatian, Hungarian, and a large array of other languages in the newly established printing presses of the north; regardless of the "ethnic" or linguistic identification assigned to such publications, the authors all claimed to be Hungarians. What nationality conflicts existed, usually occurred between the German urban population and the Slovak-Hungarian urban population and did not encompass either serious enmities among the peasants or between Slovaks and Hungarians.

Indeed, the first ethnic claims to separatism were made by Magyar authors who in the 17th century bemoaned the demise of a greater Slav era than was claimed to have existed hitherto, but even during these years, the concept of *Hungarus* remained unchallenged.[4] The fact of the lack of independence united *slavus et hungarus;* only the romantic nationalism of the 19th century began to speed the process of the development of separatist, anti-*slavus* or anti-*hungarus* ethnic settlements.

The process of ethnic revival is far too well-known to be recounted on these pages. The Hungarian writers and authors who were concerned about the disappearance of written Hungarian literature, tried and succeeded in convincing the *literateurs* of the nation to undertake the process of linguistic revival. Struggling against absolutism from Vienna, the battleground was, obscure enough, but—aided by international events that limited the power of Austria—it became the seed of further quandries. The educational reforms of 1791-1825 turned around the universalist practice and linguistic nationalism won the day for a Hungarian rather than a German or Latin language educational system, And a decade later, the same demands were raised by Romanians, Serbs, Slovaks and Croatians who lived on the territory of Habsburg Austria. Their relative lack of success was due to their smaller numbers, their more disbursed settlement patterns, and also to the fact that among the nobility their numbers were considerably smaller than their Hungarian counterparts.

The only "assistance" that the Slavs received during the first part of the 19th century came from a dubious source: pan-Slavism. I say that it was a dubious source, because during those days the "Russian danger" seemed real to the Court in Vienna as well as to other European capitals. And pan-Slavism began to be realized as a potentially destructive force in the territory where most Slavs lived outside of Russia, namely in Austria-Hungary. And during the Hungarian war of independence in 1848-1849, the same pan-Slavism, which as expressed by Jan Kollar and Ludovit Štur, was so modest and so human, suddenly was played off against the Hungarian *state* that dared oppose the concept of Austrian rule. It was a confused opposition: on Hungary's side fought such a great general from Hungary's minorities as Damjanich—against it, General Jelačić or J. Stratimirović. And as for the misuse of pan-Slavism: Generals Bem and Dembinski, recognized that they fought against a common enemy, namely Austria and Russia and did not fall for the "pan-Slavist bait."[5]

The extreme enmity between Hungarian nationalists who demanded independence from Austria stems from this period. The Compromise of 1867 created a Hungarian state whose territory was inhabited by non-Magyar nationalities, whose allegiance to the Magyar cause was highly questionable. Living in the age of nationalism, fueled by the creation of independent nation-states in areas vacated by aging Empires, during the latter half of the 19th century even enlightened Magyars vainly struggled to find an acceptable solution. On the territory of Hungary proper there were 48.1percent Magyars, 25.8 percent Slavs, 9.8 percent Germans and 14.1 percent Romanians. Aside from a very few who did not care or were assimilated totally with the Magyar population, most non-Magyars by the beginning of World War I wanted out. Caught up by the winds of independence, they too, wanted to be free. Their nationalism began to coalesce with the concept of the nation-state, just as Hungarian nationalism managed to merge the two concepts in 1849.

The result at the end of the First World War was the formation of new nation states, and Hungary was not one of the victors, Hungary lost three-fourths of its territory and two-thirds of its people, but a solution to the enormous ethnic complexities of the region was still not found. For the first time, however, it was not foreign nationalities that inhabited Hungarian territories, it was now Hungarian and other ethnic groups which formed national minorities in surrounding states. Czechoslovakia, for example, contained more than one-third "minorities" among whom nearly twenty-five percent were Germans and five percent were Magyars. In Romania, the ratio was approximately the same, with Magyars accounting for nearly ten percent of the entire population. In Yugoslavia, only 77 percent of the population could be accounted for in the category of Serbo-Croatian-Slovenian population, in Poland the Poles made up only 69.2 percent of the population. Unquestionably, the largest number of nationalities living dispersed among the newly created nation-states were the Magyars; fully 25 percent of all Magyars living in Europe did not live within the borders of the state of Hungary.

Hungary, for various reasons, some of which were just, others unjust, was treated as an outlaw by the neighboring states in the interwar years and the Magyars' feeling that they were treated unjustly, fanned the flame of nationalism during these years. They wanted a return of the ancient territories of the historic Kingdom of St. Stephen which had been stripped from her by the Treaty of Trianon. Clinging to such words as "ancient historical heritage" and "sacred lands," Hungary promoted its irredentist policy to regain control over people and lands. It is true that "the protection of Hungarian and other minorities," inserted by the Allies in the final peace treaties, was nothing more than a laughing stock of neglect.

Hungary's irredentist policies, nonetheless, aimed at the restoration of a past that really had never been. A chauvinist education system that claimed that *extra Hungariam non est vita: si est non est ita* conveniently ignored the fact that three million Hungarians were living in America where *vita* was certainly not *ita* (and those who lived there were quite thankful for that), and it demonstrated that Hungarian policy makers wanted revenge. When the opportunities for revenge were offered to the Hungarian leaders by Hitler, they eagerly accepted it. This joint collaboration with Hitler eventually cost Hungary more men, more pain, more tragedy, and more heartbreak than any decision made since the Battle of Mohács, but it ended once and for all any aspirations of Hungarians even to think, much less to dream, of an irredentist policy. The "sacred lands" were gone and Hungary would have to live in an age of grey reality, untinged by hope.

Nationalism in Hungary Since the End of World War II

The postwar assumption of power by the Communist government destroyed the bases of nationalism in Hungary: the concept of the nation and the unity of the people within the boundaries of the country, within the confines of the nation-state. A larger political community, the international workers movement, replaced the narrower community of state, while the interests of a narrower community, the working class, took precedence over the larger grouping, the nation. Internationalism thus both opened up and simultaneously constricted the definition of nationalism and reversed the positive sign before the term to a negative one. Marxism, as stated by Jozscf Révai, the most prominent theoretician of the Communist power-structure, dismissed nationalism as a progressive category and replaced it with internationalism as an organizing concept.[6]

Internationalism, of course, in itself was to be desired above parochial nationalism; provincialism should not be preferred to cosmopolitanism. An interest in other nations and other peoples is not bad as an organizing concept of one's orientation. The trouble with internationalism was that it claimed to *negate* in *toto* the contribution of the *nation* and viewed the latter as a negative concept that had outlived its usefulness. The state was expected to wither away and nationalism—viewed as having been embodied in the nation-state—was also expected to wither away.

But internationalism was not to imply merely a love for people of other countries; it was to be characterized as socialist internationalism, which implied an infatuation with the working class movement and with its embodiment, particularly in the Soviet working class movement. The Soviet working class movement, as it turned out, was not merely a movement, but bluntly stated, a state itself. Consequently, the Communist ideologues had the difficult task of, removing, on the one hand, the "bacteria" of nationalism from the minds of the people and abolishing any love of the *bourgeois* state while, on the other hand, inculcating in the minds of the people the love of internationalism and the affection for *socialist* states, notably the Soviet Union.

It was a formidable task. After all, there was little affection for the successor-states of the region even in the interwar period in Hungary; to have suddenly gained affection for them would have been impossible after a lost war. Moreover, there was no way to attain a sudden "love" for the USSR among a population which viewed generally the Soviet Union as an occupier, a nation viewed to have covered the mantle of Russians who crushed the revolution of 1848-1849 merely with red clothes. The regime, of course, realized that there was no way to politically resocialize the population overnight and the leadership did not care to what extent the population *really* internalized the value of the love of the Soviet fatherland, and eschewed its nationalism. All the regime really needed was to show outward, visible manifestations of adopting these new values.

Consequently, the Soviet government, culture, and life became the models which Hungarian national values had to emulate. Every Soviet film, theatrical production, artistic and literary accomplishment that was brought to Hungary was expected to be a new emulatable model. Socialist realism, invented as the only correct style of the new "proletcult," had to be emulated, duplicated, and admired. The ideological position of the party leadership held that even the worst Soviet film was to be preferred to the best American film and every Soviet accomplishment was held to be better than ever the best Hungarian accomplishments.[7] It is true that at the beginning the Hungarians had indeed admired to a great extent some of the accomplishments of the Russians and the USSR, but the trouble was that the Russians considered themselves peer-less even in areas where they were not. There is not a single nation in the world that can call itself perfect in every field . . . The fatal error was that the Soviet leaders declared that their people, their country, and last but not least, that they themselves, were beyond comparison.[8]

And with the notion of being perfect always there is the accompanying belittling of everything non-Russian, such as things Hungarian. Taste and art, composition or industrial planning, all had to follow the Soviet pattern because the latter was perfect, while the Hungarian accomplishments were obviously faulty. Kodály's compositions were to be regarded as inferior to those of such a tenth rate composer as that of Hrennikov; Derkovits's art—recognized as perhaps one of the most imaginative painting styles of the interwar period—was considered inferior to that of Finogenov. The native soul was being denuded in the quest of emulating everything Soviet. The nation that lasted a thousand years was not merely occupied, but for the first time in its history, denigrated by the idiocy of the occupiers, and of Hungary's leaders who were willing to emulate all things Soviet.

Outwardly, it worked for a while. Those who complained could be silenced in the prisons by the idiotic sadists who controlled the police. Ideological deviation and the praising of the native past became synonymous. It is easy to win an argument if one is willing to use the gun of terror; an executed intellectual is not likely to become a "recidivist nationalist." But guns cannot win acceptance and internalization of values, they can only sometimes force outward compliance. After 1954 few people, if any, took the leading role of the USSR in all fields seriously; instead of the desired effect, the compliance by the people carried with it a *contempt* for all things Soviet, including its leadership, culture and history. The forced compliance resulted in the delegitimation of the regime; if it relied on the emulation of all things Soviet, no one could have taken its constant claim any more seriously than could those of the Soviet leadership.

The nationalism that was emerging during these years, was thus deeply rooted, negative, and anti-Soviet, not merely pro-Hungarian. The Magyars were not sure if there was anything really praiseworthy in being Magyars anymore, but they were sure that as a whole they were anti-Soviet. As Stalin's crimes have been revealed, those of Rákosi, self-styled as Stalin's best student, also became evident. When the elemental force of the revolt in 1956 broke out, its one cohesive theme was that of nationalism, re-defined now as a desire to end Soviet rule. It was not a desire to alter the social or even the political system that was most manifest in the *jacquerie* of the cities in 1956, but its anti-Soviet nature and orientation. In spite of the fact that the Soviet leadership would not tolerate anti-Soviet activities, the revolt brought together the nation against those who had denigrated the Hungarians for so long.

In retrospect, the slogan "no more comrades!" was more of a mani-festation of anti-Russian feelings than that of a desire to change the social order. "Comrades" were to be "abolished" not because they were "Communists" but because they were identified as henchmen of the Soviet Union. In this sense, the tragedy of 1956 was not merely the death and destruction, but that the two issues were not and could not be satisfactorily separated; even among the Hungarian leadership that took the reigns of power after the revolt, the issue was far from clear.

And yet the Kádár leadership faced this problem quite soon after it assumed rule; by early 1957 it became clear that their leadership would not be regarded as legitimate as long as it was identified with that of the Soviet Union. Kádár's policy had to move in the direction of "national-izing" and achieving a legitimization of his rule. As long as he was viewed largely as a Soviet puppet for at least the decade after the Revolution—Kádár could not achieve the national legitimacy he so much desired. But national legitimacy had to come from a rehabilitation of the value of Hungarian nationalism (within limits, admittedly, but nationalism nonetheless).

The stability of the regime, its relative success in economic and social areas, and its unchallenged position for leadership throughout the 1960s, assisted Kádár in his goals of legitimation. By the middle of the 1960s there appeared another term to be added to the vocabulary of socialist internationalism, namely "socialist patriotism." The most significant step in the rewording of the central proposition regarding the concept of the nation resulted from the decade-long, so-called historical debate that was carried on as part of the struggle among those who desired to profess the Marxist rather than the objective historians' view.

The debate began with Erik Molnár's studies that attempted to de-mythologize the nation, the fatherland, the people. Projecting the disutility of nationalism, Molnár suggested that nationalism was not a concept that could be or should be used to explain history, for it accepted certain illusions instead of concrete realities that could be ascertained by professional historians. The "nationalist" view, held among others by Aladár Mód, of course, did not come out in the "defense of nationalism" but proceeded to claim the value of the organizing concept of the state, the nation, the fatherland and presented its utility as a defensible concept that legitimizes the rule of the leadership as the representatives of the nation.[9]

A debate followed and, its outcome was quite clear: far more emphasis was to be placed on the concept of socialist patriotism from the 1960s onward than ever before since the assumption of Communist rule.

There was to remain a clear differentiation, however, between socialist patriotism and nationalism. While the latter was regarded to be anti-Soviet and "chauvinistic" in its character, the former had accepted the boundary that anti-Soviet manifestations of any sort could not be undertaken. One was no longer required to praise all things Soviet, but anti-Soviet manifestations of any sorts had to be negated. Yet another element of the concept of socialist patriotism was a positive view toward the socialist nations that surrounded Hungary. They too had to be viewed positively as socialist states and statements implying revanchism or extreme chauvinism could not be made against them. But specifically toward Romania, Czechoslovakia and Yugoslavia, the reason for the beneficial tone was not the fear of intervention by the USSR, but the possibility of persecution of the Magyar minorities residing in these neighboring states.

Nationalities and Minorities in Postwar Hungary

Consequently at this point, it is most significant to follow our original line of inquiry and look at the question of the treatment of nationalities in Hungary. The sobering conclusion of World War II was that Hungary became an almost homogeneous state. The forcible and brutal expulsion of around 170,000 ethnic Germans and 73,273 Slovaks diminished the minority population even further.[10] Even though these expulsions were the result of direct orders contained in the Potsdam Declaration, in the case of the Germans and at the demand of the Czechoslovak government in the case of the Slovaks, they were characterized by mutual brutality that was clearly unnecessary.[11]

The expulsions closed the worst chapters of excesses against the minorities. Since the mid-1950s there has been a general understanding that the minorities—whether they were regarded as racial, linguistic, ethnic, national or religious minorities—must be protected, assisted and aided.[12] The reason for the adoption of this policy was simple: the dream of ever recapturing lands inhabited by Hungarians outside the territorial borders of the Hungarian People's Republic was gone. If Hungarians expected that the Magyars living in the neighboring states should be treated well, the only hope to implement that expectation had to be an exemplary policy toward the small number of non-Magyar Hungarian citizens living in Hungary.

The non-Magyar minorities living in Hungary can be classified on two bases: ethnic and national minorities. The Gypsies, an ethnic minority, number around 40,000 people (exact figures are hard to come by). The break-down of the national minorities is more difficult; if we view them from the perspective of nationality alone, according to the 1960 census figures, 53,894 people claim to have a nationality other than Hungarian. On the other hand, linguistically speaking, 134,839 people claimed in the 1960 census a mother-tongue other than Hungarian. Looking at other data, however, it becomes clear that the census figures somewhat understate their number. In fact, when one compares regional and local data the number of people belonging to non-Magyar nationalities sharply increases. According to census data in 1963 there were 50,765 German, 30,690 Slovak, 15,787 Romanian, 25,262 Croatian, 4,583 Serbian, and 7,752 South Slav citizens living in Hungary.

Various national associations, however, give the following estimates: Germans, 200-220,000; Slovaks, 100-110,000; Romanians, 20-25,000; South Slavs, 80-100,000. The best estimates maintain that there are, all told, around 400-450,000 people, who belong to the category of national minorities, accounting for about four percent of Hungary's entire population.[13]

The location of the minorities is also instructive. The national minorities do not live in enclaves of closed communities concentrated in one region, but are dispersed in widely disparate areas and are integrated into villages where the majority are ethnic Hungarians. There are certain counties, however, where a large portion of the non-Magyar population resides. Tolna and Baranya counties have a high concentration of Germans, in territories that used to be called "Schwabische Turkerey," but one can find Germans in just about all the counties of Trans-Danubia, with the possible exception of Zala. In addition to Trans-Danubia, Germans also live in Pest, Békés, Bács-Kiskun and Nógrád counties as well. The Slovaks are also dispersed throughout Hungary; one half of the Slovaks live in Békés county, the rest are settled all over the nation. The position of the South Slavs is perhaps even more complicated, since they claim to belong to at least five different South-Slav minorities. Generally, the South-Slavs live along the southern and western borders of Hungary, although their colonies can be found on both sides of the Danube and in Budapest as well. The Romanians live in widely dispersed settlements along the eastern borders of Hungary.[14]

As a result of deliberately positive policies of the regime, especially since 1960, the Hungarian government has attempted to provide as much linguistic education as possible. The foremost problem among all the nationalities is that they frequently speak dialects that differ from location to location and the use of the "literary language" has to be taught or super-imposed on speech-patterns already formed. Frequently, literary language cannot be understood by the elders of the community and resentment at "idiotic translations" are frequently voiced.[15]

The Hungarian laws have guaranteed the organization of primary schools in the nationality languages wherever fifteen or more students request it. There was a small number of voluntary students between 1950 and 1960, prompted perhaps by fear of future discrimination. But during the academic year 1960-1961, dual language instruction has been introduced in these schools; since then the humanities have been taught in the mother-tongue, and the natural and social-sciences in Hungarian, although the special terminologies of these subjects were also expected to be given in the non-Magyar mother-tongue as well. There were twenty-four such primary schools in 1966-1967, and this number has remained relatively constant throughout the last decade.

Special language primary schools are also organized in Hungary, where all the subjects, except the non-Hungarian mother-tongue, are taught in Magyar. In 1966-1967 there were 225 such schools on the primary level with nearly 20,000 students but their number has increased to above 400 since then. While it is true that very few students *choose* to learn the more complex, technical subjects in a language other than Magyar, the mere fact of emphasizing Magyar even at popular request tends to work against the instruction in other languages.

There are seven so-called "nationality gymnasiums" or secondary schools in Hungary. There are German secondary schools in Budapest, Baja and Pécs, Slovak in Budapest and Békéscsaba, Romanian in Gyula and Serbo-Croatian in Budapest, with a combined enrollment of more than 700 students. Beyond the secondary schools, nationality education is more sparse. There are kindergarten and nursery teachers training for women in the Romanian, South Slav, and Slovak languages at Szarvas, and in the German language at Sopron. In the Baja Teachers' College, the Budapest Teachers' College, and the Debrecen Teachers' College, German and South-Slav, Slovak and Romanian language training respectively prepares teachers for careers in the nationality primary schools. Those preparing to teach at more advanced levels of the general schools can get a diploma in German and South Slav at the Pécs Pedagogical Higher School, and one can get similar qualifications in Romanian and Slovak at the Szeged Higher School of Pedagogy. Only the Eotvoes Loránd University of Budapest grants degrees for nationality language teachers at the secondary school level, but the university degrees generally are awarded in the philology of the language rather than in language instruction for high schools for the nationalities. Altogether in 1976 there were 447 nationality-schools with a total enrollment of 28,816 pupils which represents a 49 percent and 30 percent increase, respectively, over 1966. In addition, between 1950 and 1975 there were also 612 textbooks published in Hungary for students in the various nationality education schools.

Although most teachers now employed in the nationality language education received their degrees in Hungary, many· of these teachers have attended either summer language instruction in their linguistically native country or have actually studied in these places for one or more academic years. Generally, they are quite competent, but they must fight continuous uphill battles against apathy and the strong local pressures of assimilation. The fact that there are half-hour daily broadcasts on three radio stations on German, Slovak and Serbo-Croatian languages seems to be of little value to the nationalities. Each nationality has at least one weekly or bi-weekly newspaper that maintains its own professional interest group association, and active cultural life is attempted at many of the villages where a large number of the nationalities live. These factors, however, are of little value in an industrially complex integrated society where isolated location—native or non-native alike—is bound to disappear.[16]

Legitimacy and Nationalism

The purpose of this elaborate educational system, frequently even for people who really do not desire special education but desire to get ahead primarily by their identification with Hungary and Hungary's advanced technological system, is to convince the surrounding states to reciprocate in kind. The issue of the treatment of Hungarians in Czechoslovakia, Yugoslavia and Romania is a serious one, an issue on which the legitimacy of the regime partially rests. If, in addition to providing an acceptable standard of living, the Kádár government is able to protect the welfare of the Magyars living in these neighboring states, the Hungarian citizens' conviction that Kádár is truly a national leader and not just a "Communist puppet" can contribute to their support of Kádár's position and his policies. If, on the other hand, they believe that Kádár and his government cannot or would not protect the Magyars in neighboring states against discrimination and what many of them deem to be close to "genocide," the economic legitimacy achieved by Kádár in a remarkably short period of time may not prove to be enough.[17]

There seems to be little problem in Yugoslavia, where Hungarian cultural autonomy is preserved. After a brief period of unease with Czechoslovakia, Czechoslovak policy has also promoted a respectable treatment of its Magyar minority; its record, while not excellent, at least is acceptable in matters of minority policy and no one in Hungary is prepared to ask for more.

The greatest problem seems to be in Romania. Ceausescu's forced Romanization policy and his conviction that he will create a Great Romanian Empire has intended to discriminate purposefully and clearly against Magyars and Germans living in Romania. In his educational reforms, economic development plans, employment policies, in short in the most important areas of human existence, the nearly two million Hungarians living in Romania are sharply disadvantaged. No one, of course, talks of the return of Transylvania or of a Hungarian attack to depose the Romanian leader. But the Hungarians demand that the Romanian leadership live up to the letter of its own laws and do so in a spirit of decent accommodation. So far, the Hungarian government has refused to "intervene in Romania's domestic affairs" in any fashion involving official contacts. Even at the June 1977 meetings between Ceausescu and Kádár, a private and low-key approach had been used to ameliorate the hardship of the Hungarian population. The example of Hungary's treatment of its own minorities is viewed as adequate in gaining reciprocally beneficial treatment for the Magyars of Romania.

And yet the issue will not go away. The nation, nationality, nationalism, and legitimacy are all involved in playing significant roles in regards to the question of the treatment of Magyars in Romania. It is now an issue on which the acceptance of the Hungarian leadership by the entire Magyar population is dependent.

NOTES

1. Endre Kovács, *Szemben a történelemmel* [Contrary to History], (Budapest: Magvető, 1977), provides a detailed development of national feelings, especially in Eastern Europe.

2. On the development of Hungarian nationalism the best work is *Nemzet és törtenelem* [Nation and History] (Budapest: Akadémia, 1975).

3. In the 1930s two of Hungary's greatest historians engaged in a passionate debate over the topic of the treatment of the minorities in the Middle Ages, but came to the same conclusion that no force was used to assimilate them. For the debate see Gyula Szekfü's initial article "Népek egymás közt a középkorban" [People in Each Others Community in the Middle Ages], in *Magyar Szemle* (1935) and his *Állam és Nemzet* [State and Nation], (Budapest: 1939), and Elemér Mályusz's reply in *Századok* (1939).

4. See for example: Benedek Szőlősy, *Cantus Catholici*, 1655; Péter Révay, *De monarchia et sacra corona regni Hungariae centuriae septem* (Frankfurt, 1659); Márton Szentiványi, *Miscellanea* (Tyrnaviae/Nagyszombat/Trnava: 1691).

5. Zoltán Toth, "The Nationality Problem in Hungary, 1843-1849," *Acta Historica*, 1955, pp. 235-277.

6. József Révai, *Marxizmus, népiesség, magyarság* [Marxism, Populism, Hungarianism], (Budapest: Szikra, 1949), p. 187.

7. Tamás Aczél and Tibor Méray, *The Revolt of the Mind* (London: Thames and Hudson, 1960), p. 124.

8. *Ibid.*, pp. 125-126.

9. The best bibliography of the extensive debate is contained in István Király, "Hazafiság és internacionalizmus" [Patriotism and Internationalism], in *Hazafiság és forradalmiság* [Patriotism and Revolutionarism] (Budapest: Kossuth, 1974), pp. 355-358. Cf. Miklos Stier, "Hazafiság és internacionalizmus" [Patriotism and Internationalism] in *Századok,* 1(1974), pp. 220-261; Jenő Szűcs, "A nemzet historikuma és a történelemszemlélet nemzeti látószöge" [The History of the Nation and the National Viewpoint of Historicism] in *Nemzet és történelem* [Nation and History] (Budapest: Akadémia, 1975), pp. 13-183; Levente Csipős, "Vita a történelemszemléletről és a hazafias nevelésröl" [A Debate Concerning Historical Schools and Patriotic Upbringing], *Párttörténeti Közlemények*, 2 (1968), pp. 121-146.

10. László Kővágó, "Népköztársaságunk nemzetiségi politikájáról" [Concerning the Nationality Policy of Our People's Democracy], *Társadalmi Szemle*, 11 (1968), 29, and Dániel Czatányi, "Nemzetiségi Kérdés es történelmi hagyományok" [Nationality Question a Historical Tradition], *Népszabadság*, July 27, 1969.

11. Dr. Frigyes Wild, "Német nemzetiségek Magyarországon" [German Nationalities in Hungary], *Belpolitikai Szemle*, (July 1959), p. 21.

12. László Kővágó, *Kissebség, nemzetiség* [Minority, Nationality], (Budapest: Kossuth, 1977), pp. 61-67.

13. For the breakdown of the above figures cf. László Kósa, "Nemzetiségek a mai Magyarországon" [Nationalities in Contemporary Hungary], *Valoság*, pp. 12-14.

14. "Nemzetiségek helyzetéről" [Concerning the Situation of the Nationalities], *Népszabadság* (October 6, 1968).

15. Lajos László, "Anyanyelve? Nemzetisége?" [Your Mother-Tongue? Your Nationality?], *Élet és Irodalom* (August 21, 1971).

16. László Kővágó, "Nemzetiségi szövetségek" [Nationality Associations], *Népszabadság* (June 14, 1970).

17.   On the official nationality policy of the regime cf. *Nemzetiségi kérdés–nemzetiségi politika* [Nationality Question–Nationality Policy], (Budapest: Kossuth, 1968); and Ferenc Herczeg, *Az MSzMP nemzetiségi politikájáról* [Concerning the Nationality Policy of the Hungarian Socialist Wokers' Party], (Budapest: Kossuth, 1976).

Z. Anthony Kruszewski

VII

NATIONALISM AND POLITICS:
POLAND

Historical Overview of the Factors Affecting Polish Nationalism

The conflict and coexistence between nationalism and politics within the Communist political system of contemporary Poland is a vast and complex subject largely predetermined by the difficult and tumultuous history of that country with the millenium of her national history. Contrary to still quite often propounded statements appearing in print in the West, Poland is not a "new" country as it is so often described.

The very fact that her establishment and consolidation as an independent kingdom in the tenth century was due to the national struggle against the German nation largely determined the politics of Poland's first dynasty, the Piasts, until the end of the fourteenth century. Although the pressure of the Holy Roman Empire (of the German Nation) on Poland ceased by the second part of the twelfth century, the subsequent two centuries witnessed intermittent struggles against the Teutonic Knights who, invited by the Mazovian dukes in 1226 to fight the Ancient Prussians, subsequently conquered vast areas from the Prussians (whom they absorbed), Poles and Lithuanians.[1] Thus, the German threat, real or perceived, did not recede from the Polish political scene and public opinion until the beginning of the sixteenth century when the Teutonic order was secularized and became the fiefdom of the kings of Poland in 1525. Ironically enough, the emerging new kingdom of Prussia largely revived the memory of those deeply seated anti-German feelings by her participation in the eighteenth century partitions of Poland and the subsequent organized attempts at the denationalization of the Poles within Prussia's borders prior to 1918. Prussia consistently glorified the history and exploits of the Teutonic Knights[2] which were so bitterly and totally differently perceived by the Polish nation.

The horror of the Nazi legacy of 1939-1945, which was to cost Poland over six million of her citizens or over 22 percent of the nation, formed in the Polish public opinion but a link in the chain of the Polish-German confrontation. As did the Prussians of the nineteenth and twentieth centuries, the Nazis again stressed the German anti-Polish policies going back to the early medieval times, the "Drang nach Osten" and the heritage of the Teutonic Knights.[3] Hence, tragically enough, the Polish-German antagonism largely contributed to the formation of the Polish nationhood in the beginning of its history and in recent centuries it considerably shaped the foundations and subsequently molded contemporary Polish nationalism.

The impact of that antagonism had not only expected cultural and political repercussions but, since the sixteenth century, also religious ones. The border between the Slavic and Germanic ethnolingusitic groups of Europe was much more in conflict than the western border between the Germanic and Romance groups. The former since the middle of the twelfth century divided Poland from Germany and later Catholic Poland from Protestant Prussia. Whereas the formation of European nationalism, expressed in linguistic and cultural terms, is generally traced to the beginning of the nineteenth century and the impact of the Napoleonic period, the Polish history of the early medieval period, the tenth through the fifteenth centuries, is replete with nationalistic feelings, cultural biases and linguistic restrictions following the "Drang nach Osten"[4] of the German nation, which later were only strengthened by the religious biases on both sides. Those events set the stage in Polish-German relations for the advent of the modern nationalism of the nineteenth and twentieth centuries, with disastrous results which culminated in the tragic events of World War II and its aftermath.

An appreciation of Polish-German political interactions is necessary if one is to understand the depth and ramifications of passionate Polish nationalism and to unravel its roots, idiosyncracies and cultural-political-religious connections. But that monumental impact of the German pressure on Poland which provided the formative (although obviously undesired) stimulus in deepening Polish national feelings is but only one element, however complex, of that passionate vortex of nationalistic perceptions without which one could not understand Polish past and present. The other element of Polish nationalism was tempered by the Polish-Russian conflict which was also expressed in the political, cultural and religious terms.[5]

The Polish-Russian conflict, which also over the centuries resulted in strengthening and molding the Polish nationalism, began initially in political competition for regional supremacy. In contrast to the situation on Poland's western border, which did not become a religious one until the sixteenth century and even then not completely clear cut,[6] the fact that the Poles obtained their religious and cultural heritage from Rome and the Eastern Slavs from Constantinople had far-reaching consequences. From the beginning of their respective national histories, the political conflict between the Poles and the Eastern Slavs was reinforced by cultural and religious differences. That conflict did not, however, possess semblance of confrontation over national identity and struggle for ethnic survival, which characterized the Polish-German clash since the beginning of Polish history.

The fusion of the political, cultural and religious elements in the Polish-Russian and Polish-Ukrainian conflict can be traced only to the struggles of the sixteenth and seventeenth centuries, for for domination over vast areas inhabited by the Orthodox population and considered by the Russians to be part of their patrimony, but at the same time part of the Polish-Lithuanian Commonwealth. The subsequent continuous efforts on the part of the Poles to "Catholicize"[7] these areas brought the Polish-Russian conflict to its peak, even if these areas were not systematically subjected to planned polonization. Nevertheless, individual and then mass polonization, especially of the upper classes in Lithuania, Belorussia and the Ukraine, added another dimension to the depth of the Polish-Russian conflict.[8]

These historical developments did not, of course, have the pronounced impact on the characteristics and strength of Polish nationalism until the eighteenth century reversal of the political roles of the main protagonists in the contest for political power in Eastern Europe: the Polish-Lithuanian Commonwealth versus the Russian Empire. The subsequent partitions of Poland, in which Russia obtained an overwhelming portion of the territory of the old Polish Kingdom and by 1815 also its central territorial core with Warsaw, predetermined the depth of that conflict.[9] The pressure brought about by the partitioning power, Russia, against the Polish upper classes and subsequently all the Catholic Poles culminated in the nineteenth century in the deep-seated antagonism between both nations.[10]

The political, cultural and religious elements were fused in the course of this conflict on a scale comparable, if not deeper, to the previously sketched Polish-German conflict in the opinion of those Poles who were directly drawn into and victimized by that conflict. The attempt, initially quite successful, on the part of the Russian Empire to remove and absorb by partition and denationalization the previous challenger for regional hegemony resulted subsequently in deepening the determination, then resistance, then despair, of the Poles vis-a-vis Russia and everything Russian. Series of desperate, brave, futile, and brutally suppressed uprisings (which characterized the Polish-Russian relations of 1793-1918)[11] resulted paradoxically enough not only in the survival of the Polish nation, which existed without its state for 123 years under pressure of cultural annihilation, but speeded up the fusion of social classes into a modern nation.[12]

These policies, ruthlessly if not crudely pursued by the Tsarist Russian occupying authorities, have progressively resulted in drawing other classes, apart from the nobility and intelligentsia, into the vortex of Polish nationalism. Religious and cultural suppression, which was ironically enough a tit-for-tat for the previous Polish attempts to "Catholicize" the Orthodox faithful, has contributed more than anything to the drawing of the peasants and the workers to the cause of Polish nationalism.[13] Thus both the Prussian an the Russian cultural-religious pressures and the Polish response to them have resulted in molding the contemporary Polish nationalism. Hence, in spite of the 123 years of division into three foreign jurisdictions, the Polish nation re-emerged in 1918 relatively unscathed to be further tempered and solidified by the experiences of the Polish-Soviet War of 1919-1920 and World War II.[14]

These circumstances, deeply rooted in the past and recent history of the country and the interaction with Poland's both powerful and numerous neighbors, have predetermined basic attitudes prevalent in Poland even now, in vastly different ideological and political contemporary conditions. Such peculair interrelations of nationalism and religion are seldom to be observed in other countries. The nonexistence of the Polish state apparatus and suppression of Polish language and culture and restrictions imposed by occupiers on the Catholic Church for over a century by both Russia and Prussia have further reinforced the long-standing pivotal role of religion in the Polish political attitudes. It was especially during the period of partitioned Poland (1795-1918) that the Polish Catholic Church became *de facto* the only public national institution where the Polish language, so deeply interwoven into the matrix of Polish nationalism, could be freely spoken and enjoyed. This peculiarity, coupled with the leadership provided by the priests (active in all the Polish uprisings and liberation movements in the country and in exile), has endowed the Polish church hierarchy with secular authority not usually enjoyed by religious leaders in other countries.[15]

Furthermore, the long-standing Polish parliamentary tradition during the period of elective monarchy (1572-1795), whereby the primate of Poland was the acting king or *interrex* in the time between the death of the duly elected king and the election of his successor, is translated into responsibilities of leadership taken seriously and not merely symbolically by the contemporary head of the Polish Catholic Church.[16] In the reconstituted Poland of 1918 the Church was accorded a very special position, influencing not only the nationalist Right in politics, but the masses generally, including even members of the socialist Left. Those foundations for the political role of the Church on one hand and its impact on the minds of the Poles on the other was furthermore augmented by two developments during and after World War II, which irrevocably affected the political and religious climate of Poland. Without the understanding of these events one cannot explain the delicate balance between the Church and (Communist) State in contemporary Poland.

One purely political development was the treatment by the Nazis of the priests and the church hierarchy in particular, who were subjected to exactly the same treatment accorded by the German occupation authorities to the Polish nation at large. The jails, execution squads and the concentration camps at Auschwitz, Dachau, Mauthausen, etc., took a heavy toll—about 2,000 or ca. 20 percent of all the Polish priests and bishops, some of whom were tortured before they were executed.[17] The Catholic hierarchy was throughout the war supportive of the Polish war aims and deeply involved in the activities of the resistance movement and the Polish war effort in exile under the allied command. There were chaplains even in the Polish Army under Soviet command irrespective of the treatment accorded to the priests, and the Polish priests in particular, in the USSR.

This phenomenon of total integration of the nation and its religious leaders in the all-out struggle for survival against the Nazis was of momentous importance for the relations between the church and state in Poland after World War II. The anti-church policies pursued in Poland by the Soviet authorities during the Soviet-Polish war of 1919-1920 and again in the eastern part of the country annexed by the USSR from Poland under the Soviet-Nazi pact of August 1939, had to be modified. The moral authority with which the Polish Church emerged from the ashes of the war was immense and formidable, even in spite of the terrible losses on all levels of religious leadership from the village to the capital city. The Church actually entered the new era of post-World War II Communist politics stronger than ever in the recent history of the country.[18]

The proud record of leadership from the seminarians[19] to the bishops who provided shelter for the freedom fighters and proudly dealt with Frank, the Nazi governor of Poland (who was "treated" to the starvation ration allowed by the Nazis to the Poles, by the archbishop Sapieha of Cracow) made the post-World War II Polish Catholic Church into a national institution, which even the full pressure available to the modern, Communist government could not dislodge from the Polish religious and political scene. In fact, the Church became the *de facto* opposition party after the take-over of the Polish political system in 1947.[20]

The second element which contributed in an unforeseen way to the added strength of the Catholic Church in post-World War II Poland was the tragic surgery performed on the body politic of Poland—the westward shift of her ethnic and national territory. It set in motion a chain of events of tremendous proportions, a mass migration of nearly five million Poles to the Western Territories along the Oder-Neisse and the Baltic Sea.[21] The Polish population of pre-1939 eastern Poland was reduced from ca. 3.8 mil. to ca. .75 mil. by war losses and the population exchanges ordered under the Soviet-Polish agreements of 1944.[22]

Catholics had composed only 64 percent of the population of Poland in 1939.[23] But after the elimination of the Germans, mostly Protestants, by flight or postwar expulsion, and the wartime Nazi genocide of three million Polish Jews, post–World War II Poland unexpectedly emerged as a Communist country with 98 percent of its population Catholic in background. This was surely an unintended outcome of the joint actions of both neighbors of Poland who inadvertently contributed to the strengthening of the role of the Catholic Church in Poland, during and after the war.

The historical overview of the factors affecting Polish nationalism has hitherto dealt exclusively with the Polish-German and the Polish-Russian relations in the context of political, cultural and religious aspirations, confrontations and conflict. The overwhelming, uniform Catholic character of the Polish culture was stressed (in spite of the existence throughout the centuries of the large and prominent groups of Poles belonging to other Christian and non-Christian religions who contributed immensely to the formation of that culture) only because these characteristics helped the Poles to survive as a nation for 123 years without their own state, against Protestant Prussia and Orthodox Russia.

Poland bordered on the countries which embraced Eastern Christianity during the first four centuries of her early history and for the following six centuries the boundary between Western and Eastern Christianity ran through the Polish and the Polish-Lithuanian lands. The westward shift of Poland in 1945 paradoxically enough restored the twelfth century border, the ethnic and religious monolith.[24] The Reformation also made considerable impact on Poland in the sixteenth century when for a time a majority of the parliamentary members were Protestant, reflecting general acceptance of the Reformation by the Polish nobility. The Counter-Reformation largely obliterated this impact but many Polish Protestants remained (some of the most prominent leaders in public life).[25]

The Jewish immigration, which had begun already in the tenth century (the first Polish coin minted in 966 has the name of the country written in the Hebrew alphabet), reached the peak in later centuries during the persecution of Jews in Western Europe. The Polish rulers actively encouraged this immigration and gave extensive privileges to the immigrants such as the Statute of Kalisz in 1264.[26] Hence the population of Poland and later the Polish-Lithuanian Commonwealth was about ten percent Jewish, an overwhelming majority at that time of all the Jews in the world. Due to the peculiar value system of the Polish nobility, disdaining commerce over the years, the Jews of Poland became the intermediate class between the peasants and the nobility, concentrated in commerce, and formed about thirty percent of the population of the large cities with the smaller ones being up to ninety percent Jewish.[27]

The coexistence and subsequent conflicts between Christians and Jews have added new strains to Polish nationalism. Especially in the nineteenth century the acute economic competition in a generally under-developed country with few job opportunities resulted in anti-Semitism which during that period was crudely exploited and fanned by the oc-cupiers for outright political purposes. Some of the stereotypes and attitudes formed, especially in the last century, are still visible in the contemporary Polish nationalism, even in vastly different economic situations and, tragically enough, even after the Holocaust there remain vestiges of anti-Semitism in the country without the Jews.[28]

The preceding millenium of the country was shared by these two peoples for better or worse. The subsequent creation of the Polish-Lith-uanian Commonwealth in 1386 and its eastward expansion to the rank of one of the largest European powers by the seventeenth century brought the overwhelming percentage of the Jews within the borders of that State (e.g., Poland, the Ukraine, Belorussia, Lithuania). The partitions divided the Jews together with the Polish territory between Prussia, Austria and Russia, with the latter acquiring most of the Polish Jewish population.

The Poles had also been brought into large scale contact with the Eastern Slavs and the Baltic peoples through the formation of the Polish-Lithuanian Commonwealth. The Commonwealth was a pluralistic country of many nationalities and languages with the Kingdom subdivided into two "nations" (Polish and Lithuanian) and each into "families." Thus some Ruthenians (Ukrainians) classified themselves in Latin as "natione Polonus, gente Ruthenus." The Commonwealth brought for the Poles a total reorientation of ethnic perceptions. Whereas Poland before union with Lithuania was a preponderately ethnically homogeneous population, after 1386 the multinational Commonwealth included, in addition to Poles and Lithuanians, Germans, Ruthenians (present-day Ukrainians and Belorussians), Russians, Jews, Tartars, Armenians, Karaims, Latvians and Estonians plus smaller numbers of other nationalities.[29]

This "Jagiellonian" concept of a state was a vast departure from the ethnically uniform "Piast" Poland. Contemporary Polish nationalism was molded by all these influences and carried within its deep roots the contacts and conflicts with the diverse fellow citizens of the Commonwealth, whose history it shared with those groups for four centuries.

These events which shaped Polish nationalism in conflict with both the Russians and the Germans, and especially the unique role of the Catholic Church in Poland, serve as a necessary key to the understanding of the complexities of the interplay between nationalism and politics in contemporary Poland.

Factors of Ethnicity in the Leadership and the Membership of the Party

The Polish Communist Party was multi-ethnic in both its leadership and membership since its creation in 1918 until the anti-Zionist campaign of 1967-1968 and its aftermath. The Party did not function between 1938-1942 after being officially disbanded by a decision of the Comintern. Most of its leadership at that time in the USSR were tried and executed on what is now termed "unjust" charges.[30] Although the purges and execution affected representatives of all ethnic groups in the Party due to historical, social and political reasons, Jews, Ukrainians and Belorussians were the only minorities of the pre-1939 Polish Republic which were heavily represented in the membership of the pre-World War II Polish Communist Party. The Jews were by far the largest group of these three and early in the interwar period the Ukrainians and the Belorussians were regrouped into the separate West Belorussian and the West Ukrainian autonomous parties.[31]

The political parties of the interwar period, with few exceptions (the Communist Party of Poland being one of them), rarely cut across ethnic lines. Although the reconstituted Poland of 1918 resembled the shape of pre-partitioned Poland of 1772 (except for the smaller depth of her eastward extension), the relationships and consciousness of all the ethnic groups which the II Republic (1918-1939) inherited from the I Republic of the eighteenth century were completely and irrevocably changed by the nineteenth century swell of national reawakening. It was tragic that the Poles, who themselves benefited from the national reawakening of the Poles of Silesia, Pomerania and Mazuria, could not understand, except for a few politicians on the Socialist Left, the reawakening and national aspirations of the Lithuanians, Ukrainians and Belorussians.[32]

This lack of understanding was largely predicated by an acute class conflict stemming from the fact that the Polish leaders, who carved the new borders and set new political situations, were largely unable to communicate across the negotiating tables with the leadership of their Eastern neighbors, whose intelligentsia developed from the peasant class. The Polish leadership class values, life style and interests were rooted in their landed estates, whose owners were largely Polish, and the peasants in the Eastern Marches of Poland were largely Lithuanian, Ukrainian or Belorussian.[33] Hence, various ethnic groups of the interwar Poland created their own national parties.

The Communist Party of Poland cut across these ethnic lines for ideological reasons and also had a disproportionately large percentage of Jews in membership and especially in leadership. Jews were among the most oppressed people inhabiting the former Russian, Austrian, and Prussian empires, and were most hopeful for the fateful changes brought by Socialism. They wanted to abolish the old order and had little to lose. But it was precisely due to this double jeopardy—radical theory and the ethnic composition—that the Party met only with limited and mostly local successes.[34]

The people in 1919/1920 perceived themselves to be endangered by the Red Army and the workers and peasants, instead of deserting the cause of new Poland, flocked to the Polish Army by the hundreds of thousands. The crushing defeat suffered by the Soviets in the Battle of Warsaw of 1920 not only effectively blocked the road to Western Europe but also destroyed one of the favorite revolutionary tenets of class warfare because the Polish workers fought mostly against them.[35] For the Poles, Communism brought on the bayonets of the Red Army was perceived to be auguring the reimposition of the Russian rule, regardless of the ideology. Furthermore, the campaign of the Polish Communists in behalf of the Soviets was largely received as treason. The publications now appearing freely admit the amazing lack of understanding by the Polish Communists, irrespectively of their ethnic background, of the strength of national aspirations prevalent at that time in Poland and craving for independence after 123 years.[36]

Thus, the Communists were then and largely now burdened in the eyes of Polish public opinion by an insurmountable handicap. The nationalism released by the fact of recovery of independence, for which four previous generations of Poles has fought, made the task which the Communists set out for themselves in the interwar Poland nearly impossible. This occurred on the strength of their ideological goals of advocating a Polish Soviet Republic[37] (within the USSR) and ethnic composition of their membership—"foreign," to say the least, in the eyes of the Polish nationalists. But it should be stressed that that perception was espoused by large segments of the Polish public opinion, even in the working class of pre-1939 Poland.

The Polish worker was voting rather for the socialists and other center parties. These parties might have had Jews in the leadership but they were opting for national independence. Thus, the deep-seated nationalist animosities, if not outright anti-Semitim, created an image the Polish Communist Party could not shake off even fifty years after its creation in 1918.

The Nazi-Soviet pact of 1939 and the division of Poland between those two powers were juxtaposed on the above historical determinants (and the nationalistic stereotypes) and created in 1942, and since, an outright impossible situation for the newly re-established Polish Communist Party. The membership of that party was severely tested by the Nazi occupation terror afflicting the whole nation—hence, much more patriotic than the Polish Communists of the interwar party. The recently published biographies of the outstanding Communist martyrs proudly proclaim their deeds in the anti-Nazi defense of Poland in 1939, immediately after their release from the Polish prisons, or their nationalistic activities in the underground.[38] Thus, the common national platform is stressed and Communist linkages with the heritage underllned, making the Party the executor of the pround national traditions and "linear" descendants of the great leaders of the Polish insurgencies in the nineteenth century. Thus, a brave, if not futile, effort is being made to "nationalize" rather than "internationalize" the traditions and deeds of the leadership of the Party against its own ideological precepts and history.

Indeed, the resistance movement which was experienced by a large segment of the present Communist leadership and its nationalistic atmosphere was both an advantage and a handicap for the reconstituted party. It was much closer to the people and their experience, and its program was property adjusted to it by leaving off the word "Communist" on the new name of the party (Polish Workers' Party) but it was also rent

by considerable and not well-hidden disagreement between the segment
of the leadership stemming from the anti-Nazi underground and the con-
trolling (overwhelmingly just after World War II but also later to a lesser
extent) element of leaders who spent the war years in the USSR and
returned to Poland with the Red Army in 1944.

The latter group, although internationalist and ideologically pure, was
inherently unable to understand the nation they set out to rule, not
having shared with it the grim, heroic and nationalistic wartime resistance.
These elements were bound to influence the power struggles of the 1950s
and 1960s. The leaders "who returned in the uniforms," as it was ironically related to this author, more nearly resembled the cross-section of
the pre-war Polish Communist Party in the ethnic terms—large numbers
of them were Jews or perceived to be Jews. The escape Eastward turned
out to be a most judicious decision for some 200,000 Polish Jews who
returned home after the war to join some 100,000 to 150,000 survivors
out of over three million who perished at the hands of the Nazis.[39] Thus,
the underground membership core of the Party included very few Jews,
mostly in the partisan units in the forests, as most were unable to escape
from the ghettos and the extermination camps. Those who were saved
and hidden by the Poles, some 100,000, were not active in the resistance,
except for relatively few completely assimilated ones, since they would
be obviously easily detected by the Nazis (only 10 percent of the Jews
in pre-1939 Poland spoke Polish at home[40] and even fewer could "pass"
as Polish).

The new stage of tragedy was thus set. The "home" Communist party
had few Jews, assumed more and more national, if not nationalistic,
postures and although the Communist military units saved many Jews,
there was no love lost. The "Moscow" Communists who came to issue
orders and generally set policies for the country hardly knew it in its
vastly changed form, were internationalists, Stalinist and Polish-Jewish.
The unification of both wings of the party was even more painful since
the leadership had to be assumed by the second/third echelon level of
leadership, those who did not hold important enough party positions or
were at the time in Polish prisons, to be able to go to the USSR, where by
1938 most of the leadership of the Party was liquidated in the purges.[41]
The most brilliant Party theoreticians and activists could not, thus, work
for the rebuilt party in the 1940s and 1950s. And they were sorely needed

since the newly promoted leadership of the 1940s neither had the stature or maturity to avoid the pitfalls of party strife and the ensuing anti-Semitic power struggle which culminated in the mass exodus of the Jews, Polish Jews or Poles of Jewish heritage in 1956-1967 and 1967-1968, which *de facto* eliminated Jews not only from the Party but from the Polish cultural life and society after ten centuries of coexistence and common history.[42]

There were several other elements apart from the sheer power struggle involved in the events of 1967-1968 which were largely determined by the quest for the positions and apartments which were to be vacated. And apartments are still an especially precious commodity since the World War II destruction of the cities. The Party was responding to the nationalistic postures shaped by the historical and religious attitudes, even if religion was not supposed to play any role in the Communist praxis. But the Party also desperately wanted legitimacy in the eyes of the public. Hence, we saw in print such a horrendously un-Marxist statement in the party literary magazine by the head of the Central Commitee education department that "the Party had improper ethnic composition of leadership."[43] Incredibly enough, the Party was responding to the most sensitive perceptions of the public opinion: (1) that the Party was not Polish (regardless of the validity of such perception) and (2) that it came from the USSR and, hence, was not perceived to be "national."

Both charges, volunteered informally over and over to anyone, including the visitors from abroad who were willing to listen, were hitting at the roots of legitimacy of the Party ruling intensely nationalistic people for whom previous historical pressures, conflicts and experiences with other religions and powerful neighbors served as a key to assessing their contemporary rulers. Thus, the frantic attempt at the indigenization of the Party's leadership was for the "partisans" a convenient excuse to reach the pinnacle of power, and at the same time, by makeing even Communist Jews scapegoats for everything that went wrong until 1967, enabled them to appeal to the basest nationalistic elements in Poland. The perusal of the Polish press brings this out quite clearly. Although concrete proof is well-hidden, such a method of provocation *de facto* linking the Communists who failed to protect Jews and the nationalists who participated in the riot had been used in Radom in 1946.

After 1968 the Party achieved almost total indigenization but at a heavy historical and ideological price. Incredibly enough, even the 1976 "price hike" riots which united workers, intellectuals, the Church and dissidents, have been hinted to be inspired by the Jews. Afraid to confront a new phenomenon of the large scale political dissident movement uniting various social elements,[44] the Party stooped very low to the point to the time-honored scapegoats. It is indeed "Anti-Semitism without the Jews," as observed by a Western author.[45] Dredging the lowest feelings of racial hatred and misconceptions fed by tragic national frustrations of the past centuries might have been a clever short-range measure but at the same time was indeed a desperate admission of Communist ideological bankruptcy.

The Impact of Modernization on National Consciousness and the Role of the Church as Reinforcing Factor of Nationalism

Modernization had enveloped the Polish lands unevenly in the second part of the nineteenth century and the beginning of the twentieth century. Industrialization, urbanization and changes in agriculture—the forerunners of modernization—affected only part of the area of contemporary Poland for reasons of the restrictive and unenlightened political decisions and socioeconomic policies, in a rather haphazard fashion. In degree of modernization, the Polish lands included in Prussia benefited the most but even they suffered from the above-mentioned restrictive policies, and the lands included in Russia benefited the least.[46]

Urbanization and industrialization, as concurrent phenomena, were limited to the Upper Silesian region, the Dabrowa basin and the Warsaw-Lodz region. Although industry was weak and most limited to agricultural processing industry in Western Poland and Pomerania, the cities both large and small were rapidly developing throughout the nineteenth century, affecting modernization, social changes and interrelations between all classes, speeding the societal development. In Southern Poland, apart from two largest cities and a small industrial region, changes were coming about very slowly and painfully. In Central Poland, ruled by Russia until 1915, the conditions were quite backward even within the sight of the large cities.[47]

All, or nearly all, these characteristics burdened the new interwar II Polish Republic. The uneven social and economic development was the

major barrier to modernization. These conditions largely prevailed throughout the interwar period of 1918-1939 and were only partly affected by a
bold economic plan developed in the 1930s, which developed industries
in some of the most economically depressed areas, stressed building new
communication links and reoriented Polish foreign trade through the
newly-built port of Gdynia. All these efforts were just the beginning and
were largely handicapped by the effects of the Depression, which sapped
the economic resources of the country.

The Depression effects, in spite of rapid economic progress in some
areas, were such that the total output of Poland in 1939 was not much
larger than that of 1913 although many new areas of economic endeavor
were fostered and developed, new industries and techniques pioneered.[48]
One could not, however, even discuss the problems of modernization on
a large scale without solving the unsolvable (in the context of the pre-1939
economic and political realities) problems of landless peasants and some
six or more million underemployed persons in the countryside. And solutions were nowhere in sight within the inherent weakness of the Polish
industry and city employment opportunities.

The economic planning and the subsequent building of the Central
Industrial District around Sandomierz, although a reasonable departure
in the right direction, did not even begin large scale socioeconomic reforms. The lack of land, even though some land survived in large estates
until 1945, made industrialization and urbanization a necessity. Only
then could one undertake large scale modernization of the mostly rural
population of Poland. Suffice it to say that by the beginning of World
War II the urban segment of the population of Poland encompassed only
about 30 percent of the people[49] and if one further subtracts from that
figure the Jews who were far more urbanized, the urbanized portion of
the Polish nation in 1939 was not larger than 25 percent.[50] This figure
is significant since it indicates that the other three-fourths of the Polish
people were rural, parochial and deeply affected by the church in its
role as the prime agency of socialization.

The other primary agency of socialization, the Polish family, often
credited with the Church as the real preserve of the Polish nation, was
deeply permeated with the values generated and transmitted by the
latter. Thus the Church and the family were in almost total symbiosis in
the Polish villages until comtemporary times and to a large extent remain
so even in the modernized nation-state.

The third major agency of socialization, the school, practically did not exist on the large scale over vast areas of the lands of partitioned Poland (especially in areas under Russian occupation); and where it existed it served the Prussian occupiers, who used it to de-nationalize the people as late as 1905-1906 (cf. the famous school strikes in Wrzesnia) by forbidding any subject to be taught in Polish. Austrian-occupied southern Poland was the only part of the country where peasant masses had schools in Polish, in relatively non-conflict situation. A large network of secondary schools and higher education also allowed the masses to be the recipients of modernization and to allow them to aspire to higher social status through education.[51] Thus, a relatively sizable group of new middle-class people of peasant origin emerged.

In Western Poland this phenomenon appeared through urbanization and in spite of the drawback of the denationalizing influence through the schools. In the above situation the role of the Church prior to 1918 was obvious. The Church leadership molded values and controlled the impact of modernization on the minds of the largely rural community. It can be said that, in spite of the poverty generally prevailing in the majority of the villages, the Church could not and did not support any large scale social schemes such as transfer of population, even if it would have been possible, to the cities or large scale social mobility generally. Any such upheaval would of necessity mean not only dimunition of Church role in shaping the values and life of the peasants but, more importantly, it would obviously lead to the dimunition of its influence and dilution of its power over large masses of people. Moreover, it would also result in drastic changes in the belief patterns, life style and responsiveness of the peasants to the call of the Church. The social linkages of the hierarchy of the Church in Poland with the upper classes, have been furthermore traditional, existed for centuries and continued on a large scale into the 1930s and 1940s.[52] Large scale social transformation within the hierarchy of the Church came only in the twentieth century and led to different perspectives and goals of the role of the Church in the society.

These changes and the establishment of a universal school system (not quite completed because of World War II) by the II Republic prior to 1939, have led to transformation of attitudes, social mobility and slowly to modernization of Polish villages. The basic role of the Church in shaping the values of the peasants, however, has changed little. It was the Church which changed its goals and perceptions of social objectives. But neither the Church nor the state could have solved the basic problem of overcrowding of the villages and overcome the weakness of the cities. Without these basic solutions one could not talk of modernization of three-fourths of the pre-1939 Polish nation—the peasants.

Suffice it to say that the Church fostered, even in its new role, traditional values and channeled patriotism and nationalism of the devout masses. The Holy Virign of Czestochowa, the most venerable cult and pilgrimage object, was dubbed symbolically the "Queen of Poland" in the II Republic and officially crowned. Unable to create conditions for social mobility, the Church tolerated emigration overseas in the nineteenth and early twentieth centuries but supported group settlement and "emigrated" alongside the millions of peasants to, say, USA, Canada, Brazil or Agentina. In the new settlements, churches founded by priests who emigrated with the emigrants, were the first and often only public institutions which subsequently ran these communities.[53] This explains the phenomenon, for instance, of some 60 Polish parishes (churches with their schools and social organizations) in "Polish" Chicago at the turn of the century (some existing in that form even today.)

The migration from the villages to the cities, with growing urbanization, was, however, less organized and hence created more problems for the Church in the pre-World War Poland. Although the parishes were in existence in the cities as well as in the villages, the city life was so different in its life style and the controllable restraints often non-existent. Hence, even if the newly-urbanized peasant continued to attend the church, the control of the church over the organized community was vastly less effective in the cities than in the villages. Thus, the Polish peasant of the interwar period who was translocated to the cities was gradually less parochial and less controllable, becoming modernized. As for his *weltanschauung,* it was and still is largely guided but no longer controlled by the Church.

The most drastic changes occurred during and after World War II when millions of peasants were taken to forced labor in Germany, where paradoxically they were largely affected by a modernized, even though wartime, society.[54] When they returned they were largely transformed in their attitudes towards work and life. Postwar migrations to the cities, whose both Jewish and Polish population was decimated (overall almost cut by half), opened enormous opportunities for modernization. The migration of close to 5 million people, largely from the villages and small towns to the newly-acquired Polish Western Territories, was an event of monumental consequences for the modernization of Polish villages.[55] It effectively solved the problem of overcrowded villages, landless peasants and lack of mobility due to town unemployment. Poland, although totally ruined by the war, was radically and irrevocably transformed.

Recently a steady stream of peasants from the villages, equal to the total yearly birthrate increment of the countryside, has been emigrating to the cities where jobs are either plentiful or created through planning. The size of the rural population in 1977 has largely remained equal to that of 1946, some 15 million. But the cities boomed from 8 million in 1946 to 20 million in 1977 due to the influx of peasants.[56] The tremendous transformation of the peasants-turned-workers, and hence the impact of modernization on national consciousness, is the overarching phenomenon of contemporary Poland.

A certain amount of "rurification" of the towns, as the phenomenon is called in Polish professional literature, occurred due to the overwhelming peasant composition of the Polish cities. The life style and values of the new arrivals were both shaped by the cities and the cities shaped by them. The postwar mass phenomenon of migration, however, resembled to some extent the previously outlined analogy with the overseas mass migration of the nineteenth century; the Church not only maintains a hold on the minds of the newly urbanized masses but influences their politics in the new confrontation of Church and (Communist) State. This does not mean that the devout patterns persist unchanged. Many a new peasant-worker ceases to attend the church when he moves to the large city. He is less prone to be visible and feels less socioreligious pressure, but in his basic attitudes he remains truly faithful to the Church.

The example of Nowa Huta, the first so-called socialist city outside Cracow without any church planned for 200,000 of its habitants, resulted thrugh the intermittent pressures, riots and petitions under the leadership of Karol Cardinal Wojtyla, the present Pope John Paul II, in the building of the beautiful modernistic church, after a Communist delay of some 20 years on Marx Street![57] Similar examples of new churches in the new housing developments all over Poland serving the new peasant-town dwellers, are replete. More than anything, they suggest the potent force of the old values and life patterns even in the socialist framework of a rapidly modernizing nation.

The forces of modernization and religion exert an immense impact on the national consciousness of half of the nation's population, which shifted from the villages to the cities in one generation. The tenacity with which they adhere to old customs and values is visible even to the casual observer. At the same time, the events of the last forty years, beginning with the 1939 invasion of Poland and subsequent turmoil and population shifts, more than anything else contributed to the unity of the nation and basic integration of the society. This paradox occurring in the supposedly socialist society is largely influenced by the Church because of its historic and present political and patriotic role, and causes a great problem for the Communist government, whose ideology can be only superficially grafted on the body politics now overwhelming Catholic and basically rooted in the Church-community closeness of its recent peasant past.

The curious, to say the least, view of religious pilgrimages and processions through the streets of the cities, with the streets closed by the Communist traffic policemen, testifies to the political-religious dichotomy in contemporary Poland. The Church is overwhelming visible 35 years after the revolution in Communist Poland and, ironically more visible, except within the sacred buildings in capitalist Mexico.[58] The tenaacity of Church-people linkages over the chasm of migrations and sociopolitical transformation in Poland is, in the final analysis, due largely to the ability of the Church to update its image and ideology, change its leadership in the immediate postwar period and assume progressive social programs. In this the Polish Catholic Church excelled and hence it succeeded in maintaining control even in confrontation with Communism. In some other countries such as Hungary and Czechoslovakia, the Church, unable to respond to the times, faltered or failed.

In Poland the Church transplanted its rural roots and spiritual control to the cities. It migrated with the people but, amazingly enough, in the process it became an even more formidable sociopolitical force in contemporary People's Poland than it was in the prewar II Republic. Now it is influencing probably 34 million out of a total of 35 million in 1939, it attracted only 20.7 million out of 35 million. There are now 15;200 priests, but only 9,700 in 1939. There are now 27 dioceses, seven more than in 1939, and most importantly, its leadership is completely unified and very carefully selected. Currently there are 75 relatively young and extremely well-educated bishops versus 46 in 1939.[59] The Roman Catholic Church has not only stayed with the people and expanded its formidable sway over people's minds into the only *de facto* opposition party, but tested by adversity and ideological struggle with the Communists has turned into a much more political and powerful force since World War II.

Competition between Communist and Traditional Nationalist Norms

The competition between Communist and traditional nationalist norms had begun soon after the introduction of the Communist government in Poland in 1944 but did not reach a sharp confrontation until the late 1940s. Only the introduction on a large scale of Stalinist norms into Poland by 1949 caused the outright confrontation of the former with the values and norms traditionally comprising the Polish national culture and especially espoused by the rural population, which over the centuries was the depository of many societal patterns in their unchanged form.

The cities and their population were always much more open to outside influences largely due to their broader contact with other cultures. The particular difficulty encountered by the Polish Communists in spreading their norms through the countryside and later supplanting the traditional nationalist norms was compounded by the difficult situation of the Communist party vis-a-vis the Polish political spectrum of the country they attempted to communize.[60] The relative weakness of Polish Communism in the 1940s has been freely admitted in the publications now appearing in Poland. The party numbered some 20,000 to 30,000 members in 1945,[61] emerging from the underground, partisan units, and exile in the USSR.

The Polish Underground State, on the other hand, consisted of the military (the resistance movement of some 380,000 members), political (complete undergound administration of all levels directed by the "Home" component of the Council of Ministers of the Polish Government in exile in London), judicial (underground courts), and educational (underground secondary schools, colleges and universities) branches which were based on a broad anti-Communist coalition of considerable strength, far greater than that which could be mustered by the Communists.[62]

The first taks of the Communists entering the country with the units of the Soviet Army or emerging from the anti-Nazi underground, was to neutralize the influence of the Polish Underground State and then dismantle and supplant its influence with Communist norms. The task was ambitious but far from easy. The pressure (even though it turned out to be sporadic, haphazard, and short-ranged) exerted by the United States and Great Britain on the Soviet and Polish governments to fulfill the promises embedded in the Teheran, Yalta and Potsdam agreements made the goal of imposing Communist norms on Poland much more difficult than in other parts of Eastern Europe, regardless of the cultural and political heritage of Polish-Russian relations and Polish nationalism.

In view of the fact that the Western powers were interested in salvaging at least some political autonomy in Poland, for which Great Britain went to war with Nazi Germany in 1939, the first postwar Communist government of Poland had to proceed with great caution on the matter of the transformation of the Polish society. The Polish Provisional Government, formed in Lublin in 1944 and sponsored by the USSR, was not accorded Western recognition and had to reconcile itself to a slow political process in implementing its program. In fact, that government had to agree under Western pressure to a temporary self-transformation of its own into a coalition government, the Provisional Government of National Unity, before it could attempt to transform the Polish society and its traditional norms.

The coalition government incorporating the non-Communist opposition, although controlled by the Communists, was a precondition for a Western recognition of the *status quo* in Poland.[63] It lasted until 1947 and to some extent postponed the Communist plans for Poland, but by then the Communist party was in full control of all the ministries and could begin to implement its own program. The events in Czechoslovakia and Yugoslavia in 1948 also triggered a wide-ranging purge within the ranks of the Communist party members accused of "nationalist deviations." By 1949 the Stalinist norms could be implemented. Even then, outright confrontation with the only remaining *de facto* opposition group, the Catholic Church, did not bring results obtained at the same time quite rapidly in neighboring Czechoslovakia, East Germany and Hungary.

The competition between the norms aspired to by the Communists and the traditional ones deeply-rooted in Polish culture primarily took place in the forum of the institutional structures: political, cultural and economic. The cultural battle took place through the news media and the progressive changes introduced into Polish political and economic structures. The educational system, as a primary agency of political socialization, became the major tool in the hands of the government to inculcate the new norms in the society. Press and radio as well as the newly-formed, or transformed, social and civic organizations were extensively used in that period beginning in 1949, with the peak of intensity of the campaign reached in the early 1950s, before "the thaw" of the post-Stalinist period.

The 1949-1956 period was long enough and the methods used by the authorities direct enough, if not outright oppressive, to implement the program of communization and imposition of new norms. To what extent these norms are deeply-rooted and lasting, especially when confronting the anti-Communist church tradition, is a subject for debate far too large for the scope of this analysis. The Communist norms were nevertheless presented to the society in detail with full support of the authoritarian measures at the disposal of the state, which banned other views from being spread and then severely curtailed the adherence to the traditional norms. The new norms were vigorously fostered in a variety of forms and on all the levels within the society.[64] Not surprisingly the Communist norms began to gain adherence in some segments of society especially connected with the Party and in the younger generation, which was openly courted.

Much of the gains achieved by the Party were irrevocably lost during the "Polish October" of 1956, when the national Communist leadership took power and diluted some of the Stalinist norms.[65] In some areas, October of 1956 still has not been "undone" by the Party, and it laid foundations for much which has since distinguished Poland from the other People's Democracies. Even during the peak of confrontation in the early 1950s the State was unable to eliminate the Church from its role as a chief, and perhaps the only institution, which defended the *status quo ante* in terms of norms, values and usages.

The Church thus functioned as a depository of tradition and attracted people who previously espoused diametrically different ideologies, even prewar atheists, to its fold. This ironic paradox goes far to explain the polarization between the Party and the nation on the issue of traditional culture and its elements. How ineffective was the campaign to make the nation embrace the new norms and secularization could be documented in many ways. Suffice it to say that after 1956 even the "Atheist Society" had to abandon its name, so cherished by the secularizers and deeply embedded in the ideological precepts of the Party, in favor of the "Polish Society of the Freethinkers" by late 1950s and in the 1960s it became known as the "Secular Culture Society." There is both something symbolic and informative in this progression or retreat. Similar anti-religious campaigns in the USSR after 1917 almost totally destroyed the Soviet churches and instituted museums of atheism in each major Soviet city.

This phenomenon largely but not exclusively has something to do with the tenacity of Catholicism in Poland and its power over the minds of the population. The family as the basic societal unit also survived many pressures emanating from the authorities and remained the depository of the old norms.[66] The visitor to the country, after over 30 years of Communist rule, is not struck by the fact of how much it has changed, which it did, but rather how much it remained the same, especially in the area of customs, personal relations, aspirations and norms traditionally adhered to.

The very fact that after the lapse of over a generation many of these norms not only survive but flourish suggest to the incompleteness, if not outright failure of the Communist norms which have been pushed on the society with enormous expenditure of time, money and coercion. The "church-going" phenomenon which overflows all the churches and chapels and creates the pressure on the Communist authorities to allow rebuilding or building of new ones (770 in the period of 1970-1977),[67] and the very composition of the congregations in which youth (not merely children accompanying their parents) are a large component, is by far an indication of the failure of the new Communist norms. But the old norms are not only related to the religious area.

The contemporary society composed overwhelmingly of the sons and daughters of the peasants and workers clearly aspires to the same values of the classes which were phased out by the revolution and now largely removed to the societal margins. As the relative affluence of the new middle and upper echelons grows, the customs now widely adopted and aspired to are frankly those of the *ancient regime*, e.g., hunting, antiques, conspicuous church weddings and parties (even rating of the churches on the scale of prestige), and the family coat-of-arms. Much of it is camouflaged as merely "retro" style now sweeping Europe.

In the most glaring fashion, on a much more "modern" level, the overpowering urge to own a car as a status symbol also illustrates fully the retreat of the government from its initial socialist insistence on mass transit and collective patterns. The decision taken by the "new" leader Gierek in early 1970s to mass-produce small cars has been one of the most popular edicts of the government and increased its popular support.

The competition between two sets of norms and the seeming inability of the new ones to displace the old ones has resulted in a rather interesting coexistence of both sets on various levels, but often also in a curious fusion of different patterns within the same framework. This becomes one of the most prevailing characteristics of contemporary Polish society in the 35th year of its Communist history. The relentless political socialization of the country has to be kept up at least to give the semblance of Communist commitment on the national if not the international level. The coexistence of such vastly different patterns results in increased cynicism of the youth and in hypocrisy, both official and private. At the same time it should not be underestimated how many new norms pertaining to the organizational aspects of societal framework have been adopted and assimilated by many who otherwise cling to the old traditional norms in their personal lives.[68]

The overpowering ability of the authoritarian modern nation-state to "set the stage" according to its goals and policies and implement them without the necessity of going through the market-place of ideas, typical of an open society, is evident in the Polish case. In the struggle between two sets of norms the State has always been manipulating the "attractive" alternatives which were to dissuade the public through participation in practices or pursuits consistent with the traditional norms; e.g., free picnics, jazz concerts, and American movies have been offered at the time of high mass on Sundays, etc. to divert the public, especially the youth. Such methods appeared to be effective in the short range but not in the long one. The church also responded in a checkmate fashion to allow the faithful to take advantage of both by allowing to move the masses to the evening hours.

The basic uniform resistance of the public, bold demands for contact with the non-Communist world, and the strict adherence and devotion to the traditional and familiar patterns have resulted in such astonishing phenomena (by Communist standards) as the rapid spread of Western fads and fashions, direct TV coverage of American space exploits (for which people stayed up until 4 a.m. because of the time difference) not seen elsewhere within the Soviet bloc and a direct five hour transmission of the inauguration of John Paul II on the Polish television network during which the Polish streets and roads were virtually deserted.[69]

The ambivalence of the Party, on the informal level, to prevent it members from participating in religious practices and activities, for fear that such a ban could be virtually unenforceable and trigger a revolution, contributes to the existence of one more double standard. This author has yet to meet Polish Communists who do not baptize their children (often in the distant village or city), which they do "for the sake of their parents and grandparents." His first encounter with that reality was during Christmas 1959 when a party member had to leave early for the midnight mass "since he sings in the choir."

This two-tier approach is endemic. Although the State has been by far most successful in its policy to change the curriculum on all the educational levels, especially in history and philosophy, the successes were marked by policy zig-zags. Religion, dropped from the curriculum in the early 1950s during the Stalinist period, was re-admitted in 1957,[70] but dropped again in the early 1960s. It has not disappeared from the scene however, but merely "changed location" from the public schools to religious programs run by tens of thousands of parishes and churches across the country and involving a significant part of the school-aged children.[71]

The changes in the curriculum still had not prevented the children from raising the "unanswerable" questions usually omitted or falsified in the curriculum, e.g., of the fate of the deported Poles in the USSR since 1939, the lack of assistance during the Warsaw Uprising, or the tragedy of the Katyn Forest massacre of interned Polish officers in 1940. When the latter question was raised the teacher on that occasion had said, "Don't ask silly questions; you know the answer. Next question" without stating what was the "answer."

The State has had a near monopoly on the dissemination of information. An exception is the Catholic press which was not only censored but also limited in its size. The press run of the leading Catholic weekly *Tygodnik Powszechny,* which has been published in Cracow since 1945, was limited to 40,000. This kind of pressure has, however, resulted in something unexpected by the authorities and perhaps the church itself: a tremendous upgrading of the Catholic press, which prior to 1945 largely catered to a relatively low common denominator. In the history of the Catholic press in Poland never before had a publication of such ideological and intellectual quality as *Tygodnik Powszechny.* It sets and restates the traditional norms but on a high, intellectual level. The limitation in circulation has resulted in black market demand, with some copies selling for twenty five dollars.[72]

The intellectual upgrading and changes from parochialism to universalism has occurred also in the quality of discussion in the Catholic Intelligentsia Clubs (KIK) in all the major towns, which have consistently been able to attract large followings among the young people. The attention paid to the education of the leadership resulted in large groups of priests and especially bishops with advanced sociology and theology university degrees. The existence of the Catholic University of Lublin, the only private institution of higher education in the Communist world, also sets the tone of the determined effort to defend the old norms and reinterpret them in the light of the contemporary societal changes sweeping the world.

The relatively open direct contacts with the outside world but especially withe the "Polonia" community, composed of the citizens of various countries with Polish heritage (some 10 million strong, or equivalent to one-third of the size of the Polish nation), and the fairly relaxed immigration policies set by the authorities (in contrast to other members of the Soviet bloc) enable personal contact on a large scale.[73] These contacts also have an impact on the perpetuation of the traditional norms in a basically unchanged, though updated, fashion. Thus the Polish communities abroad provide an input into the competition between the traditional and Communist norms in Poland with far-reaching consequences. These contacts cannot be however merely stopped, due to the multi-level linkages between even high-level Communist leaders and their families abroad (both Bierut and Gomulka had sisters in the United States, like millions of Poles all over the country).

Elements of Discord and Harmony between the Communist and Nationalist Ideologies

The Polish Communists have been acutely aware that there are indeed few elements of harmony between their Marxist and nationalist ideologies. Whereas the Communist theoreticians and leaders in the past were much more internationalist, their contemporary equivalents pay lip service to internationalist principles but try to legitimize themselves in the eyes of the public opinion as direct descendants of grand national traditions, and they often have appealed to outright nationalist emotions in their quest for legitimacy.[74] The internationalist theories of the prewar Communist Party of Poland were precisely one of the elements, apart from the fact that the sponsorship of their ideas came from Russia, which discredited the party in the eyes of the Right and Center parties and even the Polish Socialist Party. The point at issue was the independence of Poland.

The Polish Left split on this issue within a year from the founding of the Polish Socialist Party in 1892.[75] The new party, the Social Democratic Party of the Kingdom of Poland (and Lithuania), in 1918 became one of the founders of the Polish Communist Party. It advocated internationalist socialist goals but did not believe that the independence of Poland is either justifiable or realistic in terms of socialist class struggle. They openly declared themselves against independence on theoretical grounds, thus placing themselves squarely outside the pale of Polish public opinion for restoration of independence, for which four preceding generations had fought and died. The seemingly utopian notion that independence could be restored after 123 years was expressed by almost all Polish political parties. The Communists were the exception.

Their political activity after formation of the unified Communist party in 1918, but especially during the Polish-Soviet War of 1919-1920, handicapped them from the start. The creation of the Provisional Polish Revolutionary Committee in Bialystok in July 1920, after that city was taken by the Soviets at the time of the Red Army advance on Warsaw, illustrated both their lack of understanding or of the total disregard for the burning Polish desire for independence and the public perception of their activities basically as treason. A recently published Polish history text tries to tone down these implications through obfuscation and attempts to explain the reasons for such activities to a vastly different audience, even more nationally minded with obvious difficulty.[76] It admits, nevertheless, that the leaders of the Revolutionary Committee wanted to turn Poland, about to be "liberated" by the Red Army, into one of the Soviet Socialist Republics (within the USSR). It never came to pass since after three weeks, due to the crushing defeat of the Soviet Army at the battle of Warsaw in August 1920, the Provisional Revolutionary Committee had to flee Bialystok.

How much their actions were out of touch with the traditions can be detected even from their brief three week rule. They abolished, for intance, the traditional name for the provinces, *voievodships* because of the class connotation attached to the former royal servants (*voievodas,* the noblemen), and replaced it with a translation of the Russian oblast or in Polish *obwod.*[77] Thus rather shaky, insensitive, ideological interpretations lead them astray even on such minor but symbolic points, not to mention more major ones. Nevertheless, this little episode illustrates the ideological chasm between the Communists and, not only nationalists, but the nation as a whole. In the past-World War I period, they were burdened psychologically with the Soviet debacle in the Polish-Soviet War of 1920, which although severely criticized by the whole spectrum of Polish public opinion, nevertheless rightly or wrongly was credited with saving Polish independence and cherished for being the first Polish military victory on a large scale in 237 years, since the lifting of the siege of Vienna in 1683 by King John III Sobieski, which stopped the expansion of the Turkish Empire in Europe.[78]

The Communist support of the Soviet government on ideological grounds virtually alienated them from the rest of the Poles. The Party, however, persisted in its ideology and later supported another supremely unpopular and unpatriotic policy: it favored Germans over Poles in their quest for the control of the coal mining region of Silesia, vital to Poland due to its economic value (about two-thirds of her economic potential), and German control of the port of Gdansk, at that time the only Polish outlet to the sea. If there were not enough, the Party again on ideological grounds favored giving up Eastern Poland to the Soviet Ukraine and Soviet Belorussia and the city of Wilno (Vilnius) to Lithuania.[79] These cessions would have cost Poland over half of her prewar territory. Such policies, even if they would be admired by some for ideological purity and consistency (since the Communists perceived the Polish bourgeois government to be a greater obstacle to the revolution than the Weimar Republic), were plainly suicidal political goals.

Later the Party again committed an unpardonable sin in the eyes of Polish democrats and nationalists by supporting, again on ideological grounds, the *coup d'etat* of Marshall Pilsudski.[80] It was only towards the end of the interwar period when the Party started shifting its position to more appealing national positions, but it was liquidated in 1938 by a decision of the Comintern, ironically enough, most of its leaders were summoned to the USSR and executed.

The wartime realignment of the party began at the very beginning with the dropping of in 1942 the word "Communist" from its new name —the Polish Workers' Party—and "nationalization" of its program was announced in the anti-Nazi underground. This marked the departure, at least in words, from its previous deeds dictated by ideology. In spite of its continuing support of Communist ideology, the Party from then on tried, not always successfully, to appear as a national Polish party. The need became even more urgent in view of its ascendancy to the government of Poland in 1944 and complete control of that government after 1947. In view of the very slim original base of support vis-a-vis the national government in exile and in the underground, the need for legitimacy and patriotism was overpowering.

Some of the party statements, pronouncements and the whole style of reporting on the events in the Polish post-World War II Communist papers were oozing with patriotic and nationalist phraseology.[81] This time, getting a second chance rarely given by history, the Polish Communists took a highly patriotic and anti-internationalist stand on the issue of the Polish western boundary on the Oder and Neisse and the reestablishment of these territories which had been germanized over the centuries.[82] On the issue of the postwar attitude toward the Nazis and Germany generally, the Party was in the forefront of the patriotic position, largely preempting the most far-reaching nationalist goals.[83] Thus the Party was fully attuned to the nation and received support on that issue even from the anti-Communist emigres and the hierarchy of the Catholic Church.[84]

This was in glaring contradiction to the Party political record of 1918-1938 and the policies of the Polish Communists who, after the Soviet-Nazi pact of August 1939 and in spite of the terrible fate meted out by the Soviet to the Polish party in 1938, followed closely the Soviet directions and refused to join the Polish anti-Nazi underground until the Nazi attack on the USSR in June 1941.[85]

The reversal from international to national goals was timely and needed, and it enabled the Party to achieve first real semblance of harmony with the national ideology and patriotic perceptions of those issues universally considered to be crucial in contemporary Poland. Thus the policy was transformed into highly popular patriotic programs deemed necessary for the nation's well-being, if not survival, as a separate nation-state. The ability of the Party to achieve that transformation meant a difference between getting some national support at all or footing the complete bill for the Soviet treatment of Poland and the Poles in the period 1939-1945.

The above description of the mostly political and religious discord between the Communist and national ideologies, with the resulting policy divergence, was purposely stressed due to its overrriding importance in the Polish popular perception of the policies of the Communist party since 1918. It should also be stressed, however, that there were elements of harmony between the socioeconomic goals of the Party and a large segment of the Polish Left and Left-of-Center. The programs of those political groups, although eschewing some Communist methods, techniques, and linkages to the Comintern, had advocated along parallel lines many of the same far-reaching social and economic reforms to be implemented in agriculture and had advocated nationalization of various branches of industry. Those goals were accepted by the Socialist and peasant (populist) party programs.[86]

Not all of these reforms were implemented in the interwar II Republic, largely due to the composition of the Polish parliament, but many different reforms were attempted, including the agrarian reforms. Some very enlightened programs such as the vote for women, social security, and an eight hour working day, even in the early 1920s, put Poland in the forefront of progressive countries in the world. Finally, just before the Communist takeover in 1944 the underground parliament of the resistance movement announced a bold program of socioeconomic reforms to be implemented in post-World War II Poland, many of which were more far-reaching than the reforms implemented initially by the postwar Communist government (e.g., an upper limit on the size of the farms which would remain in private hands).[87]

In those areas the harmony between the Communist and nationalist ideologies was far greater than the present Communist leadership in Poland would care to admit. The scope of this analysis does not allow the elaboration on a comparison of the various social policies in detail; however, the Communists have capitalized on the disenchantment of various sectors of Polish society from the previously-landless peasants to the intellectuals.

A great pool of dissatisfaction existed in the Polish villages and industrial regions on the issue of opportunities, especially educational, and the distribution of wealth. The goals of social mobility to be achieved were harmoniously agreed upon and widely accepted throughout the Polish political spectrum, except for the most conservative elements on the Right. The lack of achievement of these goals was due not so much to the programmatic ill will, but more to the drastic paucity of means at the disposal of the II Republic. Thus, by implementing the plans and goals developed before the war, the Party was fulfilling the wishes of the vast majority of the citizens, regardless of their political persuasion, and could appear to act as a trustee for the nation.

The Place of Minorities in the Contemporary Polish Political System

Poland was transformed, as previously described, from a multinational country with the minorities comprising one-third of the population in 1939, to a homogeneous country which became 98 percent Polish after the completion of the post-World War II migrations.[88] The transformation was total, shocking and irrevocable, putting an end to patterns respectively cherished and hated by many of its citizens. Some of the long-standing historical relationships and perceptions receded into the past but many have been lingering still in the contemporary Poland and even brutally used for political purposes, e.g., the anti-Zionist campaign.

A great deal remains to be yet researched and said about the Polish policies toward minorities in the past but what has happened can not be undone or changed by either side. The past should, however, serve as a guide to the present and future. In this brief review of the role which the minorities have within the present political system, only scant attention is going to be given to the past as some linkages between them and the dominant society were pointed out in the previous description of the development of nationalism.

The drastic reduction of the size of the minorities through the Nazi-organized genocide, shift of the borders, flight and expulsion of the Germans and the exchange of population, have also cause far-reaching consequences for the remaining minorities. The size of their pre-war communities might have also been a protective device against the Polonization and loss of their heritage, especially if they remained in compact groups. The dispersion of many minorities resulting from the war and its aftermath has put additional stress on their relations vis-a-vis the larger society.

The small size of the groups and their dispersion had also a negative impact on the efficacy of their protection and legal representation in the dominant society regardless of the formal constitutional norms. As it is, the latter have the tendency to remain on paper, when applied to an unpopular minority. In contemporary Poland some of the largest pre-war minorities, e.g., the Jews and Germans, were almost totally destroyed and/or removed from the country. Others remain only as small vestiges of their previous numbers (e.g., the Ukrainians and the Belorussians) or have small communities (e.g., Russians, Gypsies, Slovaks, Lithuanians). The only new minority is that of Greek and Macedonian political refugees from the Greek civil war of 1945-1949.

The relationship between the size of various minority groups has been also totally changed. The largest group by far are about 250,000 Belorussians (there were about 210,000 in 1967), followed by about 200,000 Ukrainians (170,000 in 1967), other groups are very small: Russians (20,000), Slovaks (20,000), Gypsies (15,000), Lithuanians (10,000), and Czechs (4,000).[89]

After the anti-Semitic Party campaign of 1967-1968 only about 8,500 Polish Jews remain in the country, almost all of whom are intermarried with Poles. There were only some 3,000 Germans left in Poland in the 1960s; practically all have left since that time, along with some 125,000 Poles of mixed Polish-German extraction or intermarried with the ethnic Germans who are currently leaving Poland under the 1975 agreement between Gierek and Schmidt signed in the aftermath of the Helsinki Agreement.[90] Thus, these two large pre-war minorities *de facto* ceased to exist after almost 1,000 years of Jewish-Polish history and some 700 years of German history of settlement in Poland.

The drastic reduction of the dispersion of those minorities have not reduced but, on the contrary, exacerbated some problems as seen from the point of view of the minorities. They all complain that their relative small size has effectively deprived them of political power, which although heavily curtailed by the Polish pressures before World War II nevertheless existed due to the size of their communities and their parliamentary representations. Currently some members of their respective minority communities represent them, usually on the local level, but only rarely on the provincial level. The traditional constitutional and legal norms largely remain unimplemented precisely because in the eyes of public opinion, Poland ceased to be a multinational state and there are pressures on the minorities to Polonize.

The recent case of the Slovaks living along the Tatra Mountains in the south of Poland, whose church services in Slovak languages were curtailed by the Polish Catholic Church, illustrates attitudes prevailing even in the Polish Catholic Church hierarchy.[91] Only the Belorussians, largely due to their compact mode of settlement in the Bialystok province and their Orthodox religion differentiating them from the Poles, can slow down their rate of assimilation, especially because of their almost exclusively rural background.

The Ukrainians, who were suspected in 1947 of supporting the Ukrainian nationalist resistance movement (UPA), were drastically uprooted and resettled in the Northern and Western territories of Poland, in small groups only.[92] They have been prevented even after 30 years from returning to their former settlements which were largely destroyed in the 1945-1947 military operations against the partisans in Southeastern Poland. Their dispersion hampers and severely restricts the development of cultural programs and schools with the Ukrainian langauge.

It is significant also that the chief Polish statistical source, the *Rocznik Statystyczny*, ceased to publish any statistics on schooling in the languages of the minorities since the early 1970s. The downward trend in the number of schools and students was previously discernible. The statistics can now be only obtained indirectly and are incomplete or outdated. On the local level the Polonization of all the scattered groups is encouraged and fostered in spite of the official denials and the passive resistance of the minorities.

In order to present the "Polish" case on the minorities the authorities point to the subsidies they give to the minority cultural organizations (one for each minority), whose existence implements, in the eyes of the authorities, the minority needs for representation, participation and aggregation in the society. Some of these programs are largely propaganda showcases maintained at great cost (e.g., the Jewish Theater in Warsaw, one of the two professional Jewish theaters outside Israel, which still performs in Yiddish even after most Yiddish-speaking citizens were forced out of Poland by 1969; the simultaneous translation is provided in Polish through earphones attached to each seat in the theater). The weekly *Folks Sztyme is still published, (obviously heavily subsidized)* for the 1,500 members of the Jewish Cultural Organization.[93]

The Belorussian, Ukrainian and Lithuanian cultural societies are nevertheless the main pillars for the cultural and ethnic maintenance of these groups. The case of the Lithuanians illustrates well another issue of largely emotional and patriotic nature, which is totally misunderstood by the dominant society. This author was able to ascertain that the Lithuanians living within a few miles of the Lithuanian SSR still bitterly resent the "Polish rule" and claim they would prefer to live in Lithuania, although their compatriots in the Lithuanian SSR can not even enjoy a fraction of the personal freedoms accorded to citizens of Poland (travel, relatively relaxed atmosphere in the villages, which are *not* collectivized).

The interplay of nationalism and politics is evident in the discussion of minorities as it was throughout the review of other contemporary political patterns in Poland. Set against the historical perspective it sheds more light on this vast and complex subject without an understanding of which one can not understand the Polish past, present and possibly future. Nationalism is no doubt *the* single most potent force on the Polish political state today to be reckoned with, even by very powerful forces in East Central Europe.

NOTES

1. *The Times Atlas of World History* (Maplewood, NJ: Hammond, 1978), pp. 140-141.

2. *F. W. Putzgers Historischer Schul-Atlas,* "Die Deutsche Nord und Ostseeherschaft (Blüte des Deutschen Ordens)," (Bielefeld: Velhagen and

Klasing, 1913), p. 176; and *History of Poland* (Warsaw: PWN, 1968), p. 116.

3. Even the Nazi elite's most modern training camp on the Crössinsee near Falkenburg (Zlocieniec) in Pomerania was a modern adaptation of the Teutonic Knights architecture with castle-shaped towers. It now, incidently, serves as a Polish Olympic team training camp.

4. *History of Poland*, p. 113, and *Historia Polski*, Vol. 1, (Warszawa: PWN, 1958), pp. 391-393.

5. Jesse D. Clarkson, *A History of Russia* (New York: Random House, 1963).

6. *Grosser Historischer Weltatlas, III,* "Konfessionen in Deutschland um 1546," (Munich: Bayerischer Schulbuch Verlag, 1962), p. 116.

7. Anatol Lewicki, *Zarys Historii Polski* (London: SZPZ, 1947), pp. 164-166.

8. *Ibid.,* p. 144.

9. *The Times Atlas,* pp. 169, 214.

10. Piotr S. Wandycz, *The Lands of Partitioned Poland 1795-1918* (Seattle: University of Washington Press, 1974), pp. 24-180.

11. *Ibid.,* pp. 195-196.

12. *Ibid.,* p. 179.

13. *Ibid.,* p. 196.

14. M. K. Dziewanowski, *Poland in the Twentieth Century* (New York: Columbia University Press, 1977), pp. 63-144.

15. Tymon Terlecki, *Tysiaclecie Polski Chrzescjanskiej,* (Chicago: Polish American Book Company, 1967), p. 15.

16. As expressed to this author by Stefan Cardinal Wyszynski, Primate of Poland.

17. E.g., Archbishop of Plock Antoni Nowowiejski, 83 years old, and Father (now Blessed) Maksymilian Kolbe, who starved to death in Auschwitz concentration camp, et al.

18. By becoming the *de facto* only religious confession of Poland for the first time since the fourteenth century.

19. Pope John Paul II, then a seminarian, was a messanger for the "Unia" military organization in the national resistance movement, Home Army, rescuing Jews from the Holocaust.

20. When the Polish Peasants' Party was taken over and later became a junior partner of the Communist Party.

21.   Z. Anthony Kruszewski, *The Oder-Neisse Boundary and Poland's Modernization* (New York: Praeger, 1972), pp. 35-77.

22.   *Ibid.*, p. 53.

23.   *Maly Rocznik Statystyczny 1939, X* (Warszawa: GUS, 1939), p. 25.

24.   *Grosser Historischer Weltatlas, II,* "Der Slawische Western vor beginn der Deutschen Ostbewegung," (Munchen: Bayerischer Schulbuch Verlag, 1970), p. 94.

25.   Some 835,000 by 1931.

26.   Lewicki, *Zarys Historii Polski,* p. 71.

27.   *Maly Rocznik Statystyczny, 1939,* p. 38.

28.   Paul Lendvai, *Anti-Semitism Without Jews* (Garden City, NY: Doubleday, 1971.

29.   Lewicki, *Zarys Historii Polski,* p. 188.

30.   *Encyklopedia Powszechna* (Warszawa: PWN, 1973-76).

31.   Jerzy Topolski, ed., *Dzieje Polski* (Warszawa: PWN, 1977), p. 685.

32.   Wandycz, *Lands of Partitioned Poland,* pp. 238-259.

33.   *Ibid.*

34.   Topolski, *Dzieje Polski,* pp. 683-684.

35.   *Ibid.,* p. 654.

36.   *Historia Polski IV,* part 1 (Warszawa: WP, 1969), pp. 396-400.

37.   *Ibid.*

38.   *Encyklopedia Powszechna, PWN.*

39.   Kruszewski, *The Oder-Neisse Boundary,* p. 60.

40.   *Maly Rocznik Statystyczny, 1939,* pp. 22, 24.

41.   *Encyklopedia Powszechna PWN.*

42.   *The New Jewish Encyclopedia* (New York: Behrman House, 1962), pp. 381-386.

43.   Andrzej Werblan, "O genezie konflictu," *Miesiecznik Literacki,* June 1968.

44.   Which after June 1976, "price riots" included workers and intellectuals who received support of the Polish Catholic Church.

45.   Lendvai, *Anti-Semitism Without Jews.*

46.   Wladyslaw Rusinski, *Rozwoj Gospodarczy Ziem Polskich* (Warszawa: Ksiazka i Wiedza, 1973).

47.   *Ibid.*

48. Z. Landau, J. Tomaszewski, *Zarys Historii Gospodarczej Polski 1918-1939*, (Warszawa: KIW, 1971).

49. *Concise Statistical Year-book of Poland* (London: Polish Ministry of Information, 1941), p. 4.

50. *Ibid.*, p. 10.

51. Wandycz, *Lands of Partitioned Poland*, pp. 377-378.

52. Only with the death in 1948 of the brave archbishop of Cracow, Prince Adam Sapieha, these personal links ceased to exist.

53. Andrzej Brozek, *Polonia Amerykanska 1854-1939* (Warszawa: Interpress, 1977).

54. Kruszewski, *The Oder-Neisse Boundary*, p. 152.

55. *Ibid.*, pp. 144-148.

56. *Rocznik Statystyczny 1978*, XXXVIII (Warszawa: GUS, 1978), p. 31.

57. *Time*, October 30, 1978; *Newsweek*, October 30, 1978.

58. In conformity with article 130 of the Mexican Constitution of 1917.

59. *Maly Rocznik Statystyczny 1939*, p. 353, and *Rocznik Polityczny i Gospodarczy 1976* (Warszawa: PWE, 1977), pp. 209-211.

60. Topolski, *Dzieje Polski*, pp. 828-853.

61. Richard F. Staar, *Communist Regimes in Eastern Europe*, 3rd ed. (Stanford: Hoover Institution Press, 1977), p. 133.

62. Jan Karski, *Story of a Secret State* (Boston: Houghton and Mifflin, 1942); Stefan Korbonski, *Fighting Warsaw* (New York: Minerva Press, 1956); Tadeusz Bor-Komorowski, *The Secret Army* (London: Macmillan, 1951).

63. It was organized on 28 June 1945, and recognized by the United States on 5 July 1945.

64. Topolski, *Dzieje Polski*, pp. 859-870.

65. Flora Lewis, *A Case of Hope* (Garden City, NY: Doubleday, 1958); Konrad Syrop, *Spring in October* (New York: Praeger, 1957).

66. Jan Szczepanski, *Polish Society* (New York: Random House, 1970), pp. 181-187.

67. *Rocznik Statystyczny 1978*, p. 24.

68. Alexander Matejko, *Social Change and Stratification in Eastern Europe* (New York: Praeger, 1974).

69. Interview with a recent visitor from Poland.

70. Lewis, *A Case of Hope.*
71. Author's interview with a religious leader.
72. Interview with a recent visitor from Poland.
73. *Rocznik Statystyczny 1978,* p. 412. In 1977, 934,000 citizens of non-Socialist countries visited Poland and 518,000 Poles visited the West.
74. *Maly Slownik Historii Polski* (Warszawa: WP, 1967).
75. Wandycz, *Lands of Partitioned Poland,* p. 298.
76. *Historia Polski IV,* part I, p. 396.
77. *Ibid.,* p. 398.
78. Dziewanowski, *Poland in the Twentieth Century,* p. 84.
79. Topolski, *Dzieje Polski,* p. 685.
80. *Ibid.,* p. 695.
81. Zbigniew Kruszewski, "Government of Poland," in A. Iwanska, ed., *Contemporary Poland: Society, Politics, Economy* (Chicago: University of Chicago for HRAF, 1955), p. 356.
82. Kruszewski, *The Oder-Neisse Boundary,* pp. 27-28.
83. *Ibid.,* pp. 197-204.
84. *Ibid.,* pp. 159-163.
85. Dziewanowski, *Poland in the Twentieth Century,* p. 117.
86. *Podreczna Encyklopedia Powszechna* (Paris: Ksiegarnia Polska, 1954), p. 694.
87. *Ibid.*
88. Dziewanowski, *Poland in the Twentieth Century,* p. 147.
89. *Maly Slownik Historii Polski,* p. 193.
90. *Christian Science Monitor,* January 9, 1979.
91. As reported in a series of articles in the Paris monthly, *Kultura.*
92. Kruszewski, *The Oder-Neisse Boundary,* p. 59.
93. *Encyklopedia Powszechna PWN,* IV, p. 473.

Trond Gilberg

VIII

MODERNIZATION, HUMAN RIGHTS, NATIONALISM:
THE CASE OF ROMANIA

Modernization, Human Rights and Nationalism in Communist Political Systems: The Conceptual Triangle

Throughout much of the post-World War II period, the literature on modernization and development made certain fundamental assumptions concerning "human rights" and "nationalism." Basically, the hypotheses advanced on the subject of the nexus between these three elements postulated a unilinear development and a set of consequences thereof: "modernization," it was said, would carry with it greater political participation, expanded social mobility, and a wider range of individual choice in the socioeconomic and cultural realms. The fundamental human right of belonging to a wider community and of participating in its affairs would be increasingly satisfied. Similarly, the parochial values of regionalism would, presumably, give way to the incessant and effective communications from the politico-administrative center, so that a national political culture would emerge, at the expense of sub-national configurations in this realm. In the field of economics, expanding communications networks, a growing banking system, and the interrelatedness of increasingly sophisticated production processes would tend to break down the remnants of *economic* regionalism and parochialism.[1]

While there was considerable agreement among students of "modernization" as to the relationship between this developmental process and the expansion of human rights as well as economic progress, the views expressed differed sharply on the question as to whether or not the modernizing tendencies in many fields would lead to political and socioeconomic nationalism or internationalism. On the one hand, some scholars argued that technical developments would so shrink the globe that national problems would immediately become international; on the other hand, the view was expressed that the nation-state still constituted the basic building bloc of the international order, and that modernization in socioeconomic and political terms would essentially serve to strengthen the position of the state and the nation, thus basically enhancing political nationalism.[2]

Communist scholars and decisionmakers have experienced no such problems concerning the relationship between modernization, human rights, and nationalism. Modernization, as socioeconomic development, is part of the necessary process of "laying the material base of socialism and communism;" *political* modernization provides for intensive re-education in this field, so that the "new socialist man" come equipped with a new and qualitatively higher set of values, thus leaving "retrograde views" such as "bourgeois nationalism" behind. Because the nature of socialist and communist society is free of class exploitation, human rights are fully safeguarded. The fundamentally new principles of international relations which presumably guide the foreign policy of socialist states will preclude a conflict between nationalism and internationalism, allowing "the flowering of the socialist nation" within the context of "socialist internationalism."[3]

Public opinion and many decisionmakers in the West have problems with all of these "models." For many, the political systems of Eastern Europe are repressive autocracies which run roughshod over the human rights of their citizenry, openly flouting the provisions of the Helsinki Agreement and other international declarations which have been signed by their governments. During the Carter Administration, the emphasis on human rights everywhere in the world has become a centerpiece of U.S. policy, thus adding an extra measure of interest to the topic at hand.

Some of the controversy surrounding the relationship between modernization, human rights, and nationalism in Eastern Europe is derived from lack of clarity in defining the terms involved. Lengthy volumes have been written on the concept "modernization" as well as the practical manifestations of it in communist and non-communist systems, and there is no attempt to summarize them here. Suffice it to say that much of this research has shown the lack of a direct positive relationship between socioeconomic modernization (defined as industrialization, urbanization, secularization, penetration of the periphery, and the breaking down of parochialism) and human rights; in fact, many modernizing regimes have eliminated or limited political participation (in the form of meaningful elections, group activity, and free speech) and have severely restricted other human rights, all in the name of historical or economic necessity. In communist systems, the regimes have often redefined "participation" and "human rights" in such a way that the concepts utilized in the study of pluralistic political systems cannot readily be employed.[4] The analyst must attempt to "get inside" the concepts ultilized in those political systems in order to make a meaningful analysis of the problems posed for our panel.

Similar conceptual problems arise over the term "nationalism." Once again, a great deal of literature exists on this subject, and it is not necessary to repeat the main points here. Instead, the concentration shall focus on the problem of "nationalism" in a multinational society.

By definition, a multinational society will contain several (and different) nationalisms. If there is a majority of ethnic groups, the "nationalism" of country X will usually be defined as the set of values, goals, and aspirations, and the appropriate actions undertaken on their behalf by that majority. But ethnic minorities have "nationalisms," too, and the very fact that the individuals in such groups consider themselves ethnically different from the majority should indicate the need to study several "nationalisms" in multiethnic systems. Finally, in the presumably "international" system of communism, with relative regional hegemony exercised (or attempted) by the Soviet Union, "nationalism" can only be studied in the context of this semi-enforced international fraternity of states.

The Case of Romania

The Romanian case is a problematical one for the examination of modernization, human rights, and nationalism, insofar as it is a multiethnic system with considerable cultural and socioeconomic differentiation among the nationalities; at times this differentiation reflects real animosity based on a perceived hierarchy of group "worth." At the same time, the Romanian regime, especially in the Ceausescu era, has been staunchly nationalistic, in the sense that it has emphasized traditional *Romanian* values (albeit presumably in socialist garb) and has conducted a foreign policy which clearly has emphasized the national over the international inside the parameters of communism. The hectic pace of socioeconomic modernization in Romania is coupled with a continuous ideological offensive dedicated to the eradication of "retrograde" values and the establishment of socialist views. This massive program of social transformation has strengthened the authoritarian aspects of Romanian society and imposed upon the citizenry one of the most repressive regimes in all of Eastern Europe, considered with regard to traditional Western civil rights. This complex relationship, then, constitutes one of the major facts of contemporary Romanian life.[5]

Since 1965, when Nicolae Ceausescu assumed the position of First Secretary of the Romanian Communist Party (PCR), and to the present, when the positions of this individual leader include the Presidency as well as the General Secretaryship of the Party, both socioeconomic and political modernization processes have been accelerated. It is the *political* modernization process, as interpreted and executed by the PCR leadership under Ceausescu, which has had the greatest impact on human rights, while socioeconomic development has created a complex and increasingly sophisticated society in which individual and group concern over personal freedom (or the lack thereof) is on the rise. The main problem for the General Secretary is the tendency of the general population (or at least its articulate spokesmen) to define "human rights" along lines strikingly familiar to inhabitants of "bourgeois-liberal" democracies, while the PCR leadership is attempting to establish, defend, and communicate a "Marxist" concept of the rights of individuals. In this context, the signing of the Helsinki Agreement, and in particular the so-called "Basket Three," gave rise to an intensified campaign against "nefarious" and "alien" influences which is still under way. This campaign, which has represented perhaps the most ambitious and intensive effort of political socialization and indoctrination in Romania during the last decade, nevertheless represents merely the climax of a trend which may be termed "continuous ideologization" in the era of Ceausescu. Central to the General Secretary's concerns and programs during the last twelve years have been his commitment to societal transformation, the remaking of individual consciousness, the re-interpretation of the relationship between the individual and the state, and the creation of a "socialist" culture which exists at a qualitiatively higher level than "nationalist" culture, thereby removing the problem of ethnic separatism and "bourgeois nationalism" in the future Romanian society. All of these considerations produced an approach to political decisionmaking which can best be labeled "Ceausescuism." It is the imposition of this personal style upon Romanian society which provides the main motor force of political life in contemporary Romania, and it is therefore "Ceausescuism" which sets the parameters for human rights and nationalism in that country.

The following basic aspects of Ceausescu's political program are crucial to an understanding of individual and nationality rights in contemporary Romania:

a) The position of the individual in society is dependent upon the needs of the collectivity, and the sole interpreter of that collective need is the PCR, under the leadership of Nicolae Ceausescu. Since the PCR, as "the leading force of society," is a communist party, the development of individuals and groups must take place within the confines of Marxism-Leninism as it applies to Romanian conditions. Individual rights can therefore only be discussed within the parameters set forth above; reference to such rights without due concern for societal needs becomes meaningless.[6]

b) Individual rights can only be realized within the confines of "the multilaterally developed society," which is said to be the stage of future development closest to fulfillment in contemporary Romania and a ncessary stage preceding socialism and communism. According to this outlook, only a socialist society (or one developing in the direction of socialism and communism) can offer the individual the opportunity to realize his or her potential. Whereas capitalist society operates with phony individual rights, based upon an inequitable system of exploitation and unequal opportunity, socialism offers the individual maximum opportunities for being the best *he* can, without fear of exploitation and unfair and inadequate remuneration. In socialist society, each individual contributes according to his or her ability, and is remunerated according to his contribution—the only completely fair system devised by man. While capitalist individuals, furnished with impressive paper guarantees of human rights, in fact relate to their society with resentment and anger, because their rights set them apart from society, socialist men and women enjoy *their* rights as integral members of society, engaged in fruitful and mutually beneficial interactions with the collectivity in a higher form of symbiosis.[7]

c) While considerable progress has been made towards the creation of the "new socialist individual," whose individuality exists in the closest symbiotic relationship with the rest of society, there are still "retrograde values" in existence in Romanian society, and, what is more, the rapid socioeconomic development of the country has produced certain contradictions of its own, even in the stage of the multilaterally developed society. Some of the remaining retrograd values are egotism, greed, concern primarily for one's own immediate family, and outright theft and other economic crimes, overt or covert. Furthermore, "bourgeois" tendencies are manifested through such remaining values as ethnic separatism and the activities which are associated with this attitude, and other negative manifestations include emphasis on the right of the individual to "opt out" of the nation-building program of the PCR and its General Secretary as well as the tendency to emphasize practical negative events in contemporary Romanian life, while the great achievements of the last generation go unnoticed.[8]

Such an outlook on the relationship between the individual and the collective is bolstered by the twin mechanisms of political and socioeconomic control and the existence of a set of laws which safeguards the rights of the individual within the confines of socialist society and law as well as the Marxist-Leninist program of the PCR. The extensive control mechanisms employed by the Party in all areas of human life have been discussed in considerable detail elsewhere and need no repetition here; suffice it to say that the PCR appears determined to execute its program of "citizen education" in the political realm to an extent rarely found elsewhere in Eastern Europe.[9]

The complicated laws safeguarding individual rights in contemporary Romanian society represent a curious mixture of traditional liberties and special restrictions reflecting the definitions of the relationship between the individual and the collectivity discussed above. Thus, freedom of assembly, of speech, and of religion are all guaranteed, provided they do not harm the socialist order; on the other hand, citizens are not accorded the right to question openly, disavow, or seek actively the destruction or fundamental change of the socioeconomic and political systems now in existence. Stringent laws prohibit the open discussion of "state secrets," of which there are many. Activities associated with ethnic minorities are only permitted insofar as they take place within officially sanctioned bodies. It is expressly a crime to avoid service to the republic in military and paramilitary formations, and the new law on defense, adopted a few years ago, makes it a crime of treason not to defend the homeland ("patria") actively in the case of general war, invasion, or other armed conflict. The President of the Republic possesses wide powers to declare a state of emergency, which automatically suspends the code of civil rights, and martial law may be imposed in numerous situations, with or without the declaration of a state of emergency. Refusal to participate in the "building of a socialist Romania" as well as refusal to take officially proposed work constitutes a crime which is punishable in a variety of ways. "Hooliganism" is a broad and flexible concept which can be applied to a wide range of activities which are considered detrimental to society, as defined by the regime.[10]

In addition to the formal system of law, the political leadership of contemporary Romania has access to a wide array of administrative powers which in practice function as formal law. Furthermore, the extensive network of organizational control which exists through the PCR's sponsorship of virtually all groups in society provides informal sanctioning mechanisms of the first magnitude. Finally, the widely used "comrades' courts" provide ways of enforcing conformity in a variety of situations without the need for the application of the formal legal system.[11]

All of this is very familiar to the student of East European political and legal systems under Communist rule. What *is* rather unique in Romania is the intensity with which these mechanisms have been employed and the *range* of the regime's concern with individual human rights and behavior. As this author has stated elsewhere,[12] there is an extremely high "regime profile" in Romanian life which allows for less purely private behavior than most of the other fraternal systems of Eastern Europe.

The Growing Discrepancy Between Public and Private Views on Human Rights

Remaking mass attitudes about the state and the individual is a massive undertaking of political socialization, and much of the literature on Eastern Europe agrees that this attempt has been only moderately successful; in fact, it may be said that it has failed to reach the most ambitious goals established by the regimes of the area.[13] During the last few years, the increasing concern of the regime with this problem hints at the dimensions of it. There are several major aspects of it, as follows:

a) Substantial segments of the public have refused to accept the ambitious definitions of the symbiotic relationship between the individual and the collective and have apparently opted for alternative interpretations of this relationship. Specifically, "privatization" and withdrawal from public activity have become major problems in Romania during the Ceausescu era, precisely at a time when the forceful efforts by the General Secretary to remake society through political socialization and indoctrination became the major motor force of the political realm. It may be said that while the PCR leadership hammered home its message of "socialist human rights," significant proportions of the population adhered to a much more individualistic definition of these rights, essentially emphasizing the view that one must be able to retreat from the public to the private—that individual rights should be employed to *protect* and *insulate* each person from society and its formal and informal power structures, not to help *mobilize* each citizen for the fulfillment of some predetermined goal. This discrepancy in definitions of the term "human rights" has become markedly more pronounced since the Carter Administration's offensive in this field, and this development has become proof positive for the regime of its fears that expanded contacts and socioeconomic intercourse with the "bourgeois" West could lead to dangerous consequences for the stability of the political order under East European socialism. The "protective" interpretation of civil rights, emphasizing the individual rather than the collective, is essentially the emphasis of the liberal-democratic West; the fears of the East European regimes of "Trojan horses" in this field seem well founded.[14]

b) Because of greater access to Western publications and more information on such major political events as the signing of the Helsinki Agreement and President Carter's preoccupation with human rights, increasing numbers of individuals have become willing to risk *expressing* their views, whereas their earlier inclination was to remain passive (even if hostile to the regime). In a much publicized move earlier this year, several prominent Romanian citizens published manifestoes supporting the basic ideas of the "Basket Three" at Helsinki and were promptly jailed for this activity. The subsequent campaign by the regime against such "retrograde" views hurt Romania's prestige abroad and soon subsided in intensity, although it is still going on.[15]

c) The modernization process, which has created a complex, stratified society with universal literacy and a large population segment with considerable education, coupled with an increasingly sophisticated and technologically advanced economy, has in itself made society more unruly. It is one thing to run an authoritarian political system in a relatively undifferentiated population existing at a low level of economic development, and quite another to attempt basically the same style of leadership in a "developed" citizenry. Highly educated technical cadres, possessing vital information for political leaders and citizens alike, are bound to begin defining individual rights in terms of increased latitude for experimentation, individual discovery, societal change based on *these* discoveries, rather than on political fiat, and perhaps also active political participation. All of these tendencies are fraught with real or potential dangers for the autocratic *apparatchiki* currently in charge of Romania, and the clash between these different views of human rights, sparked by the very success of the PCR's modernization program, is bound to become one of the main headaches for Nicolae Ceaucescu in the years to come.[16]

d) Human rights in a multiethnic society cannot be separated from the question of *nationality rights,* both for individuals of non-Romanian origin and their primary groups of ethnic connotation. This is a potentially explosive area of civil rights, for it combines both individual and group rights as perceived against a backdrop of old animosities, perceived cultural hierarchies, and a well-developed tradition of ethnic jokes and slurs, now confronting an ever-increasing tendency for the PRC leadership to expand its legitimacy in the masses of the population through emphasis on the "organic ties" between the current regime and traditional *Romanian* nationalism. As this author has pointed out elsewhere,[17] socioeconomic modernization has the tendency to expand individuals' consciousness of their past and will, most likely, enhance ethnic separatism rather than alleviating it, at least in societies where there are no major economic or social reasons for abandoning one's ethnicity and adopting the mantle of a "higher" culture. In Romania, where the modernization process has created considerable personal hardships for many (despite the impressive results in "gross" categories), there appears to be no such overriding interest of assimilation, and thus, ethnic separatism continues to exist as a major problem. And once again, the concern of the external world with individual and group rights in a multiethnic society has helped fan the flames of this issue, especially since the US represents only one concerned viewer of the Romanian situation—the center stage of scrutiny is in fact occupied by fraternal Hungary and nearby, powerful West Germany, representatives of the "ethnic homeland" of the two largest minorities in contemporary Romania.

The existence of a dual set of considerations concerning human rights and nationalism in a modernizing society makes evaluation and analysis doubly difficult. From the regime's point of view, many activities are punishable as crimes and violations of human rights as defined *under socialism.* From the point of view of the Western observer, with his built-in biases based upon a quite different interpretation of "human rights," the *regime* appears to be the culprit, in that it unduly restricts the exercise of presumably *universal* rights of citizens *everywhere.* For many of those who are currently suffering incarceration or other problems as a result of their "brush" with the regime on this question, the principles challenged and argued simple revolve around the question of whether or not the regime lives up to *its own* laws, statements, and promises. In a way, therefore, these citizens are charging that the regime, having accepted certain aspects of human rights as valid in their own countries as well as elsewhere, must now make serious efforts to *implement* these principles. A systematic evaluation of the regime's performance, then, must examine all three of these bases. Because nationality policy and the human rights of minorities include more elements of this "evaluation set" than any other area discussed above, it will be selected for an empirical investigation.

Nationality Policy and Human Rights in the Period of Multilateral Development

Any political system containing significant ethnic minorities will be confronted by a set of problems deriving from the situational and perceptual differences between the majority and all other collectivities. From the majority vantage point, ethnic political separatism must be avoided or at least reduced so that the danger of irredentism and secessionism can be contained, and the social and political order can be maintained. This requires some restriction of minority activities, be it in a positive or negative way; one may utilize control mechanisms to forbid or otherwise forestall the concerted use of minority group symbols and activities such as flags, festivals, educational programs, or political rallies designed to insulate the group from the larger society; conversely, ethnic separatism may be reduced by assimilation, integration, or direct absorption through a variety of mechanisms such as intermarriage, socioeconomic privileges, or political and educational indoctrination. From this vantage point, individual and group rights can only be upheld as long as they do not seriously endanger the interests of the majority, from whose midst the political leadership is most likely to spring.[18]

From the vantage point of the ethnic minority, the basic question of human rights must be posed differently, provided such a group has maintained a basic commitment to its distinctiveness in cultural and perhaps also linguistic terms (on occasion also its geographical, economic, and political autonomy). For such a minority group, "human rights" will involve *culture maintenance,* i.e., the ability to maintain such basic aspects of the group's distinctiveness as language, literature, the remembrance of a collective past which is different from that of other groups, including the majority. Furthermore, culture maintenance is dependent upon common symbols, heroes, and villains, perhaps also dress, certainly mores and folkways; occupational separateness, on the other hand, is increasingly difficult to maintain during a period of rapid socioeconomic modernization.

Similarly, for the individual member of a minority group, "human rights" has several meanings. First, such an individual is concerned with possible *individual* discrimination against him, based on ethnicity; this would be a case of violation of his or her human rights. Second, if the cultural autonomy of the ethnic group to which he or she belongs is somehow impaired, this has an impact upon the individual as well, insofar as it creates a conflict in his conception of membership and of "belonging." It may well be that an individual considers such restrictions on *group autonomy* a violation of his *individual* rights.

This complex problem is exacerbated during periods of rapid change in which a determined political leadership attempts to break down many of the established values of society for the purpose of instituting new values and new collectives of "belonging." If this effort is directed at creating a "new culture" for everybody, alienation from or support of this venture may be fairly equally distributed among all citizens, regardless of ethnic group connotation; if, on the other hand, it becomes clear that the so-called new culture is somehow just an extension of the symbols and values of an existing ethnic group, the reaction among members of *other* groups, now subjected to the political and ideological offensive of the majority, is likely to be negative.

During the Ceausescu era it has become clear that the PCR leadership officially dedicated to the creation of a "socialist culture" is in effect engaged in an attempt to gain acceptance of the most fundamental aspects of *Romanian* nationalism, even among the ethnic minorities. For the Romanian majority, the problems of execution of this program revolve around integration of minorities or at least their acceptance of the basic parameters of "Romanian socialist" culture, while the minorities have become increasingly concerned with culture maintenance both at the group level and among individuals. During the last twelve years, the following aspects summarize the basically *Romanian* policy vis-a-vis the ethnic minorities:

The regime's nationality policy during the Ceausescu era has undergone several important changes. During the first few years after the change in leadership, necessitated by the death of Gheorghe Gheorghiu-Dej, the new PCR head moved cautiously in his relationship with the ethnic minorities in Romania. In fact, Ceausescu attempted to improve his ties with these groups as a counterweight to his important rivals who remained at the central level as carryovers from the previous regime. As a result of this political rapprochement, the Ceausescu nationality policies during this period were markedly less stringent then had been the case during much of the Gheorghiu-Dej era. The new First Secretary assured the minorities of expanded educational facilities in their own languages; there was a temporary increase in the number of publications (as well as print runs) in German, Hungarian, and Yiddish; minority literature, plays, and movies were encouraged, and a major effort was made to expand native folklore among the ethnic groups.[19] The economic reforms, implemented in 1967, presumably assured greater autonomy for regional and local decisionmakers in the economic field, wiht a view towards increasing the industrial capacity of underdeveloped regions (among which there were some heavily Hungarian-populated areas) and improving the standard of living in such regions.[20] All of these policies, taken together, represented a trend towards some decentralization and expanded autonomy which seemed to bode well for ethnic group rights in the cultural field and also seemed to increase the economic viability of such entities.

During 1967 and 1968, further policies of the Ceausescu leadership seemed to promise even greater opportunities for the maintenance, or even expansion, of the human and economic rights of the minorities. A territorial reorganization of the country, which re-established the prewar system of *judets*, provided opportunities for minority party cadres to move rapidly to important political and economic posts in the new administrative *apparats* established as a result of the reform, and several individuals of Hungarian and German origin actually became first secretaries of the *judet* PGR organizations.[21] At the same time, however, the reorganization did have the effect of breaking up large units with heavy minority organizations into smaller units, thus undermining the possibilities of maintaining cultural autonomy, and this tendency makes it difficult to speak of the administrative reform as overly favorable to the interests of cultural maintenance.

Another development, unfolding simultaneously with the events discussed above, tended to further weaken the possibility of cultural maintenance among the ethnic minorities. The process of modernization, so relentlessly pursued by the regime, had the effect of mobilizing hundreds of thousands of individuals for industrial occupations and urban residence, and the socioeconomic structure of Romania, with its large, untapped reserve of essentially ethnic Romanians in the rural areas, ensured that most of the new industrial workers were Romanians. These masses of "recruits" now moved into the cities, and in the areas traditionally inhabited by minority populations they constituted a new element, which would ultimately tend to break down the cultural, occupational, and residential autonomy of the ethnic groups of these areas.[22]

The two somewhat conflicting tendencies described above have coexisted in an uneasy fashion in Romania ever since, but there have been occasional shifts in the balance between the two. After the Polish uprising of December 1970, Ceausescu's concern with the national minorities in Romania increased, and several steps were taken to improve their economic plight, maintain their cultural autonomy in noncrucial areas, and ensure the continuation of educational programs in Hungarian, German, and other minority languages in areas where the concentrations of non-Romanians would warrant it.[23] The activities of the nationality councils were expanded, and Ceausescu made repeated (and well-publicized) visits to minority areas, in which he held his famous "dialogue with the masses" in order to assure that regional and local authorities, both Party and state, would behave "correctly" towards the minorities.[24]

This trend, too, soon came into conflict with other major policy developments. In the summer of 1971, after a lengthy visit to the People's Republic of China and other Asian communist countries, Nicolae Ceausescu launched the so-called "little cultural revolution," an integrated program of ideological and organizational offensives designed to raise the political consciousness of Party cadres and the general population alike. At the same time, the strong nationalistic overtones of the Ceausescu regime's foreign policy were considerably intensified on the domestic scene as well. The General Secretary and the top PCR leadership increasingly associated themselves with the traditions of *Romanian* nationalism and the heroes of the past, especially Stephen the Great, Michael the Brave, and, more recently, Vlad the Impaler.[25] This program, designed to enhance the regime's popularity among the Romanian masses, had a detrimental effect upon the cultural aspirations of the ethnic minorities, whose historical *epos* was tied in with the experiences of *their* ethnic brothers in Hungary, Germany, and, to some extent, Israel. This highly charged nationalistic campaign has continued unabated up to the present time; indeed, it was significantly strengthened during 1976 and so far in 1977, as the PCR leadership launched a renewed campaign of mass participation in the so-called "Hymn to Romania," which was designed as an integrated series of artistic performances, literary events, and song festivals throughout the country, in which citizens of all nationalities, occupations, and social strata would join in a patriotic outpouring of love for the fatherland. At the apex of this mass-orchestrated mobilization effort stands Nicolae Ceausescu, who has made many important speeches during the last two years in which he had repeatedly compared himself to Stephen the Great, Michael the Brave, and, increasingly, Dimitri Cantemir, educator and statemean of a fateful period of Romanian history.[26]

In addition to the ideological and cultural offensive at the mass level, the Romanian intelligentsia (and those among the minority intelligentsia who have remained loyal to the regime) has been mobilized for a campaign of *scientific discovery* in fields such as archeology, anthropology, and history, with an emphasis on the organic ties between the past and the present; imbedded in this offensive is the political need to prove the continuity of civilization and a national culture on Romanian soil during extended periods of time, even during the dark centuries of foreign occupation. Thus, massive excavations in various areas of the country have uncovered a great deal of evidence concerning previous civilizations in the areas which now constitute Romania. Furthermore, anthropological research has concentrated on showing the ties between the present-day inhabitants of the country and the old Geto-Dacian civilization which preceded the Roman conquest. In historical research, the main emphasis has been on the continuity of social systems and cultural manifestations as well as political forms; of particular importance here is the felt need to show that the Romanians inhabited Transylvania and Bessarabia long before the Hungarians, Germans, or Russians arrived.[27]

During the last few years, there has been a subtle change in the emphasis of this research. While earlier Romanian historiography (as well as Ceausescu's pronouncements on the matter) emphasized the Latin origins of Romanian culture and language, the stress now is on the pre-Roman civilization, most often called the Geto-Dacian cultures, and its organic ties with contemporary Romanian culture. Some historians have even claimed that the Geto-Dacians had developed a civilization superior to that of the Romans, and that the latter, having conquered much of Dacia, in fact became culturally absorbed into this higher culture, thus producing a fusion of great cultural value and impact.[28] This interpretation is currently sponsored by the General Secretary himself. Ceausescu is also increasingly emphasizing the concept of "free Romania," which is a description of those areas of Transylvania which escaped the Roman conquest and were only marginally touched by the Turks or the Habsburgs. Here, presumably, is the core of the Romanian nation and its culture, and it is this core which constitutes the historical underpinnings for the "scoialist culture" of the present and the future.[29]

For the ethnic minorities, as groups, this heavy emphasis on *Romanian* hsitory and civilization must appear as a threat to their group autonomy in the cultural field. For the Germans, the Hungarians, and the Jews, the cultural heritage is not centered on the Dacian kings Burebista and Decebal, but on the origins of their respective nations in the territory of present-day Germany or the Hungarian plain; for the Jews, the focus remains a dual one, emphasizing both the geographical heritage of past generations in *some* areas of Europe and the overriding cultural affinity with the Diaspora and "next year in Jerusalem." In many cases, the Romanian national epos is filled with the description of fundamental struggle *against* the Germans and Hungarians as well as their culture; this is especially the case for Transylvanian Romanians, who suffered for centuries under Habsburg rule. In addition to this basic contradiction between the cultural heritage of the major ethnic groups in Romania, contemporary historiography as well as official Ceausescu pronouncements tends to be rather chauvinistic on this topic, especially since the Romanians now claim that they represented a bulwark of European civilization against the onslaughts of Asiatic Islam—a bulwark which received precious little help from the rest of Europe, especially the German princes and the rulers in Vienna and Budapest. In this context, it is important to note that Vlad the Impaler is being upgraded as a legitimate hero of Romanian history—a leader who maintained internal law, order, and justice in the face of external pressure. It is not an accident that Vlad successfully resisted several major Turkish offensives by establishing a "people's army" and by maintaining internal cohesion, albeit by fear. The message for contemporary citizens of Romania should be fairly clear: As long as "imperialistic" powers (certainly including the Soviet Union) are threatening the self-realization of a national road to soicalism (and thus a nationally based socialist culture), internal cohesion is necessary. Cultural and other autonomy for ethnic groups must be curtailed in order to bolster national unity, much as Vlad did (but the methods, to be sure, are less drastic nowadays).[30]

While the increasing emphasis on Nicolae Ceausescu and his lieutenants on Romanian nationalism in the cultural field has served to put the national minorities *as groups* on the alert, it has also had certain effects upon individual members of the non-Romanian nationalities. First, individuals of Hungarian, German, or other minority origins have on occasion voiced concern over the cultural and ideological offensive of the

Romanian-oriented leadership, and many more certainly harbor such views without expressing them.[31] Second, the malaise among many individuals in these categories has given rise to increasing pressures for exit visas and individual (if not group) emigration. The latter issue became a rather hot one by 1976 and the General Secretary has hit hard upon the tendency of individuals to look for the solution to their problems outside the fatherland rather than attempting to solve such questions inside Romania, for the benefit of all.[32] Ceausescu has made it absolutely clear that he will not permit any mass emigration, and that individual exit visas will only be issued for good cause, the most important of which is reunion of families. Even within this rather restrictive interpretation there are tendencies towards tougher positions, insofar as the PCR leader repeatedly emphasizes the fact that families can also be united by having individuals elsewhere emigrate *to* Romania.[33] On several occasions during the last six months, Ceausescu has gone so far as to characterize emigrants as "traitors," and the law on Romanian citizenship, passed a few years ago, has certain provisions which mandate the loss of such rights if an individual attempts to cross the state border without the proper permission and documentation.[34] All of this has become a major source of international controversy now that the Belgrade conference on the performance of the Helsinki agreement provisions is getting under way. There is no sign that Ceausescu is about to relax his firm stand on this issue.

For the individual member of an ethnic minority group, the right to emigrate has increasinly become a touchstone of the regime's adherence to international agreements (to which it is a signatory). If the regime attempts to promote a "socialist culture" which is heavily laden with *Romanian* nationalism, emigration to the ethnic (and thereby cultural) homeland may be an act of last resort for an individual. In most cases, other motivations are probably also important; it so happens that the ethnic homelands of all the major minority groups in Romania are considerably better off than the latter country economically, and the social and cultural systems are much less restrictive—facts which constitute considerable attractions for a would-be emigrant. In the end, most of those who do ask for exit visas are probably motivated by all of these considerations as well as others. Whatever the motive, the regime's refusal to allow emigration in cases other than the fairly exceptional is increasingly seen as a violation of human rights, especially among those seeking such a solution.[35]

The increasing restrictiveness of policies in this field may be more apparent than real. In total terms, more individuals are leaving the country than was the case prior to 1970, and Romania is by no means the most restrictive of the East European states in this field. The recent concern over the problem is rather derived from a combination of rising expectations among increasing members of individuals inside Romania, the massive publicity given to the topic by President Carter's stand on "human rights" as a fundamental issue of international relations, and the stridently nationalistic tone of Nicolae Ceausescu's political and cultural programs. This combination of factors has raised the question of emigration and human rights above the "threshold of salience" for a great many people inside Romania and out, and the regime must therefore deal with this issue. For Ceausescu, with his profound convictions about nation-building and the organic link between the individual and the collectivity, the issue of emigration probably appears to be limited to treason or abandonment of the common nation-building effort; in a way, abandoning "the ship" is a form of violation of the General Secretary's *personal* human rights, as summarized in his perceived mission as *the* nation-builder in Romania.[36]

The regime's rather restrictive policy on emigration is not matched in other fields. An examination of educational and occupational statistics indicate that the ethnic minorities, especially the Jewish segment, have occupied a rather privileged position in these two dimensions, and the relative equalization now taking part among the various ethnic groups of the country is rather a function of the Romanians catching up, as mass education and employment changes take place in the general modernization process.[37] There are cases of individual discrimination against ethnic Germans, Hungarians and Jews (as well as other "ethnics"), and some of these have received a great deal of publicity in the West, but one fails to see a concerted campaign on the part of the regime. Only insofar as members of minority groups perceive the nationalistic cultural campaign of the Ceausescu regime as a threat to their autonomy as individuals or members of groups can one talk about a "campaign." This conclusion should be emphasized, for it tends to lend some perspective to the current discussion in the Western press.

The Confluence of Group Rights and Individual Concerns:
The Dissident Movement

While the problems surrounding human rights and the ethnic minorities is a serious one, it is of necessity limited in scope, since it does not affect the vast majority of the population, who are Romanians and appear to stand solidly behind many of the nationalistic aspects of Nicolae Ceausescu's domestic and foreign policy. There is, however, a potentially much broader problem for the regime in the field of human rights, a problem which could involve large numbers of individuals without regard to ethnic background. This problem area is the entire question of the relationship between the individual on the one hand, and the state and collectivity, on the other hand, in a communist system. As discussed above, the Ceausescu era has been remarkable for the intensity with which the regime has emphasized the symbiotic relationship between the individual and the state and the subordination of the former to the latter. Furthermore, the 1970s have also been remarkable for the ideological campaigns instituted to carry out the General Secretary's vision of society and nation-building. All of this amounts to a restrictive political and socioeconomic system in terms of individual "elbow room" and, conversely, a large and interventionist profile of the Party in many areas of human activity which have essentially been left alone in many of the other East European states. These factors, taken together, provide a larger area of potential conflict over individual rights and duties than is the case in less interventionist regimes; at the same time, the extensive control mechanisms employed in Romanian society have succeeded in limiting any really general open controversy, even if feelings of dissent should be relatively widespread.

Several events triggered popular interest in the issue of dissent and thus provided the basis for increased political activity on the subject. First of all, the US stand on human rights, reflecting deeply held convictions concerning the individual in a pluralistic society, were given massive publicity everywhere, and some of it also reached the East European countries. The American position was tied in with the Helsinki Agreement ("Basket Three") to which Romania was also a signatory. In addition to this, the Carter Administration was willing to give weight to its convictions by linking human rights to economic relationships and aid, thus complicating the issue for regimes in need of the

latter but dubious about the former. For Romania, this connection between civil rights and economic relations was particularly disturbing
in view of the fact that Bucharest had been attempting to obtain most-
favored-nation treatment in trade with the United States for a considerable time.

Second, the dissident movement in Poland, and especially the GDR
and Czechoslovakia, had a major impact on Romania. In two of the
most orthodox regimes of Eastern Europe massive manifestations of
discontent with the cultural policies of the regimes and their stand on
emigration, freedom of speech, and freedom of conscience became the
order of the day. In East Berlin, thousands of people applied for exit
visas to the Federal Republic; in Prague and elsewhere, many individuals
signed petitions which demanded adherence of the regime to the civil
rights provisions of Helsinki. These events brought home the point that
even in restrictive systems, there was a possibility of voicing one's views
on the subject and making an impact, both in terms of public opinion
and in the regime.

Third, the increased "national culture" of the Ceausescu regime reached
extremely high intensity during the summer and fall of 1976, and an
important aspect of the campaign was increased control of writers, artists,
theater directors and others in the arts and in literature, a fact which
created considerable resistance among the intelligentsia.[38] Furthermore,
much of the cultural activity of Romania during 1976 was dominated by
"commissioned works," i.e., plays, novels, and theater pieces by politically safe but artistically mediocre writers, a situation which infuriated
many important writers.[39]

Finally, the massive social and economic dislocation caused by the
earthquake may have prompted certain individuals to become "dissidents" in order to receive exit visas. By and large, the quake and the firm
handling of the crisis by the authorities had a positive and solidifying
effect upon the population, but there are always exceptions, and the
dissident movement was widely perceived as a "ticket out" during the
spring of last year, a perception which undoubtedly increased the size
and scope of the movement.[40]

The movement started modestly. At first, there was merely a small
circle around the writer Paul Goma, whose earlier works had often been
highly critical of Romanian society and the main ideas of the regime on

state and society. In the beginning, only a dozen individuals signed statements referring to the Helsinki Agreement, Basket Three, and the "bourgeois" conception of human rights. The regime's reaction was also moderate at first. Goma had an interview with Cornel Burtica, the PCR's chief ideological overseer, a meeting unique so far in the annals of recent East European dissident movements. Burtica apparently held out the possibility of early publication of some of Goma's censored works in exchange for the author's cooperation on civil rights.[41] Goma's reaction was unfavorable, and the regime's reaction became ominous. Police cordons were thrown around Goma's apartment building, there was other harassment of him and the first signatories of the civil rights manifesto, and, eventually, the famous author was jailed, albeit only for a short time.[42] Subsequently, the relative tolerance of Ceausescu gave way to much harsher treatment, and the General Secretary repeatedly castigated the dissidents as "traitors." Furthermore, the ideological campaign was intensified. The press carried daily articles on "nefarious forces" abroad whose activities were not designed to help maintain individual rights but rather to destroy the social fabric of Romania. This criticism of the West was quite outspoken; the General Secretary and others especially condemned emigre organizations of German-Romanians in the Federal Republic, but left no one in doubt that the Carter administration was also a target. There were also hints that Bucharest considered the ferment among some elements of the Hungarian minority as possibly inspired in Budapest.[43]

As regime repression grew duing the summer of 1976, so did the dissident movement. Over one hundred individuals signed various manifestoes demanding human rights, and the scope of the protest, large by Romanian standards, has caused considerable regime concern. Up to this point, however, there has been no significant modification of Ceausescu's stand, which continues to characterize the dissidents as potential or real traitors.[44]

The controversy revolves around the familiar problem of individual freedom versus societal and collective needs. Goma and his associates essentially maintain that the modernization of society, with improved material and social conditions and thus enhanced choice possibilities for the individual should be matched by increased choice in other fields as well; in the latter category should be included the individual's right to be "different"—different in the sense that he or she could choose (without fear or recrimination) to opt out of the nation-building process and simply remain psychologically on the sidelines. The main thrust of the argument, therefore, is not rejection of "socialism" per se, but rather the regime's unwillingness to expand the parameters of personal choice in the relationship between the individual and the state. Conversely, the Ceausescu approach to the question emphasizes the view that the individual can only reach self-fulfillment in interaction with the collectivity (under the leadership of the Communist Party), and that the new socialist society is qualitatively superior to "private" society precisely because the former emphasizes the symbiotic relationship between the unit and the collectivity.[45] With such fundamentalist views and little willingness to compromise, it is unlikely that the dissident movement will wither away in Romania. Conversely, the high profile of the PCR in society, replete with major control mechanisms, probably ensures that the size of the movement will be modest, at least for the time being.

As it moves toward the end of the decade, the Romanian society and polity will experience increasing problems from the relationship of modernization, human rights, and nationalism. Specifically, it seems that socioeconomic modernization will carry with it greater demands for a freer exchange of ideas, both in terms of necessary exchanges in a sophisticated economy, and also in purely personal terms. This demand, which will have to be met in the exchange of technical information if economic progress is to continue, is likely to reinforce dissidents' claim that human rights demand freer communication and greater parameters of personal choice in *all* fields. If this train of thought is granted, the next step is not far-fetched: The ethnic minorities, both as groups and also in terms of individual preference, will most likely claim the privilege of expanding their *cultural* autonomy. This may not automatically mean *political* nationalism, but to the present PCR regime, with its strong emphasis on the *integrated* nation, whose symbols and values tend to be traditonally Romanian, even the quest for increased cultural autonomy is likely to be interpreted as unwarranted *political* nationalism. On this basis it is logical to predict continuing, perhaps increased, controversy in this field in the years to come.

Conclusion

What does the Romanian case contribute to our understanding of the relationship between modernization, human rights, and nationalism in communist political systems? It is possible to argue that "Ceausescuism" is a unique phenomenon, and that the Romanian case therefore has little to contribute to our understanding of the *general* nature of this relationship. On the other hand, it is certainly true that Romania and Ceausescu, despite their special features as a system and as a leadership personality, have several features in common with other East European states under communist rule. First of all, the Romanian experience has shown that socioeconomic modernization, which produces a more highly stratified society with a generally higher level of education and general socio-political consciousness, is likely to raise demands for greater personal autonomy and some political choice, including the choice of remaining *outside* of the mainstream of nation-building and development. Second, the modern world with its instant communications systems, has indeed shrunk to such an extent that events in one contry (particularly a major one such as the United States) will have immediate repercussions elsewhere, as was the case with President Carter's stand on human rights in *all* countries. Third, in a multiethnic society such as the Romanian, the complexity of the concept of "human rights" is such that provision of these rights for all citizens becomes exceedingly difficult. The reason for this difficulty is the relationship between "human rights" and nationalism. For the majority group of a multiethnic society, (especially one ruled by local leaders of an allegedly *international* movement) the expression of nationalistic feelings and values is one of the most fundamental of human rights. But for the ethnic *minorities*, such nationalistic expressions on the part of the majority group appear as infringements of the formers' individual or group rights.

There are two basic solutions to this problem: either the regime allows for greater cultural autonomy for *all* ethnic groups, or it attempts to integrate all of them into a "new" culture. For communists in charge of socialist states, the integrative solution is preferred, as a natural element in the progression of mankind towards a predetermined goal of full integration of everybody (Communism) and because of the Communist propensity for centralized rule which allows for little autonomy for individuals or groups. Thus, a change in the existing policies on human rights and nationalism in Eastern Europe would demand both a fundamental switch of political philosophy as well as an alteration of the basic premises of political rule, which emphasize centralization and control. Add to this the function of the Soviet Union as the "watchdog" of authoritarianism in Eastern Europe with the Brezhnev Doctrine as a ready fig leaf of intervention, and the prospects of basic changes in communist policies on human rights and nationalism remain rather dim for the immediate future.

NOTES

1. The classical "model" of modernization in this respect is still Karl W. Deutsch, "Social Mobilization and Political Development," *The American Political Science Review* (September 1961), pp. 493-575.

2. E.g., Charles Gati, ed., *The Politics of Modernization in Eastern Europe* (New York: Praeger Publishers, 1974), esp. chapter 1 by Vernon V. Aspaturian and chapter 2 by Cyril E. Black.

3. See, for example, Nicolae Ceausescu at the Eleventh Congress of the Romanian Communist Party (PCR), November 1974, in *Congresul al XI-lea al Partidului Comunist Roman* (Bucharest: Editura Politica, 1975), esp. pp. 15-16, 68-79.

4. In the Romanian case, this view is stated in considerable detail in *Programme of the Romanian Communist Party for the Building of the Multilaterally Developed Socialist Society and Romania's Advance toward Communism* (Bucharst: Meridiane Publishing House, 1975), esp. Part VI, VIII.

5. See, for example, Trond Gilberg, "Ceausescu's Romania," *Problems of Communism* (July-August 1974), pp. 29-44.

6. I am basing this on an extensive research on Nicolae Ceausescu's speeches and public statements, as they are found in his *Romania pe Drumul Desavirsirii Constructiei Socialiste* (Bucharest: Editura Politica, 1968), 8 volumes. See also Ion Florea, *Dialectica Democratiei Socialiste* (Bucharest: Editura Stientifica, 1973), esp. pp. 195-204.

7. *Ibid.*, esp. pp. 86-89.

8. For recent regime criticism of "individualism" in the arts and literature, see *Luceafarul,* July 31, 1976; "retrograde" views among the ethnic minorities were castigated by the General Secretary in *Scinteia,* June 19, 1976.

9.   For a detailed discussion of these control mechanisms, see Trond Gilberg, *Modernization in Romania since World War II* (New York: Praeger Publishers, 1975), esp. chapter 2.

10.   The powers outlined above are found in the constitution of the Socialist Republic of Romania. The rights and duties of Romanian citizenship are exhaustively discussed in Ion Deleanu, *Cetatenia Romana* (Cluj-Napoca: Editura Dacia, 1976).

11.   Ceausescu discusses this organizational network frequently, e.g., in his report to the eleventh PCR congress, in *Congresul al XI-lea,* esp. pp. 68-79.

12.   Gilberg, "Ceausescu's Romania."

13.   See for example, Ivan Volgyes, ed., *Political Socialization in Eastern Europe* (New York: Praeger Publishers, 1975).

14.   During April and May 1977, the problems of beginning open dissent combined with Ceausescu's malaise over lacking ideological commitment among the masses, and gave rise to a massive campaign against "bourgeois values" (cf. *Scinteia,* April 10, 1977).

15.   One of the strongest statements on dissent and lacking ideological commitment was made by Nicolae Ceausescu, speaking to the congress of collective farmers (*ibid.,* April 21, 1977).

16.   The General Secretary has attempted to counteract this tendancy by frequent reorganizations and regime transfers, in preparation for the eleventh PCR congress, during November 1974 (*ibid.*).

17.   Gilberg, *Modernization in Romania,* chapter 8.

18.   The "symbiotic" relationship between the individual (no matter what hsi ethnic background) and the collectivity is spelled out in great detail in the *Programme fo the Romanian Communist Party,* esp. chapter VI, VII, and VIII.

19.   This effort was especially pronounced in early 1971; see for example, *Scinteia,* April 11 and May 7, 1971, and *Lupta de Clasa,* March 1971.

20.   This effort continues, as witnessed by Ceausescu's visits to such areas during 1976; see, for example, *Scinteia,* June 19, 1976.

21.   For a detailed discussion of this, see my "Political Leadership at the Regional Level in Romania: The Case of the Judet Party, 1968-1973," *East European Quarterly,* IX, 1 (January 1976), pp. 97-118.

22.   This massive movement of population categories can be seen in the 1956 and 1966 census figures, as follows: Republica Populara Romania,

Directia Centrala de Statistica, *Recensamintul Populatiei din 21 Februarie 1956,* (Bucharest: 1959), 556, and Republica Socialista Romania, Directia Centrala de Statistica, *Recensamintul Populatiei si Locuintelor din 15 Martie 1966* (Bucharest: 1968), p. 113.

23. Ceausescu discussed some of these measures, with special reference to the Hungarians, in *Scinteia,* March 14, 1971.

24. These visits have continued, e.g. visits to minority areas in Transylvania (cf. *Scinteia,* June 19, 1976).

25. The re-evaluation of Vlad the Impaler is also taking place in Romanian academia, e.g., Constantin C. Giurescu in *Magazin Istoric,* No. 3 (March 1974).

26. E.g., Nicolae Ceausescu in a speech at historical Alba Iulia, in *Scinteia,* May 29, 1975.

27. The General Secretary discussed this at a congress on Thracian history, in *Magazin Istoric,* No. 10 (October 1976).

28. E.g., Mircea Musat and Gheorghe Ionita in *Anale de Istorie,* No. 1, (January 1976), p. 57.

29. *Ibid.*

30. The emphasis on Vlad as a great stateman creating national unity is especially strong in Dumitru Almas in *Munca,* December 10, 1976.

31. An example of this is found in the writings of the so-called "Banat Action Group," where writers of German origin discussed Romanian society, e.g., *Neue Literatur* No. 7/1976, and also in the *Neue Banater Zeitung* during the last two-three years.

32. *Scinteia,* April 19, 1977.

33. *Ibid.*

34. See, for example, discussion of the law on citizenship in *ibid.,* December 18, 1971.

35. Ceausescu's condemnation of the motives behind application for exit visas is clearly stated in *ibid.,* April 19, 1977.

36. Based on his collected speeches and articles, in *Romania pe Drumul Desavisirii Constructiei Socialiste,* and other published sources.

37. See Gilberg, *Modernization in Romania,* esp. chapter 8.

38. In this resentment, some of the intelligentsia was apparently joined by Bucharest youth, according to C. Stanescu, in *Scinteia,* October 27, 1976.

39. The political reasoning for this selection process was repeatedly furnished by Ceausescu, e.g., in *ibid.,* October 23, 1976.

40.   These perceptions have been voiced to me by observers on the scene and some Romanian officials.

41.   Reported in *Le Monde,* February 23, 1977.

42.   Goma's release was discussed in *ibid.,* May 10, 1977.

43.   These were merely hints, however; cf. *Scinteia,* February 18, 1977.

44.   In this respect, the General Secretary has followed the path he established in his February 17, 1977 speech (see *ibid.*).

45.   *Ibid.*

FEDERAL SYSTEMS

Milan J. Reban

IX

CZECHOSLOVAKIA: THE NEW FEDERATION

As a multinational state undergoing rapid transformation since its inception in 1918, Czechoslovakia pursued its development under a unitary system until 1968. Its brief history has been marked by a series of dramatic events. There was its plight in the darkening shadow of Hitler's Germany and the ignominy of the Munich Pact and its aftermath. It was the only democracy transformed into a Communist party-state. Most recently, there was the heady "Prague Spring" of 1968. The very real ingredients of tragedy in all these events easily evoke sympathy which in turn is apparent in the resultant analyses, often presenting Czechoslovakia in an unduly romantic perspective. Indeed, the lofty values of independence, democracy, self-determination, and the like, which were being challenged throughout much of the post-1918 evolution tended to detract attention from several fundamental problems besetting the Czechoslovak polity. Above all was the crucial question of the role of the nationalities and ethnicity in general within the system. It is Yugoslavia which immediately comes to mind when such problems are noted in Eastern Europe, but Czechoslovakia's reality is second only to Yugoslavia's in its complexity. The vexing problems of the minorities, notably the German, remained a major challenge to state-building. The participatory status of Slovakia continued to be a fundamental question which was to be aired again thoroughly and openly in the mid-1960s. The imperfect solution of the federalization of Czechoslovakia was formulated in response.

Yet, problems remain. Although in many respects the most highly developed system of Eastern Europe, Czechoslovakia was not immune

215

to the problems besetting other systems of the region on account of widespread authoritarianism and uneven and delayed modernization. Moreover, as noted by some, it is a region tending to favor collectivist views of human rights. As in other systems, Czechoslovakia witnesses clashes between the official doctrines of the ruling party and its political traditions. In Czechoslovakia, which in many respects constitutes an exception in the region, conditions for civic civility and liberties existed on a large scale. But as Tökés observed recently, most "alternative concepts of individual rights as advanced by nationalist, radical, Christian, Socialist, ethnic and, in Czechoslovakia alone in the interwar period, by communist party spokesmen, were formulated in collectivist, class, ethnic and linguistic terms."[1]

The intensity of ethnic identity in the modern world needs no elaboration; yet, some of its forms were devastating for Czechoslovakia. It was hoped that the process of rapid economic development would bring about the ultimate amelioration of nationalist inclinations, thereby solving the problem. Although Slovak nationalism revolved around the traditional Roman Catholic forces before the war, it flourished at a time when Czechoslovakia ceased functioning as an entity during World War II.

The German minority prior to the war was another issue, although some have argued that Czechoslovakia sought to pursue policies of justice and equality toward its nationalities, and the German democratic element may have been strengthened by the appeasement policy of Czechoslovakia's allies, especially the British.[2] The process of including the German-populated sections into Czechoslovakia after World War I was laborious, for it involved conflicts between the ideals of democracy for all and the tendency "to transform that State into an instrument of Czech and Slovak nationalism."[3]

The Czech policy toward Slovakia was characterized by rigidity, and indeed, President Beneš' intransigence on the question of decentralization permitted the Communists to stand out as the sole supporters of the idea that Slovakia was a national unit.[4] However, no fundamental changes occurred until 1968. Its antecedents, along with the free flow of ideas during the year 1968, produced a watershed in the history of the Czechoslovak polity, in that it witnessed a determined attempt to end decisively the Czechoslovakism-dominated centralist policy, and the birth of a federation.

Slovakia in the Events of 1968

The issue of Slovak nationalism and the nature of Slovak participation in the Czechoslovak system was, in conjunction with the whole economic performance issue, at the heart of the tumultuous events leading up to 1968. It witnessed the activation of critical groups whose demands had an impact reaching beyond the nationality question, adding emphatically to large-scale demands for pluralization of the system as a whole. The treatment of the Slovak issue had been closely interwoven with the shaky economic performance in timing; the first evidence of large-scale dissatisfaction by various significant segments of the Slovak society as well as of the Slovak Communist Party came into the open at the same time as the national economic crisis, that is, in the early 1960s.[5]

Unlike the Czechs, however, the Slovaks sought to deal with the hitherto unresolved nationality problem first. The demands for reforms, although varied in their point of origin, ultimately raised fundamental questions about the legitimacy of the Czechoslovak system as a whole. Sidney Verba identifies the linkage when he argues that there exist certain problem areas which have close ties to the making and enforcement of decisions, the key problem areas being identity, legitimacy, participation, penetration, and distribution. The problem areas—or crises, as some prefer to call them—are interrelated, and, in Verba's judgment, they all "imply questions of legitimacy: are they (government actions) accepted because of normative beliefs as to their rightness? All imply questions of participation: who took part in making the decision?"[6] Indeed, with reference to Slovakia we may speak of a crisis of political development, a crisis whose significance must not be underestimated for the entire period of 1963 to 1967, and one which the reformers left compelled to address in their concrete proposals during 1968, albeit the Czech involvement was belated and most reluctant.

That, in the end, it came to be treated by the reformers as one of the fundamental problems is shown in the fact that the Action Program of April 1968, contained extensive references to it. The principal solution advanced in the same document and the one finally accepted—the plan to federalize Czechoslovakia—reinforced anew the overall political reform plan of 1968 to create a plurality of political subjects. Whereas the economic reformers saw the necessity for pluralization in order for the economic reform to succeed, the issue of Slovak nationalism contributed to the demand for pluralization along the nationality dimension.

Professor Brzezinski speculated some time ago that the complex nationality claims in the Soviet Union are becoming more pronounced and will constitute one of the principal challenges to the Soviet system in the coming years.[7] This is so despite the fact that nationalities had been at the forefront of concern for Russian revolutionaries, and resultant formulations of the question were close to the core of their revolutionary strategy, widely emulated in Eastern Europe. The Soviet Union is still wrestling with this problem, exacerbated by some unexpected ethno-demographic trends, and it is not surprising that the much younger Communist inheritors of the complex nationalisties mosaic of the Austro-Hungarian Empire came to experience major problems. Despite much justified attention accorded the almost exotic pattern of Yugoslavia, Czechoslovakia has nationality problems nearly as vexing in Eastern Europe. Before the war, due to the rise of Hitler in Germany, it was the German minority that received the most attention. After the war, the magnitude of this problem was reduced by the massive deportation of some two and one-half million Germans from Czechoslovakia.

Ironically, the very war leading to the "resolution" of the prewar German minority issue had created propitious circumstances for the flowering of Slovak nationalism, the fulcrum of the current concern with nationalities and ethnic groups in Czechoslovakia. The genesis of the problem must be sought at least partly from within the framework of the truncated Slovak state during the war years, which in its way satisfied some of the existing nationalist sentiments. It was brought into sharper focus in the significant Slovak National Uprising of 1944. As often happens, the treatment of this event ultimately enabled a fundamental debate about the future in terms of the past. Not surprisingly, the uprising turned out, upon closer examination, to have been much more of a nationalist undertaking than had been officially admitted during the subsequent years. Its strong nationalist outlines and its basically Slovak, not exclusively Communist, leadership, had been denied or distorted in the Czechoslovak Communist historiography. After 1945, the uprising had been portrayed as having been led by Communists, and principally Czech Communists at that, who acted under Moscow's direction in a military campaign directed against the German armies and their collaborators. The nationalistic impulse of numerous Slovak leaders and intellectuals was exacerbated by the deep-seated and growing resentment over the continued charges of "bourgeois nationalism" leveled against their activities throughout the 1960s by the top Centralist party leaders. In the 1950s, it should be recalled, several principal leaders of the Slovak CP found themselves charged with "bourgeois nationalist" deviations, while Novotný himself in 1954 accused some Slovak leaders of conspiring with the Habsburgs and other lackeys of imperialism.[8] In combination with other features of nationality policy—or lack thereof—these conditions thrust Slovakia into the role of catalyst in the 1968 transformation.[9]

The intensity and magnitude of the Slovak assertiveness in the early 1960s served notice that, in the long run, Slovakia and its place in the Czechoslovak political system had become a fundamental issue for the future of Czechoslovakia as a state, and not merely a test of the primacy of the party within the system.

The transformation of any political system is an uneven process, and the attendant problems may be examined in terms of the differing rates of social mobilization or, specifically, in terms of the process whereby different strata are integrated into the modernizing sector of society. This particular perspective may be fruitful in our consideration of the participatory demands of Slovakia. Its problem is to some extent related to the issues of economic reform, but has been in fact exacerbated by the marked degree of underdevelopment of Slovakia in contrast with the Czech lands.

The wide gulf in levels of development separating the Czech lands and Slovakia came to influence numerous relationships between the Czechs and the Slovaks.[10] It existed in the Communist Party character as well; the Party had been an elitist party in Slovakia before the war, whereas it functioned as a mass party in the Czech lands. This fact allowed the leadership of the Slovak organization to function with a relatively high degree of unity, especially on issues of importance to Slovakia. The Slovak intelligentsia, too, had been smaller in number, and therefore quite homogeneous on issues affecting Slovakia. As we shall see, the interaction between the Slovak intelligentsia and the Party in the events dealt with here was extensive, and the positions of the two, not unexpectedly, were mutually reinforcing.

The basic relationship of development and nationalism is an intimate one, and Paul Shoup suggests one facet of this linkage in his analysis of the Yugoslav case, where the economic problems became involved in the national question in numerous and subtle ways, but the tendency for economic disputes to assume a national character was particularly evident in two respects: first, in efforts to deal with the great contrast between the developed and underdeveloped regions of Yugoslavia; second, in competition between territorial units, either local or regional, which came to be known as particularism, but very often took the form of national rivalries as well.[11]

Shoup's conclusions hold well to the case of Slovak nationalism, although the economic factors are but one aspect of that nationalism. The central Czechoslovak leadership's approach to the rapid nation-building of Czechoslovakia proceeded along more centralized lines, thus coming into conflict with the particularist demands of the Slovaks. In Communist systems, nation-building entails the building of a unit according to an overall plan, especially in the realm of planned management of social and ethnic groups, so that the social consequences of industrialism and modernization may be controlled by the leadership. Obviously the demands of the Slovaks were beyond the parameters defined in Prague.

We need not dwell on the details of Slovak development, but it might be appropriate to mention a few of the objections raised by the Slovak intellectuals, obviously speaking with the support of important segments of the Slovak Communist leadership. They pointed to the many differences stemming from the unequal development in the two sections of the country, despite massive efforts designed to alter that situation.

For example, the differential levels of wages and of the economic structure were shown to be unfavorable for Slovaks. Not unlike the developing countries, Slovakia found itself with a labor surplus, although exact estimates of its size differ. Thus, the Slovak Union of Women claimed there were some 180,000 job-seekers in Slovakia, although the planners perceived that figure as something of an exaggeration. Standard measures utilized by the Czechoslovak Communist Party had been successful in raising the level of economic development, but the argument had been made by critics that the heavy subsidies in Slovakia only weakened the potential influence of the market pattern. In other areas, the picture was quite dismal. The neglected Slovak spas, for example, were not expected to reach the capacity they enjoyed in 1937 until 1980. Furthermore, services throughout the land were judged wholly inadequate.[12]

There has also been a disparity between the share of national production and the level of exports (22.6 percent during the first six months of the critical year 1968, as contrasted with 16.2 percent for imports) so that the many problems of Slovakia allegedly had become exacerbated by the very measures slated to ameliorate the conditions of backwardness. In other characteristics, too, the area contrasted with the Czech lands and showed the classical indicators of underdevelopment: low productivity, heavy reliance upon agriculture, a large proportion of children in the population, and a rapidly increasing productive population sector.[13]

Some arguments became intensely anti-Czech. One Slovak writer, in an angry analysis, described the conditions of inequality between the key parts of Czechoslovakia as shameful, for they reflected nothing but neglect of Slovakia. Charging that standard solutions for the problem such as the shifting of surplus labor from the less-developed Slovakia to other labor-short regions of Czechoslovakia were wholly undignified and exploitative, Anton Hykiš saw the political significance in these terms:

> The renewal of contemporary ČSR is inseparably united with the wish of the majority of the Slovak nation. How would the map of Europe look had the Slovak insurgents declared the continuity of the Slovak republic and fought for some Democratic Slovak Republic and not for the Czechoslovak Republic? In 1944 the Slovak nation voluntarily gave up a part of its sovereignty for the united, not yet existent state of Czechs and Slovaks, and theoretically can any day change its decision and again ask full sovereignty, to decide for the other constitutional alternative, return of its own state.[14]

Vladimir Minac, in a still more outspoken position, labeled the Czech policy toward Slovakia as "genocidal." To be sure, he referred to prewar times, but his words were intended to have a contemporary ring.[15] These few statements indicate the intense sentiment of nationalism among some members of the Slovak intelligentsia.

Shils, like Kautsky, agrees that, in the developing setting, the spirit of opposition is very strong among the students and the intelligentsia in general, substantially affecting the existing public opinion, Clearly, the Slovak intellectuals with their articulation of strong charges fit the mold, thereby producing a potentially explosive situation, for their sentiments challenge the very legitimacy of Czechoslovakia.

Gabriel Almond suggested that an important test of whether a given nation has evolved a common "secular political culture" is in the response of individuals to key symbols. A public opinion survey addressed indirectly to this point showed sharp differences between Slovaks and Czechs. Whereas the most positive times of the past for the Czech sample were the Hussite period, the reign of Charles IV, and the years of the First Republic, for the Slovaks the three leading events were the Štúr period, the first months of 1968, and the Slovak Uprising. The obverse for the Czechs consisted of the Protectorate of World War II, the post-White Mountain period, and the summer of 1968. For the Slovaks, the times of the Slovak State, the Austro-Hungarian domination, and the 1950s represented the most difficult times. For the greatest leaders of the past, the Czechs named Thomas G. Masaryk, Jan Hus, and Charles IV, while the Slovaks designated Ludovít Štúr, Dubček, and Štefánik.[16] While reflecting to some extent the scenario of the times, these replies attested to a deep division which no leadership of Czechoslovakia will ever again be able to ignore or neglect. For where political divisions are reinforced by other lines, especially linguistic or cultural, political sociologists see potential for serious conflicts, especially should issues polarize along these lines as in the situation studied here.[17]

Students of comparative politics have addressed themselves to the question of political "fit" between political culture and the system, and the problem is indeed very complex in the Communist systems generally, for they have been committed to the radical alteration of the political culture existing at the time of their coming to power at the end of World War II.[18] Nonetheless, the poll in question, especially in direct comparison with the poll taken before 1948, shows continuities with the pre-Communist era, and so highlights the gap between the system of rule and the context of that rule.[19]

The nationality problem was but one where the search for identity and increasing assertiveness took place. Other relatively dormant ethnic groups came into focus during 1968 after a long period of neglect. These groups posed not only internal challenges, but since they included sizeable numbers of Hungarians, Poles, Ukrainians, and Germans, their small size would have been magnified to produce international repercussions well beyond their numbers.[20]

On ethnic problem is illustrated by the Hungarians in Slovakia. They number around 500,000 people and in some districts they constitute the dominant group. During 1968, their spokesmen publicly demanded equality and other concessions on matters of schooling, the language of instruction, and other bread-and-butter issues. But it appears that the events of 1968 did not necessarily engender overt concern over democratization among them; rather, they stimulated heightened ethnic demands. As one Hungarian official in Galanta succinctly put it, "the whole regeneration process of the January plenum bypassed our district. We simply have not time for anything; only the nationality problem is being solved."[21]

Similar pluralistic articulation was evident in the religious sphere, where some previously suppressed groups made themselves heard again. The Roman Catholic Church, an especially potent group in the more traditional Slovakia, became much more dynamic as a political force. The nationality and ethnic demands furthermore triggered a whole host of ancillary pressures, articulated by representatives of the territorial divisions of Czechoslovakia, notably those of Moravia and Silesia. In fact, some of their spokesman called for the creation of a "tri" and "quad" federation in 1968, in place of the one that was actually created. Other spokesmen feared that Brno, the principal city of Moravia, would be at a disadvantage vis-a-vis Bratislava and Prague, slated to be the capitals of the two federation components. Even the most cursory examination of the Moscow-Leningrad Party organization rivalries shows the possible consequences of such enmity.

Some demands for fundamental reform had been heard for years, although no Slovak leader came forth to advocate publicly a federal solution to the problem. In fact, not a significant national Slovak leader advocated the federal solution as late as the historic December-January 1968 session of the Central Committee. Instead, there were some suggestions made for a return to the Košice Program of 1945. The Košice Program, adopted as the war was coming to a close, enunciated the plans for postwar Czechoslovakia with one of the principal provisions advancing some autonomy for Slovakia. This demand for a return to the Košice Program represented a call for the reinstatement of a relationship that had been abrogated almost as soon as it had been forged. The Czech lands and Slovakia, with the support of the Slovak Democratic Party, were united into one Czechoslovakia with the latter receiving a ·semi-autonomous role. In the Košice Program promulgated in April 1945, the Slovaks were promised equal treatment in the resultant unitary state. While the national government administered all of Czechoslovakia, a Slovak regional administration functioned on a basis that made it subordinate to Prague. Almost immediately, but especially after the coup of February 1948, the relationship of Czechs and Slovaks was subjugated to the Soviet model of nationality policy, with some regional autonomy allowed for "Slovakism," and with a program of equalization in the Communist Party.[22] Thus, the remains of the Košice Program, with some transmutation, were permitted to continue until the announcement of a new constitution in 1960, which for all practical purposes abrogated once and for all the remaining formal autonomy possessed by Slovaks at that time.

There is evidence that the 1960 constitution which declared the arrival of the stage of socialism in Czechoslovakia had been drafted hastily, and that such key questions as the relationship of the Czechs and Slovaks were decided without discussion by experts. The Czechoslovak leadership at the time committed itself to a policy of integration as a solution to the problem of Slovak participation in the system. The constitutional document stripped the Slovak National Council of its remaining rights and the Slovak Board of Commissioners was further weakened.

In view of the strong nationalism that permeated not only the truncated Slovak state during World War II, but the very strong nationalist sentiments motivating the Slovak Uprising of 1944, it becomes evident that the centralism sought by the Prague leadership would frustrate Slovak aspirations. It is evident that the Slovak Communist Party leadership succeeded in articulating certain demands for Slovakia in the wake of the frustrating abrogation of its remaining administrative autonomy as a direct result of the rising economic crisis throughout Czechoslovakia. The crisis undermined the authority of the leadership in Prague. In this context it became not only possible but in fact necessary as part of the belated destalinization campaign to reopen the trials of the early 1950s.

Specifically, in the Slovak case, this meant the exhumation of the "bourgeois nationalism" campaign waged by the Prague leadership against the Slovak Communist leaders, some of whom (Vlado Clementis, for instance) had been executed in the 1950s for their alleged transgressions. Because of the politically sensitive nature of the destalinization campaign, the reexamination of the trials was of limited scope and duration. When it was officially announced as having ended, many unanswered questions about the past were being raised in various quarters. In Slovakia, the frustrations broke into an open and critical discussion in various journals.

Riveles concluded that the central objections raised by the Slovaks stemmed from the incomplete nature of destalinization. The individuals responsible for Stalinist practices were left untouched, including the head of the Czechoslovak government at the time, Viliam Široký, a Slovak. And, second, "although those accused were themselves rehabilitated, the heresy of 'bourgeois nationalism' as an ideological deviation within the SCP remained under official interdiction." Široký's continued tenure had become offensive, and, as a consequence,

> Slovak intellectuals, clearly acting with the consent of the Slovak
> Party, reacted vigorously. Miro Hysko, a prominent journalist,
> attacked Široký in the Bratislava *Pravda* for having initiated
> the purge at the 9th Slovak Party Congress in May 1950.

Although Novotný counterattacked in strong language, in the fall of 1963, Široký was removed from the Presidium and lost his post as Premier.[23]

The special new conditions permitted moves not as readily available to leaders within an effectively centralized system. As the removal of Široký attests, the capacity for maneuver on the part of the Slovak CP became increasingly possible when the CPCZ leadership, and Novotný in particular responded to the modified Prague-Bratislava relationship repressively and ineptly.

The party leaders reflected views that were symptomatic of many inequalities. In the context of the larger issues here, numerous measures assumed greater significance than would have been the case under less charged circumstances. For example, even the designation "Slovak" was deleted during the 1950s in favor of a "Comrade from Slovakia," and the grammatical rules imposed Czech spelling. These demeaning gestures were accompanied by other moves against the Slovaks. Lakatoš recalled that, after 1945, whole areas of the Czech borderlands emptied of their former German residents were occupied by Slovaks, and in the initial stages of their residence in these areas they maintained their own schools and publications. These were, however, discontinued after 1949. The Slovaks, too, noted that when their compatriots assumed posts with the central administration in Prague, they were only able to assimilate through the adoption of Czech ways. These and other comparable slights contributed to the highly explosive character of Slovak nationalism,[24] which had been of recent origin. How recent may be seen in a figure mentioned by Vlado Clementis, a Slovak leader executed as a "bourgeois nationalist deviationist" in the early 1950s, that before 1918 in all of Slovakia there were but some 500 families taking Slovak publications.[25] Clearly, this was a modest foundation for nationalist communication.

The opposition to Czechoslovak centralism had become more insistent, with strong overtones of "anti-colonial" nationalism, although this particular approach was not embraced by all. Gustav Husák in mid-1968 cautioned the Slovaks that all blame for their plight could not be placed on the Czechs, and called for changes in the Slovak attitude. The Gallup institute in Bratislava showed that in the minds of most Slovaks, the political arrangements that would be satisfactory to them took precedence over economic well-being, a sentiment that is not surprising for it is commonly found in all the developing areas.[26]

Although it was not always unified, the Slovak CP, operating within the context of a reawakened Slovak national sentiment, increased its assertiveness and turned into an independent power center. For all practical purposes, the key Slovak representatives in Prague became divorced from their home bases, and by default relinquished political control to those closer to home. So strengthened, the Slovaks made increasingly vehement demands for elimination of the entire "bourgeois nationalist" campaign carried on by Novotný as late as 1967. In addition, there were the sensational reappraisals of the Uprising occasioned by its twentieth anniversary in 1964, which vocalized complaints against the inadequacies of the constitutional provisions in the 1960 document. These objections blened into an attack on Novotný personally and on the centralist direction of the Party as a whole.

Ushering in the year 1968 was the selection of Dubček as Novotný's successor in the leading party role. This news, which spread around Prague just before four o'clock in the afternoon of January 5, was the shot at Sarajevo for the Czechoslovak "socialist humanism" experiment. The Slovak Dubček was the choice largely on account of Slovakia's new role. As late as October 1967, Novotný resorted to the "bourgeois nationalism" accusation, but it was his last. It was possibly his disposition towards the Slovaks that was even more objectionable than his Czechoslovak commitment. At this critical juncture, the Slovaks in effect functioned in the role of a second political party within the system, with Dubček standing at its forefront.[27] Czechoslovak multinationalism prompted this development, for it now stood in direct conflict with the prevailing centralist tendencies. One observer evaluated the alarming consequences:

> If then the just efforts of the Slovaks to negate the centralism of Prague had reached in January a certain, if symbolic, victory (what happened then was not) an opening of a crack but an actual catastrophic gap, which resulted in that in January the monolithic system began to collapse like a house of cards. The infection of pluralism, be it only "nationalism," was deadly for it.[28]

There is no doubt that the economic reformers within the Communist Party were welcoming the change in leadership and came to support Dubček. This is no indication that the Slovaks were pleased with every facet of the economic reform; indeed the dislocations caused by the new reforms in 1967 worked to the detriment of Slovakia. However, the common desire for change prevailed over the principal reservations held by both groups in question.

As shown in the preceding analysis, the Slovak involvement in the reform activities before and during 1968 was complex. While many Slovaks were committed to genuine liberalization, many others perceived liberalization as a vehicle for the attainment of Slovak goals—namely, an effective participatory role in the system. Federalization in Czechoslovakia came to be seen as allowing for the latter. It is possible to say that the willing Czechs gave more support to the creation of an effective model of democratic socialism, whereas the Slovaks sought primarily the realization of nationalist aspirations. Although their motivations differed, both groups viewed with favor a reform designed to give power to a variety of actors. The Slovak leaders found such a solution attractive because it promised to strengthen them in their dealings with the central government in Prague.

Some students of the development have expressed misgivings about the rapidity with which federalization was implemented, pointing out that other Slovak ventures of the past toward self-determination were accompanied by regression. We noted before that the pressure for reform of the asymmetrical Czech-Slovak relationship became so strong by 1966 that the only question that appeared to have validity concerned the nature of that reform. While at the 1967-1968 Central Committee session federalization was not openly advocated, the Action Program of the Party (announced on 5 April 1968) contained a frank recognition of the past problems in nationality relations. It explained that in order to have an orderly development in the future, it had become necessary

> to effect a crucial change in the constitutional arrangement of the relations between Czechs and Slovaks and to carry out the necessary constitutional changes. It is essential to respect the advantage of a *socialist federal arrangement* as a recognized and well-tested legal state form of the coexistence of two equal nations in a common socialist state.[29]

This momentous program was being undertaken without adequate study, without proper planning, and without much preparation. Furthermore, when some of the Slovak leaders who were in opposition suddenly switched sides to become ardent supporters, they provoked suspicion among the Czechs.

After the invasion, too, some Czech critics charged that the Slovaks were able to commence their participation in the new federated state with some semblance of effective representation. Although the Slovak representatives elected were of the traditional Communist state variety, they were nonetheless legitimized. Unlike the Czech Party, the Communist Party of Slovakia had held its Fourteenth Congress shortly after the invasion, and utilized the opportunity for strategy planning. Perhaps because of this, the Slovaks were able to ensure the selection of one of their men as the top leader of the Czechoslovak Communist Party—Dr. Gustav Husák. Additionally, the Slovaks had an early opportunity to shift some unwanted officials into numerous national organs that remain largely honorific under present conditions. A fundamental question, raised by a number of observers, was encapsuled in this observation:

> No one has attempted to formulate even roughly what will hold together the newly created republics, the Czech and Slovak, and why we must continue in the contemporary European political and moral reality to persevere with each other.[30]

One of the younger intellectuals who had taken an active role in the drafting of the economic reforms explained the overall motivation of the reformers as being aimed at the creation of a plurality of political entities. The calculations with respect to the federalization of Czechoslovakia were as follows:

> The setting up of separate Czech and Slovak parliaments and Czech and Slovak governments under a weaker federal parliament and federal government meant the devolution of state power into three centers. The intention was to federalize the Communist Party in the same way as the state, so that there would be a Slovak Communist Party operating in Slovakia and a Communist Party of the Czech lands in Bohemia, Moravia, and Silesia, each with its own Central Committee, Praesidium and Secretariat. These national Communist parties would then share political power with the federal Communist Parrty of Czechoslovakia. This political pluralism with the Communist movement would itself have meant a great step toward the democratization of public life. For the triangular arrangement of both state and Party organs, as well as of other social and special-interest groups, would create a diversity of power centres and control centres in mutual balance. The federalization of the Republic therefore, was intended to play a cardinal role not only in settling the nationality question but also in converting the centralized power system into a democratic one.[31]

The expectations of the federalization were obviously far-reaching, and its implementation was perceived by its key advocates, the Slovaks and the reformers, as a variable-sum game. Interestingly, too, this part of the Action Program was the only part committed to a definite implementation schedule.

The federal arrangement was seen by others as a means of eliminating specific inequities. Implicitly equating the Czech and Hungarian domination of Slovakia, Laco Novomeský, one of the principle targets of the "bourgeois nationalism" charge, expressed the hope for an end to Slovak subservience in these terms:

Hundreds of thousands of people had to depart for America
because they were dying of hunger at home. Then came the
Masaryk republic, but it did not solve the social question, and
again the Slovaks had to leave for foreign lands so that they could
find livelihood; and because emigration to America was curtailed, left for France where they worked in mines. Then there
was the independent state and the Slovaks again went after
work, this time to Germany. Then came the socialist republic
—and again the Slovaks go after work in Moravia and Bohemia.
We want it so that the Slovak would not have to leave, so that
he could work and be well at home. And that, we await from the
federalization.[32]

For the post-1968 evolution, the orientation of the Slovak leaders
was most significant: Dubček and Husák were much more nationalists
in their outlook than Vilém Široký, Julius Ďuriš, and others, who found
the Soviet version of internationalism as interpreted in Prague more
acceptable. Early in 1968, Gustav Husák, siding with the reformers, supported the expansion of the rights of individuals, an important part of
the Czech program, although there were to be in his view definite limits
to liberalization after August. But, in the first days of 1968, Husák stated
an unmistakable position on Slovakia:

The modern European wants to know what are the issues of state.
He wants to understand, to have a say, to help decide his fate
and living conditions, to elect his leaders, and then according to
their deeds to praise them or even to criticize them. In short, he
wants to see the constitutional principle that "the people are the
source of all power" implemented in everyday practice. The citizen wants to realize his civic and national self through his national and state representatives. He wants guarantees that he is free
of civic responsibility.[33]

These debates took place against the backdrop of a strong anti-Soviet
sentiment expressed in many quarters, accompanied by rumors that the
Soviet union had in fact gone so far as to contemplate the separation of
Slovakia from the rest of the country, and appending it in some manner
to the Ukrainian S.S.R.[34] The threat of Soviet domination may have

served a useful function by securing unity in the uncertain early stages of federalization. Many new nationalist movements seem to require outside threat to achieve objectives set forth by modernizing elites; the leadership of Czechoslovakia may actually have welcomed the invoking of such a threat as the emergency means for the execution of their maneuvers so necessary to reestablish legitimacy and unity in the system.

Just as at the conclusion of World War II, Slovak particularism soon came under pressure from Prague. Gustav Husák, a major proponent of federalization, feared initially the potential influence of strong federal organs, but in January 1970,[35] argued that factors of unity must have precedence. The measures since 1970 were to "strengthen the functions and the integrating role of federal bodies, to solidify the management of a unified Czechoslovak economy, and to fortify the control functions of the federal center."[36] Alois Indra, Communist Party Presidium member and Central Committee Secretary, identified generally as one of the leaders seeking the Soviet intervention of August 1968, stated unequivocally in August 1970, that insofar as the demands of Slovakia were concerned, "the requirements of a united state come first always. They must prevail over the artificial, narrowly national interests of both the Slovaks and the Czechs." Other critics of Slovak demands also charged that their separate interests were the products of "slogans" gravitating "toward anarchism."[37] Indra's remark contained within it the seeds of the limitations of an effective federal pluralism for an organization whose definition of legitimacy throughout its history had included the necessity for central direction: the Communist Party. It was a heritage which numerous party officials found difficult to alter, and which the Slovaks found advantageous in the changed context.

The patterns of nationality are discernible in the most significant movement of dissent in recent Czechoslovakia, known as Charter 77. Dating to January 1977, the movement's initial document, signed by three well-known figures, Professors Jiří Hájek, Jan Patočka, and writer Václav Havel, called for adherence to Czechoslovak laws, including the two international covenants published in the Czechoslovak *Collection of Laws* in October 1976. Shattering the post-1968 "normalcy," its supporters became openly critical of various facets of the human rights policy of Czechoslovakia, but with their methods and activities seeking to·remain within the parameters of Czechoslovak legality. Prosecution was initially virtually impossible, and although only various extra-legal methods have been utilized against the Charter activists, trials were at last held in 1979.

There are apparently about 1,000 signatories of the Charter in 1978, mostly from the intelligentsia, but interestingly, "of the 750 signatures available, only eight could be identified as Slovaks, and most of these even live in Prague. This fact cannot be explained solely by the difficulties in communication."[38] One reason may be advanced—that the party-population links in Slovakia had been traditionally lower than in the Czech lands. Also, an area where there appears to be some dissent in Slovakia is in the religious sphere, again an activity, although reported, that remains beyond the scope of the basic Charter concerns. Most importantly, the federalization, however emasculated in recent years, continues to be perceived much more positively in Slovakia, whereas, to many Czechs, there have been no tangible gains at all—indeed, setbacks instead.

In 1968, the Communist Party organization was to be likewise federalized. To overcome the previous asymmetric model, a Czech Communist Party was to be formed alongside the already-existing Slovak Communist Party as another territorial entity of the CPCZ. As a compromise, a Czech Party Bureau was then established on November 16, 1968. The Party organization was to be the key integrating institution, superseding in importance the state administration. The membership and statutes were to be uniform for the Communist Party of Czechoslovakia as a whole, thus safeguarding some central authority.[39] In the original form, the CPSL would have maintained effective control of the state administrative machinery in Slovakia, giving a more substantial degree of control than that enjoyed by the Czech organization. After August 1968, however, this potentially far-reaching proposal was scuttled, presumably for negating the Soviet definition of the principles of democratic centralism, for it technically opened the possibility of "factionalism." Not only on account of Soviet desires in the matter, but perhaps also because of the requirements of consolidation, Husák in effect gave up on the federalization of the party, declaring that it was unified. The process of consolidation, ably described in other works, notably that of Vladimír Kusín, not only restored fully by 1971 the party's "democratic centralism," but also took the form of a massive purge of the entire party

organization. In their total effect, the measures limited the room for purely Slovak initiatives within the Party.

The purges assumed a different form in Slovakia than in the Czech
lands; whereas in the latter nearly 22 percent fell in the purge, the Slovak
percentage was 17.5 percent.[40] Moreover, it is generally agreed that the
fate of the purged individuals, especially the intellectuals, was less hard
and demeaning than that of their Czech colleagues. Of course, in having
some goods that society had to offer, they are thereby subject to effective
control, lest their unwanted activism should cause them to lose what
little they possess. On the whole, except for the religious sphere, Slovakia
appears to be more tranquil and in some respects remarkably prosperous,
a condition within which the Slovaks, in the quest for national self-as-
sertion, will not likely wish to seriously impair.

The federalization process spread throughout the institutions of the
state and in a checkerboard pattern, the ministers and their deputies
altered the basis of their nationality. Prague and the rapidly-growing
Bratislava, which became in 1979 the second largest city in Czechoslovakia, are seats of government.

The Chamber of the People consists of 200 deputies chosen on the
basis of proportional representation, and the Chamber of Nations consists of 75 Czechs and 75 Slovaks. In the two, the Czech National Council has 200 members and a Slovak National Council, 150. The Presidium
of the National Assembly is divided equally: 20 Czechs and 20 Slovaks.[41]

It is not, therefore, that the federation arrangement is the only significant survival of the heady year 1968, and should be viewed with considerable satisfaction in Slovakia, a decade after its implementation. The
numbers of Slovaks in important positions alone, with Husák as the first
Slovak President of the Republic, are a far cry from the nineteenth century when the Slovaks fiercely resisted intense Magyarization, or the
interwar period when some 250,000 Czechs came to run Slovakia, often
in paternalistic ways. Federalization is an arrangement commonly resorted
to in situations of ethnic discord, for it addresses above all a point of
major grievances, that of an access to the system; and, however imper-
fectly, the Slovaks gained in the 1970s.

The Slovaks pursued a pragmatic course in 1968. Reflecting on that
eventful year, and the subsequent divergencies in the Czech and Slovak
developments, Jiří Hájek, the former Foreign Minister, saw this picture:

In Slovakia the "normalised" repression has been substantially
more moderate than in the Czech Lands. Slovaks are the smaller
of the two nations, people are closer to one another there, and
their bonds of solidarity are stronger. Moreover, the Bratislava
political leaders are evidently cleverer than their colleagues in
Prague. They have no desire to destroy their creative intelligentsia. After the defeat of the Prague Spring, repression in Slovakia
was almost exclusively directed against active "reform Communists," and not against large groups of people outside the
party. Communists have never been as numerous in Slovakia
as they were in the Czech Lands. Furthermore, federalization
of the country has been preserved as the only large-scale reform
of the Prague Spring. It marked a big step forward on the national
plane for Slovakia, and it has survived "normalisation." The
Slovaks have no national reason to add to the general disappoint-
ment as the Czechs have. These may be among the reasons which
have made fewer people in Slovakia feel that they should sign
the Charter.[42]

The Position of Minorities in the Federation

With the Law on Federalization, a Law on Minorities was promulgated.
Not only were additional rights given to the already established ethnic
groups of Poles, Ukrainians, and Hungarians, but the Law on Minorities
reestablished formally the status of Germans as an ethnic minority, a
status they had lost after World War II.

Even a cursory examination of data on national minorities reveals
considerable discrepancies, the reconciliation of which is beyond the
scope of this essay. It is to be noted, however, that Czechoslovakia—
unlike Hungary, Poland, Romania, and the German Democratic Republic—compiles data on national minorities in its statistical publications.
As of December 1974, the official figures revealed the figures found on
the following page.

Under Czechoslovak law, Jews do not constitute a nationality or
national minority and are not included in these figures. During a census
Jews must declare themselves as belonging to one of the recognized
nations (Czech, Slovak) or nationalities (Hungarian, German, etc.).

Minority Group	Number	Percentage of Population
Hungarians	583,000	4.00
Germans	77,000	0.50
Poles	71,000	0.50
Ukrainians	51,000	0.30
Russians	10,000	0.07
Others	48,000	0.03

In 1975, there were, according to some figures, 266,000 gypsies in Czechoslovakia, constituting 1.8 percent of its population. Slovakia has 183,000, and the Czech lands 83,000. Those deemed to be fully integrated are no longer counted as gypsies; the rest must declare as members of one of the legally recognized nations or nationalities.[43] (There are substantial discrepancies in census figures. For instance, some estimates of the Hungarian minority reach 750,000.)

Ethnic Germans have been diminishing in numbers, and only about 77,000 remain. The official policy has been one of assimilation rather than resettlement, and although recognized as a minority, Germans do not have German language schools and presumably, most of the younger generation speaks Czech. Some outside observers suggest that in twenty years there will be no Germans left in Czechoslovakia. In recent years there has been some emigration under close scrutiny in the post-Helsinki period. Although there are discrepancies in the Czechoslovak and the German figures regarding the numbers wishing to resettle in Germany, it appears that there are still many hundreds wishing to do so. Whereas in 1969, 15,306 Germans left Czechoslovakia, in recent years the numbers have fluctuated around 500 annually. It appears, however, that Czechoslovakia is a somewhat reluctant participant in the process.[44]

Today's situation stands in dramatic contrast to the immediate postwar period, when Czechoslovakia had nearly three million Germans. However, the plan to transfer this large minority was formulated during the war, with the reluctant assent of the Great Powers, excepting the Soviet Union, which endorsed the plan without equivocation. No doubt the Soviet leaders appreciated the geo-political consequence of such a vast transfer, for it would almost inevitably guarantee Czechoslovak dependence on the Soviet Union for security against expectedly strong pressures for return from Germany. Although the question remains to be studied in detail, it appears that in Slovakia, unlike the Czech lands, the animosity against the Germans may not have been as intense and uniform, in part due to their smaller numbers there and in part to the role of Germany in wartime Slovakia. On the other hand, they harbored strong feelings against the Hungarians, in part because of the experiences of the Slovaks included under Hungarian control in the period of the Slovak state. The transfer of the Germans proceeded rapidly, and by 1947 only 250,000 remained in Czechoslovakia. The transfer also deflected attention, especially in the Czech lands, from the other nationality problem, that of Slovakia, in the immediate post-war reconstruction.[45]

During 1968, the demands of some of the other minority groups tended to be modest, but in 1968, as since 1950, the ethnic situation was considerably less complex in the Czech lands. In Slovakia, however, the Ruthenians, Hungarians, and also the gypsies wished to attain separate national entity status, each group seeking nationality rights. The Ukrainians, or Ruthenians, about 30,000 strong, live around Prešov. This group has been pressured to become Ukrainians, and their sensitivities were further affected by the forcible elimination of the Greek Catholic Church, which showed some signs of awakening during 1968.[46]

Although recognized as a separate nationality in 1921, the gypsies saw major changes in their fortunes in the following decades. Many perished in World War II, but many survived, especially in Slovakia. After the war, many survivors went to work in the Czech lands, often ending up in the ghetto-like conditions of the industrial centers. A group of nomads, called Vlachs, continued to move about. This was clearly in conflict with the policy of the government, determined to effect assimilation, and, over a period of five days in 1958, nomadism was formally halted. Many problems of dislocation ensued, as when the nomads returned to their original settlements only to find them abolished. The policy of dispersion, pushed after 1965, sought to identify those to be dispersed, mostly those with regular jobs, those whose children attended schools, and simply those who were seen as leaving their gypsy setting.

The effort collapsed in 1968, and gypsies were moving in the direction of forming their own associations, one for Slovakia and one for the Czech lands. As often happens with movements of cultural revitalization, those farthest along the continuum of assimilation appeared to be at the forefront of the efforts. These associations appeared to gain momentum, especially in the realm of culture, but by 1973 were ordered to cease their activities, lest they should seek nationality status. Serious problems remain, exacerbated by the gypsies' exceptionally high fecundity.

Whereas the Potsdam conference concentrated on the question of the German minorities, the other minority matters were left to the various states involved. Therefore, the Hungarian minority problem was up to the Czechoslovak government, which applied the harsh principle of collective responsibility. Presumably, this verdict was justified by that minority's desire to join the country of their origin at the time of the Munich Pact, and the consequent pressuring of the reeling republic. The Košice Program included the removal of the Hungarian minority, affirmed by the political parties of the National Front in 1946, and affirmed thereby the principle that Czechoslovakia as a national state was to be for Slovaks and Czechs.

The plan to expel the Hungarians was hampered from the outset by the unwillingness of Budapest to cooperate, and this one-sided approach, after some second thoughts and negotiations, envisioned the process of resettlement as reciprocal, becoming in effect a program of exchange, with Slovaks from Hungary moving into Slovakia. The delaying tactics of the Hungarians bore fruit, as the Paris Peace Conference in August 1946, did not endorse the original Czechoslovak intentions. The "solution" was postponed, and other, less inclusive, measures such as the dispersal of the Hungarians into the Sudeten region were tried in late 1947, ending withe the coup in 1948. The campaign was bitter, as considerable force had been used, but obviously unsuccessful in the long run, because the Hungarian calculations for the Hungarian minority in Czechoslovakia still show it some 200,000 higher than the official Czech figures.

The animosities evident in the Hungarian question, especially in Slovakia, assumed major significance for Slovak nationalism, and overtly in its earlier stages of the 1960s was possibily even more important than the hostilities toward the Czechs. Slovak nationalism has had a strong anti-Hungarian component from the nineteenth century onward and was one of the major factors for the willingness to participate in the Czechoslovak state in 1918. To be sure, as Robert R. King observes, it is possible that much of the hostility was deflected toward Hungary because anti-Czech sentiments could not be expressed openly. Indeed, in the marathon debates between the Slovak and Hungarian historians about Ludovit Štúr's role, especially during 1948, the Slovak historians became especially vehement in the mid-1960s, given that the Hungarian government renounced any irredentist claims to Slovakia. King argues persuasively that the Slovak historians praised Štúr as a champion of Slovak national rights against the Hungarians, who also sought recognition for Slovak national identity vis-a-vis the Czechs.[47] As on some many occasions, the future is examined in terms of the past: the anniversary of Štúr's birth triggered an especially intense debate.

> At the same time the Hungarian party, with the Soviet leadership's approval if not at its request, had become the chief advocate of "internationalism" in Eastern Europe. It was the Hungarian party leadership which openly criticized the nationalist position taken by the Rumanian party, and Hungarian historians were the principal opponents of the Rumanian historians' emphasis on the sovereignty and independence of the national state.[48]

The Hungarian internationalism coincided somewhat with the Hungarian position, King argues, and the Hungarians chided the Slovaks for nationalism, a position with which some Czech leadership undoubtedly could agree.

During 1968, the demands of the Hungarians were controversial, holding, for example, that nations and nationalities should be treated equally, and the constitution revised accordingly. Another set of demands by the Cultural Union of the Hungarian Working People (*Csemadok*) called for more education, along with the readjustments of the districts to produce greater homogeneity. Other Hungarian rights were called for, such as the repudiation of the pertinent sections of the Košice Program, the repressive treatment of the Hungarians after the war, and the like. Hungarians were to be appointed to various posts according to the principle of proportional representation, and a Slovak ministry for Hungarian nationality was recommended. These demands were bitterly resisted by the Slovaks and countercharges were expectedly made about the Hungarian separateness, unwillingness to learn Slovak, and acts of discrimination against the Slovaks in the Hungarian districts of Slovakia. Obviously, the basic problems remain, and many demands are unmet.

Ján Gregor, Deputy Chairman of the Slovak Government and Chairman of its Council for Nationalities, recently proferred an appraisal of the current status of the nationality question, focusing upon the Hungarian minority, and defending current policies. Although implying reservations about the adequacy of the level of the international consciousness of the nationalities, Gregor presents a picture of progress in which the dynamics of industrialization are seen to continue a constructive role. Thus, not unlike many social scientists in the West and the Soviet planners on the other hand, Gregor sees the rapid industrialization as an appropriate vehicle for the overcoming of the differences in levels of development between Slovakia and the Czech lands. Thus between 1946 and 1975, the number of industrial workers in the southern districts of Slovakia increased sixfold, and the heretofore minuscule industrial group of Hungarians increased to 150,000. This growth, evaluated positively, is expected to increase still further.

With respect to education, Gregor cites numbers designed to elicit approbation; but, given the size of the minority, they are not intimidating. For example, in the 1977-1978 academic year, 13,604 children of elementary grades attended schools in Hungarian instruction, an increase of 1,840 over the academic year 1970-1971. Hungarian language instruction, while available in the higher grades as well, does not involve large numbers of students, for they expectedly decrease in the higher grades. In the institutions of higher learning, there were only 2,600 students of Hungarian nationality, 2,094 of them in Slovakia.

Ambivalence greets the goal of bilingualism: teachers, parents, and students themselves are charged to master either the Slovak or Czech language, "on account of its societal function, from the viewpoint of an equal fulfillment throughout the territory of the republic." The process may be hampered by the quality of instruction, for the report implies that the quality of teachers must be raised. Of course, in addition to schooling, a modest cultural life exists as well, with numerous publications in Hungarian, theaters, and the like. Much remains undone, however, and the problems acqurie new dimensions. Ján Gregor states that, insofar as the new constituional guarantees are concerned,

we must give attention to the solution of such special questions as the formation of further expectations and guarantees, which would secure to the members of the Hungarian and Ukrainian nationalities the full use of their mother tongue in contacts with officials, so that they would not suffer losses on account of the usage of their civic rights.[49]

Beyond the 1970s

With its complex population mosaic, the Czechoslovak Communist leaders pursued a policy not unlike their democratic predecessors with regard to the nationality policy. Moreover, they had to cope with Slovak nationalism against the background of Titoism and its potentially threatening appeals. Although Slovakia in some respects is seen from an economic standpoint as the biggest gainer among all the Communist-led Eastern European nations, its remarkable attainments did not produce the anticipated unity. As is well known, rapid economic development can be destabilizing and tends to trigger sentiments betraying a sense of relative deprivation on the part of some Czechs, which suggests that Slovakia benefited disproportionately at the expense of the Czech lands. Yet, its special economic dynamism under the existing conditions may yet facilitate the germination of ideas for economic reforms. The development in Czechoslovakia, and not only those affecting the Slovaks, suggest anew that the advances of interaction and communication, rather than bringing about the "flowing-together" of different people, produces a heightened cultural awareness of separate ethnic groups within the state, exacerbating inter-ethnic conflict.

During the 1970s, many refinements in the policy of Czechoslovakia toward its nationalities had taken place, but even in the most significant outcome, the federalization, the Slovaks have not been able to fully assert themselves. The basic outline of the system still follows the patterns commanded from Moscow. The Yugoslav alternative, for example, is an impossibility for the time being.

No doubt, with a political culture that once sustained the Czechoslovak democracy, the Czechs are being compelled to rethink their own role in the system, but it would seem that they have a long way to go. The Czech liberals in 1968 did not fully grasp the significance of Slovak nationalism, and their manifestoes and other pronouncements reflected little understanding of Slovakia. The cultural developments appear to be proceeding along separate paths. One sign of new thought was Jan Příbram's reflection on 1968, observing that the Slovaks were not as "masochistic" as the Czechs in their demands. Under existing conditions, the Slovaks are pursuing an eminently realistic line, with no significant dissent, no conspiracies. They are, instead, "engaged in achieving the best possible goal, i.e., they are trying to 'save the Slovak people, and they do not allow themselves to be disrupted from within."[50]

The post-war evolution of Czechoslovakia brought to question the very character of that system. The consideration of human rights encompassed in its ethnic mosaic guarantees that rigid centralism will no longer be acceptable, not only to the Slovaks, but to the other smaller nationalities as well. Possibly, the groundwork for a meaningful discussion of the larger questions of human rights will have been at last created in the new Czechoslovakia.

NOTES

1. Rudolf L. Tökés, *Opposition in Eastern Europe* (Baltimore: The Johns Hopkins University Press, 1979), p. 9.

2. For example, J. W. Bruegel, *Czechoslovakia before Munich: The German Minority Problem and British Appeasement Policy* (New York and London: Cambridge University Press, 1973).

3. *Ibid.*, p. 65.

4. An excellent overview is Eugen Steiner, *The Slovak Dilemma* (New York and London: Cambridge University Press, 1973).

5. It is interesting to note that Alexander Dubček became a member of the Slovak Communist Party Presidium in 1962, starting his rise toward 1968. See William Shawcross, *Dubček* (New York: Simon and Schuster, 1971).

Some materials on Slovakia are based on Milan J. Reban's dissertation, "Czechoslovakia in 1968: Some Aspects of Pluralism and Change," Michigan State University, 1972.

6. See Sidney Verba, "Sequences and Development," in Leonard Binder et al., *Crises and Sequences in Political Development* (Princeton: Princeton University Press, 1971), pp. 299-300. For our purposes we shall accept Seymour Martin Lipset's definition that a system must engender

and maintain that existing political institutions are "the most appropriate or proper ones for the society." See his "Some Social Requisites of Democracy: Economic Development and Political Legitimacy," *The American Political Science Review*, LIII (March, 1959), p. 86.

7. Zbigniew Brzezinski, "The Soviet Political System: Transformation or Degeneration," *Problems of Communism*, XV (January-February, 1966), pp. 1-15.

8. Milan Hübl, "Konflikty nebo jednota?" (Conflicts or Unity?), LIterární listy, I (March 14, 1969), p. 1.

9. See an illuminating article tracing the recent developments in Slovak nationalism by Stanley Riveles, "Slovakia: Catalyst of Crisis," *Problems of Communism*, XVI (May-June, 1968), pp. 1-9.

10. Although narrowing in the prewar period, the gap between Slovakia and Bohemia remained wide. Thus, the percentage of population engaged in agriculture and industry was as follows:

		Bohemia	Slovakia
Agriculture	1921	29.7	60.6
	1930	24.1	56.8
Industry	1921	40.6	17.4
	1930	41.8	19.1

The pattern was not substantially altered in the ensuing period. From: *Annuaire Statistique de la République Tchécoslovaque*, (Prague: Orbis, 1938), p. 15, reproduced in Karel Černý, "Historical Background to Czechoslovak Economic Reform," *East European Quarterly*, VIII (September, 1969), p. 340.

11. Paul Shoup, *Communism and the Yugoslav National Question* (New York: Columbia University Press, 1968), p. 228.

12. These figures are drawn from several sources, including Jiří Baudiss, "Slovenské obavy a naděje" (Slovak Worries and Hopes), *Práce*, December 5, 1968, p. 4.

13. For example, Štefan Gronský, "Jsme nevděční?" (Are We Ungrateful?), *Kulturní tvorba*, April 25, 1958, p. 9.

14. Anton Hykiš, "Proč chce Slovensko federaci?" (Why Does Slovakia Want Federation?), *Reportér*, XXX, No. 26 (June 26-July 7, 1968), p. 15.

15. "Federace, demokratizace abdikace" (Federation, Democratization, Abdication), *Literární listy,* I (May 9, 1968), p. 7.

16. "Žijeme minulostí?" (Do We Live by Our Past?), *Práce,* November 27, 1968, p. 4. This extract from a survey by the Institute of Public Opinion Research, an organization of the Czechoslovak Academy, won the approval of *Práce* "Such research. . . is needed like salt (to serve) as a barometer which helps us to get rid of superstitions and illusions and takes us closer to reality." Interestingly, Štúr, a Slovak nationalist, was explicitly condemned by Marx and Engels for his support of the Habsburgs against the Hungarian Revolution of 1848.

17. Gabriel Almond, "Comparative Political Systems," *Journal of Politics,* XVIII (1956), pp. 391-409.

18. A provocative discussion of the question is presented in several essays by Alfred G. Meyer, including "Authority in Communist Political Systems," in Lewis J. Edinger (ed.), *Political Leadership in Industrialized Societies* (New York: John Wiley, 1967), pp. 84-107. We agree with Meyer's observation that to measure legitimacy of the existing system by comparing it with the criteria they seek to destroy is a problematical matter. That the traditional culture elements persisted is also a fact, and these criteria were for comparison by the intellectuals. Thus, in this particular case, the Stalinist practices with their emphasis upon integration of Czechoslovakia conflicted directly with the Slovak search for national identity.

19. See reference to the matter in Vladimír V. Kusín, *The Intellectual Origins of the Prague Spring* (London: Cambridge University Press, 1971), pp. 15-16.

20. The Ukrainians, for instance, had a radio station broadcasting in their language in Prešov in Northeast Slovakia. Its activity was objected to most strenuously by Soviet authorities during 1968.

21. During 1968, some Slovaks began to object openly to the treatment accorded them by the Hungarians, and by moving out left numerous villages completely Hungarian. And, in some cases, teachers refused to teach their children Czechoslovakian history, rationalizing their stand by stating that there was little interest in it among their Hungarian children. See Pavel Pokorný, "Vášně na jihu Slovenska" (Passions in South Slovakia), *Reportér,* XXX (June 12-19, 1968), p. 14.

22. For a summary of the Košice Program, see W. Diamond, *Czechoslovakia between East and West* (London: Stephens, 1947), pp. 1-7.

23. Riveles, "Slovakia: Catalyst or Crisis," pp. 2-3.

24. "Co si myslí Češi o Slovácích?" (What are the Czechs Thinking about the Slovaks?), *Reportér*, III (May 22-29, 1968), pp. 5-6.

25. Zdeněk Eis quotes the remark Clementis made to Ehrenburg, who visited Slovakia in the 1920s. *Ibid.*, p. 6.

26. See *Práce*, July 13, 1968.

27. See a perceptive commentary by Petr Pithart, "5. ledna 1968?" (January 5, 1968?), *Listy*, II (January 9, 1969), i. To mark the break with the 1968 weekly, the Union of Czechoslovak Writers dropped the 1969 word *Literární* from its masthead, while letting commentary on contemporary political happenings.

Illustrating the Slovak leverage later and this time in opposition to Dubček is the statement by Vasil Bilak, one of the principal conservatives of 1968, who let it be known that he did not support the summoning of the Extraordinary Congress of the CPCS. At the regional conference of the Slovak CP in Bánská Bystrica he stated pointedly and in retrospect rather ominously, that "we, the Slovak part will not attend it." *Kulturný život* (Bratislava), June 7, 1968.

28. Ratislav Volf, "Nevědomost hříchu neviní?" (Ignorance Does Not Made Sins?), *Kulturní tvorba*, IV (April 25, 1968), pp. 10-12.

29. "The Action Program of the Communist Party of Czechoslovakia," in Robin Alison Remington (ed.), *Winter in Prague: Documents on Czechoslovak Communism in Crisis* (Cambridge, Massachusetts: The MIT Press, 1969), p. 107.

30. Zdeněk Eis, "Oddělujema se a zůstanene spolu" (We Are Separating and Remain Together), *Reportér*, XXX (December 28, 1968), p. 5.

31. Radoslav Selucký, *Czechoslovakia: The Plan that Failed* (London: Thomas Nelson, 1970), pp. 132-133.

32. Stanislav Budín, "S Novomeským o federaci" (With Novomeský about Federation), *Reportéer*, III (June 19-26, 1968), p. 12.

33. *Kulturný život*, January 12, 1968.

34. Interestingly, similar rumors were circulating at the conclusion of World War II; even President Beneš was reported to have expressed concern over such a possibility, lest the nascent regime fail to cooperate with the USSR. Indeed, the underground Slovak Communist Party in 1944 prepared a report which alluded to the possibility of a Slovak state, and suggested that "With regard to the state arrangement, the best would

be a combination with the USSR; if a ČSR, then it should be federalized on the basis of the national principle. . . ." *Právnické studie,* 1971, pp. 107-108.

35.   *Rudé právo,* January 31, 1970.

36.   Viliam Plevza, *Nové slovo,* No. 44 (October 28, 1976).

37.   *Rudé právo,* August 12, 1970, in *East Europe,* XX (January, 1971), p. 54.

38.   H. Hájek and L. Nižnaský, *Czechoslovak Dissent: Sources and Aims,* RAD Background Report/143, June 29, 1978, pp. 1-11.

39.   *Rudé právo,* November 18, 1968.

40.   Radio Prague, December 14, 1970, and Radio Bratislava, May 13, 1971, in Ladislav Nižnaský and William F. Robinson, *Slovakia after a Decade of Federation,* RFE/RAD Background Report/5, January 10, 1979, pp. 18-19.

41.   For the documentation and an extended descriptive introduction to the system, see Jiří Grospič, *Československá federace: zákony o federativním uspořádání* CCSR (Prague: Orbis, 1972), 263 pp.

42.   *Svenska Dagbladed,* November 13, 1977, quoted in Vladimír Kusín, "Challenge to Normalcy: Political Opposition in Czechoslovakia, 1968-77," in Rudolf L. Tökés, *Opposition in Eastern Europe* (Baltimore: The Johns Hopkins University Press, 1979), p. 53.

43.   In William F. Robinson (comp.) RFE/RAD Background Report/ 225, November 3, 1976.

44.   See *End of German Resettlement from Czechoslovakia?* RFE Situation Report, August 3, 1977, pp. 1-2.

45.   For discussion of some of these issues, consult H. Gordon Skilling, *Czechoslovakia's Interrupted Revolution* (Princeton: Princeton University Press, 1976); also Ludvík Němec, "Solution of the Minorities Problem," in Victor S. Mamatey and Radomír Lɒža (eds.), *A History of the Czechoslovak Republic, 1918-1948* (Princeton: Princeton University Press, 1973), pp. 416-427.

46.   See Peter A. Toma and Milan J. Reban, "Church-State Schism in Czechoslovakia," in Bohdan R. Bociurkiw and John W. Strong (eds.), *Religion and Atheism in the U.S.S.R. and Eastern Europe* (London: Macmillan, 1975), pp. 273-291. It should be noted that, with respect to the numbers of adherents of different groups, there are no reliable figures for the religious groupings after 1930.

47. Robert R. King, *Minorities under Communism: Nationalities as a Source of Tension among Balkan Communist States* (Cambridge: Harvard University Press, 1973), especially pp. 176-178.

48. *Ibid.*, p. 186.

49. Ján Gregor, "V spoločnej socialistickej vlasti" (In One United Socialist Land), *Pravda* (Bratislava), January 3, 1978.

50. Jan Příbram, "Slovaks with Czech Eyes," *Svědectví* (Paris), No. 52, 1976, quoted in Ladislav Nižnasky and William F. Robinson, *Slovakia after a Decade of Federation*, RFE/RAD Background Report/5 (Czechoslovakia), January 10, 1979, p. 20.

George and Patricia V. Klein

X

NATIONALISM VS. IDEOLOGY
THE PIVOT OF YUGOSLAV POLITICS

Political Culture

The Federal Socialist Republic of Yugoslavia is a multinational state. Unlike other multinational states in Eastern Europe it does not contain a majority nationality. The plurality nationality, the Serbs, comprise only 40 percent of the total population. Modern Yugoslavia in the Tito era has represented a reaction to the unitary regime which prevailed during the interwar period. The war of national liberation was a multifaceted conflict; on the primary level it was resistance against brutal occupation regimes, which animated most of the combatants on the Partisan side. On the lower levels of awareness there was also the promise of social revolution which would reconstitute the country both as a socialist state and a state in which equality between the various nationalities would prevail. It is difficult to separate the elements of utopia and *real politik* in the Partisan Movement. Nevertheless, the promise of equality made it possible for the Partisans, unlike the Četniks, to become a truly national resistance movement which drew support from all ethnic elements comprising the population. The Communist Party even then was the only national organization which transcended the bounds of narrow ethnic particularism and which could base its appeals on ideology rather than tribal allegiances. It was this combination of ability to mobilize heterogeneous populations into the task of national resistance which was responsible for its rise to power.

247

The Communist Party known as the League of Communists of Yugo-slavia (LCY), never forgot that it was the guardian of a frequently tenu-ous national concensus. It has vacilated between a greater or lesser centrali-zation since it came to power, but after 1948 and expulsion from the Cominform, it has never opted for centralism as a viable political doctrine. The fundamental question of Yugoslav governance remained as to what degree of decentralization was consistent with the Party's retention or control over major policy matters. The answers differed during various periods and coincided with stages of constitutional reforms. During the period from 1945 to 1950 Yugoslav institutions drew on the Soviet model for inspiration. The Constitution of 1946 treated the issue of centralism and nationality in the same way as the USSR Constitution of 1936. Ever since the 1950s, the Yugoslav leadership was divorced from any reliable outside source of support and had to base its political viability and legitimacy entirely on the support it could muster amongst its own population. As a result, the system was reorganized to place the major responsibility for decisionmaking in the hands of republican leaderships which were ethnically based. The system of workers' self-management became the key for major experimentation in the realm of industrial management and in local and regional self-administration. The balance of power between the various regions of Yugoslavia and the federal government has swung like a pendulum. Since the 1953 pro-mulgation of the Fundamental Law of Yugoslavia, there has been a steady devolution of federal powers. This devolution was formalized in the Constitution of 1963, which resulted in relatively untrammeled, non-partisan elections. The level of political liberty was significantly expanded in 1966 with the downfall of the vice president of Yugoslavia, Alexander Ranković, who had until then controlled the Uprava državne bezbednosti (UDBA), the Yugoslav secret police. With the downgrading of the security organs Yugoslavia embarked on a far-reaching experiment in liberalism which affected every political aspect of life. The permissible level of dissent reached near Western proportions and market socialism became an officially approved goal and method of the Yugoslav economy.[1] There were numerous institutional adaptations to conform to the ever-wider powers wielded by the political leaderships of republic on both federal and local levels. These were reflected in the constitutional amendments of 1968 and the proposed constitutional amendments of 1971.

This state of affairs also contained the seeds of a move toward reassertion of centralistic control. The more permissive atmosphere of the late 1960s also brought many of the dormant ethnic conflicts to overt expression. This is the natural result of any liberalization movement in Yugoslavia. Particularistic nationalism is an ever present force, a constant, in Yugoslav politics. There are merely those circumstances in the general political climate which support it, and others which keep it below the level of overt expression. With the dismissal of Ranković in July 1966, and with the downgrading of the organs of coercion, the secret police, it did not take long for the results to be felt in the political arena. In March 1967, a number of leading Croat intellectuals published a petition demanding that Serbo-Croatian be abolished as an official language, and Serbian and Croatian be constituted into separate official languages. This formed the backdrop of the linguistic dispute which in effect commenced with an equally vocal Serb response.[2] A foreigner might be perplexed about the passion generated between the two lingusitic groups which are so close, but the underlying passions deal with the preservation of the parameters of profound cultural chasms which separate the two leading nationalities. Moreover, when these enter into the paroxysm of overtly expressed nationalism they cannot expect to remain the sole parties to the dispute for long. Any breach is quickly utilized by other groups, the Albanians, the Macedonians, or the Moslems, to present demands which would grant their respective groupings greater security in the maintenance of their separate identity as expressed through the republican leaderships.

All multinational states are balancing acts. Only the fiercest form of repression can obliterate the demands for inter-ethnic arbitration. Even Stalin, at the height of his most ruthless repressions, had to recognize that he was dealing with a special political constituency in the Ukraine in the 1930s. He alternated between murder and bribery to maintain control. In the Second World War he fell back on appeals to traditional patriotism, and particularly great Russian patriotism, to bolster the morale of the Soviet forces. The German racist policies in the occupied territories merely tended to underscore the cogency of the appeal. The Yugoslav leaders refused to depend on oppression for the attainment of national goals in the 1960s. In the immediate aftermath of the Second World War particularistic nationalism in Yugoslavia was not a permissible topic, not only because it was not tolerated by the government, but because the memory of internecine massacres inspired by the Axis occupation was still fresh. Yet, with the maturing of a new generation, and with the restrictions placed on the organs of coercion, particularistic nationalism could make its appearance on the Yugoslav political scene overtly. The Yugoslav League of Communists tried to create through the constitutional amendments of 1968 and the proposed amendments of 1971, a political framework which could cope with such disputes on an institutionalized basis, without overt and direct intervention by the administrative organs of the federal government.

The assumption on which the League leadership operated demanded a great deal of self-restraint from the republic political leaderships. The Ninth Party Congress of the League of Communists in 1969 decreed in accord with the constitutional amendments, which made the republics the principle loci of power in the system, that the federal organs of the League be entirely delegated from the republics including its highest organ, the Executive Bureau. If the newly reorganized institutions were to perform as expected the republican leaderships could not place them under conditions of institutional overload. Yet, this is precisely what happened during the Croat crisis from October to December of 1971.

This was the logical result of the system which the Yugoslavs had created during the previous twenty years. It was based on the unprecedented freedom of movement into and out of the country. It was further based on "contested" elections. The republics had an ever-expanding freedom to dispose of investment funds generated within their respective areas. Under these rules of the game, local politicians were no longer dependent on the League for their position, but rather on their republican electoral constituencies. They acted like any power brokers within the political and economic market place, namely, they tried to mobilize the constituencies, representing themselves as the champions of their aspirations. This meant that they tried to enlarge their political constituency across narrow League lines and to appeal to the entire population of the republic on a nationalistic basis. This united many normally mutually hostile elements under the banner of the League leadership. The Matica Hrvatska and the Catholic Church became partners with the League leadership in demanding ever greater economic concessions from the federal government.[3] This occurred first in the realm of economics, which quickly spilled over into the political arena.

The authors are not prepared to explore the relative justice of the perceived rights and wrongs of all the contending nationalities, but as outside academic observers it is plain that cogent arguments can be entered on many sides. The issue which the Croat political leaders targeted was the right to the retention of the foreign exchange earned within Croatia for investment purposes. The previous practice was to convert the "valuta" in the National Bank in Belgrade at rates deemed unfavorable by the Croats.[4] There were many other voices which articulated demands ranging from the abolition of a Federal tax structure, to separate Croatian representation in the United Nations.

The federal government and Tito responded predictably by an administrative crackdown. The federal leadership demanded and obtained the resignation of the Croat leaders and punished those who were in the second line of nationalist agitation with questionable legality. The object was to put nationalism and its most vocal expressions beyond the political pale and to return Yugoslav politics to the limits acceptable to the League. In this, the federal leaders were aided by the firm hold they retained on the armed forces and the police network. The balance had shifted once more. The federal leadership had decided that in Yugoslavia there was no alternative to the League of Communists, since it has been and remains the only supranational organization within the State. The institutions had to be recast in such a way as to permit greater control of the candidate selection process by the League and to return Yugoslav politics to a more direct party control.

The League had to be revitalized because it had lost most of its cogency in the previous era. In communist states the Communist Party is generally the policymaking body, while the executive organs of government are organs of execution. In Yugoslavia, in the latter 1960s, the League of Communists had largely lost this role because, in a state in which the selection of politicians takes place outside of direct League channels and where most of the decisionmaking functions have been de-politicized (because they were placed under the jurisdiction of the organs of regional and workers' self-management), the League had lost its sense of identity and mission.[5] Even influential League members chose to exercise their authority through non-League organs and channels. The result was non-

attendance at League meetings and a general sense of lethargy. The phenomenon, called "embourgeoisement," was observed at all levels of the
League, with declining working class participation (working class members of the League were the least frequently admitted and the most
frequently expelled).[6] The result was that Tito resolved through the
Tenth Party Congress to revitalize the role of the League. Older politicians were called out of obscurity or retirement to head up the plethora
of republican offices as the more autonomous and liberal leaderships
were purged. The logical Yugoslav response to all such changes was to re-
write the Constitution once more, the fourth constitution in a thirty year
period. The new constitution gave rise to the system of delegation which
abolished the system of direct elections. While the Constitution of 1963
provided for direct elections to the National Assembly, at present the only
direct elections held in Yugoslavia are those electing representatives to the
Communal Assemblies. All higher bodies above that level ranging from the
Republican Assemblies to the Federal Assembly, consist of delegated candidates. This restricts the political process to a much narrower circle of
participants and facilitates League control over the political process.

It would be incorrect to state that this restriction represents a repudiation of the evolution which occurred during the previous era. On the
contrary, the leaders constantly reaffirm their commitment to workers'
self-management and the rights of the various nationalities. The Constitution merely tried to confine the political process within those parameters considered legitimate by the top leadership.

The balance of power between communal republican and federal
institutions has never been satisfactorily or definitively resolved in the
post-World War II Yugoslavia. All the constitutional changes were designed
to institutionalize new channels for conflict resolution, and thereby
channel nationality conflicts along acceptable paths. The difficulty is
that each constitutional reform upset the institutions set up under the
authority of the previous document. The best example of this is the role
of the Council of Nationalities which was established by the Constitution
of 1946 as the upper chamber of the Federal Assembly. Under the Fundamental Law of 1953 it was merged with the membership of the lower
chamber, the Federal Council. Under the Constitution of 1963 it was an
upper chamber, only to reemerge in the amendments of 1968 as the lower
chamber. In the Constitution of 1974 it again emerged as the upper

chamber of the Federal Assembly, the status it held in the Constitution of 1946. These precipitous changes in the status of institutions never gave their membership a chance to regularize their work; such institutional processes, judged by the standards of established democracies, take decades. These institutional changes in the role of the Council of Nationalities reflect the ambiguities and uncertainties in the minds of those who have shaped Yugoslav institutions for the last decades. The alternating role of the Council of Nationalities merely illustrates that the perceptions about a proper institutional balance between the federal state has fluctuated and that in each political era leaders have yielded to the political pressures of the day.

Flux in institutions in Yugoslavia has become an institution in itself. There is little to support the belief that the present constitutional framework would survive radical changes in the composition of the present leadership. Yet, with it all, it is important to remember there have also been major continuities.

While there have been repeated reorganizations of the policymaking structures within both the League and the government, the bureaucracy, as expressed in the Federal Executive Council, has manifested a remarkable stability, both in design and personnel. Despite mandated rotation, the changes have been limited within fairly predictable parameters. In the constitutional amendments of 1968, great emphasis was placed on equal proportional representation for all nationalities, both in the policymaking bodies of the League and the Federal Executive Council of which all republican chair persons of Councils of Ministers and the Autonomous Provinces are ex officio members. While institutional names change with every reorganization, the faces and institutional context remain the same. In a country with a limited pool of organizational and political skills with the requisite proper background and experience, the same faces continue to staff the same desks with almost every twist of reorganization. The principle of rotation has been more symbolic than practical.

The principal change from the 1960s is that all Federal institutions have to be staffed along the lines of one Serb, one Croat, one Slovene, and if any positions remain, one Macedonian, one Montenegrin, and one representative from Kosovo and Vojvodina. This solution, if it is one, finds sanction both within law and practice. If there are five bank directorships in Belgrade, this formula will be usually applied; should a new organization and directorship be created, it is usually assumed that it will go to the nationality which had been left out previously. With the system of delegation, all legislators are supposed to be the directly instructed delegates of their constituencies, which may lead to administrative deadlock since the representatives of each nationality wants to claim a slice whether or not there are personnel or physical resources to carry out the objectives of the fund allocation. The leadership's pursuit of ethnic balance minimized the sense of relative deprivation amongst all nationalities but it also lessened efficiency. Personnel has had to be drawn into many managerial positions in the name of equal treatment for all nationalities.

Communism and Nationalism as Competing Ideologies

The interrelationship between communism and nationalism is usually viewed as inherently conflictual. The communists have viewed nationalism as inextricably tied to the bourgeois class as it sought to overturn aristocratic rule during the eighteenth and nineteenth centuries. Nationalism was viewed as an ideological device to establish a triumphant bourgeoisie in separate national states, which then were subjected to the sham of formal parliamentarianism to legitimize the *de facto* rule by bourgeois interests. Communism had the self-image of proletarian internationalism appealing for the liberation of all working individuals from class oppression. The proletariat was viewed as an international class whose sense of allegiance was maintained by common economic and political interests which were stronger than those imposed by the bonds of religion, culture or even language. The nationalists, in turn, viewed communist ideology as the worst form of dehumanization which would have divorced individuals and entire nationalities from the bond of a common culture or family. In actuality, the historical record establishes that neither creed acted in line with its maxims.

The communists all too frequently used nationalistic symbols to render their cause more appealing while nationalists sought to impose the dominance of their own particular nationality over others. National Socialist Germany, during the Second World War, sought to establish a dominance over a plethora of *Untermenschen* and tended to accept the collectivist argument for all non-Germans.[7] Both Marx and Lenin argued that nationalism was an inherently destructive force since the excessive competition for markets between competing national bourgeoisies could lead to nothing but war and their mutual destruction.

The reality was far more complex than that. During the Second World War, the Yugoslav Communists used both class concepts and the promise of national equality to mobilize their constituency to resistance against the occupying Fascists. Their task was made relatively easy because the German and Italian invaders showed little regard even for their nationalistic allies, the Ustaši of Croatia.

The Partisan movement was left in the field as the only representative of a specifically Yugoslav solution for the South Slavs. The other resistance movement was the Četnik Movement of General Draža Mihailović, which appealed to a strictly Serb constituency. The Yugoslav Communist Party was the only supranational party in Yugoslavia before World War II which promised relief from Serb super-ordination in the then prevailing social order. Its appeals were a mixture of revolutionary rhetoric and Yugoslav nationalism with the aim of creating a revolutionary new state. Its organization was to test out the equality of all nationalities. The documents of AVNOJ (*Antifašističko veče narodnog oslobodjenje Jugoslavije*) embodied the rhetoric of both nationalism and revolution. AVNOJ itself tried to create a common platform for all elements which wanted to resist Axis occupation and effectively obscure the communist leadership of the Partisan Movement.

The question arises whether the Yugoslav communists used nationalism for purely opportunistic reasons to mask and conceal the core of communist ideology which animated the movement. If this was only a strategy, then it remains as the most constant element of Yugoslav foreign and domestic policy since the inception of the Partisan movement. The only period which might cast a shadow of doubt on the Partisans' decision on nationalism is the period between 1945-48, during which Yugoslavia nominally submitted to the leadership of Stalin. It is now established by historical record that these years were dedicated to a subterranean struggle in which the Yugoslavs bid for autonomy in conducting their own affairs.[8] This conflict spanned many issues from ideology to politics. These ranged between the establishment of a Balkan federation, the settlement of the Trieste issue on the international scene and the establishment of joint stock companies to the Yugoslav Five Year Plan and its agricultural policies. Since both states were interested in obscuring their vital interests, the correspondence between the Central Committees was confined to ideological exchanges which concealed the *real politik* issues which separated the parties and states.[9] At the bottom of it was the Yugoslav refusal to subordinate their national policy to Soviet interests, as practiced in other East European states. The Soviets, in turn, would not tolerate an exception which might become a model for separate roads to socialism for the entire bloc. After the Cominform resolution in June of 1948, the conflict broke into the open. The Yugoslavs, until 1950, hoped to find some *modus vivendi* with Stalin and the Soviet Union. When this proved futile, the Yugoslav leaders had no choice but to put their independent stance on their own ideological basis because it is ultimately ideology which justifies the "dictatorship of the proletariat" to its own constituency, the Yugoslav Communist Party. The Yugoslav leaders had to find justification for both their choosing a separate road to communism and their claim to continued power.

Unlike the Soviet ideologues, the Yugoslavs had never claimed in their official writings that they had found the ultimate and universal solution to the nationality problem. They accepted the possibility that a multinational socialist state would have to live with the tensions generated by its inherent situation.[10]

Workers' Self-Management and the Problem of Nationalism

In the *dirigiste* states of Eastern Europe the issue of nationalism was kept under control by a surfeit of central institutions ranging from state planning to the police. Such institutions had their branch offices in the territorial subdivisions of the country and were truly national in scope. Yugoslavia possessed such a regime until 1950, and elements of it survive to the present. The introduction of workers' self-management created a Yugoslav ideology which in time led to the downgrading of most of the agencies of the central government, and substituted pluralized patterns of decisionmaking.

The authors of the new Yugoslav ideology considered the object of building socialism to be the direct participation by workers in the management of their enterprises. Yugoslav citizens would also be encouraged to participate in the politics of the commune in which they resided (a commune is a territorial unit akin to a county). Thus, Yugoslav citizens would vote and participate politically in many communities defined by work or place of residence. This was seen at the time of proclamation as a pathway to the withering away of the state, which would leapfrog socialist developments in the Soviet bloc. Yugoslav theory led to a depoliticized economy by making each enterprise self-managing through elected representatives. Such productive units would then participate in a socialist market on a competitive basis. The Yugoslav economist, Branko Horvat, labeled this system "market socialism" in the late 1960s.[11] Over the years the state planning machinery eroded away to a level which is lower than some Western states possess. The ideology also led to the acceptance of differential stages of development among the various republics. Since these disparities were ethnically bounded, it in effect represented the acceptance of the burdens of past history with no clear relief in sight.

In 1945 the Yugoslavs announced the Kidrič plan, which was based on the theory that the most developed areas of Yugoslavia should be reconstructed first. After the reconstruction of these areas they were slated to return development capital to the underdeveloped areas. In the heady years of revolutionary fervor, it was felt that living standards throughout the country would be quickly equalized and that national differences would wither away like the state.[12] In hindsight, these expectations were rather naive because even in states which were far more successful in leveling down differentials between nationalities, this did not lead to a noticeable decline of particularistic nationalism. A case in point is Czechoslovakia, where Slovak nationalism asserted itself despite a substantial narrowing of the gap between the two parts of the country.

The workers' self-management movement contradicted the notion that there will be a quick leveling out of economic differentials between the nationalities, and it was transformed into the belief that a socialist market in which all sections of the country will be able to participate with a free flow of men and resources will accomplish this task at lesser cost. The hope was that all parts of Yugoslavia would compete freely in a Yugoslav market and that enterprises in the more developed republics would branch out into the underdeveloped areas to capitalize on their natural resources and cheaper labor force. The federal government also promoted projects in the less developed areas, by traditional strategies utilized in market economies; e.g., the government provided infra-structures for development ranging from communications to viable educational systems. The government also funneled subsidies to industries in underdeveloped areas through re-distributive strategies. All of these policies have been followed to a greater or lesser extent.

The Yugoslav Ideology and Foreign Policy

The period of administrative socialism in Yugoslavia in the years 1945-1950 took place within an international context, which enabled the leadership to follow unpopular domestic policies and agressive foreign policies. Yugoslavia, as a member of the Soviet bloc, assured of Soviet military and economic assistance, collectivized agriculture domestically, subjected the economy to a vast bureaucracy, and placed demands on Italy and Austria under the mantle of Soviet protection. When these circumstances changed between 1948 and 1950, Yugoslavia became a state in search of a viable foreign policy. It broke out of virtual isolation with the policies of nonalignment between the years 1953-1955; President Tito became one of the principal advocates for the group of non-aligned states. This policy remaind a constant for the twenty-six years from 1955 to 1981 and is ideally suited to Yugoslavia's ethnic diversity.

The foreign policy sympathies and preferences amongst the Yugoslav nationalities are far from homogeneous. Almost any foreign policy has its larger constituency within the Yugoslav community. While there is a sprinkling of pro-Soviet sympathizers in all parts of the country, the base of such tendencies lies amongst the republics of the underdeveloped South, i.e., Southern Serbia, Montenegro, and Socialist Austonomous Province of Kosovo. Such sympathies have historical roots in the South and antedate the present regime. At the other end of the spectrum the population of Slovenia and Croatia and particularly the people inhabiting the Dalmatian coast share ties to the West through tradition, the Catholic Church, and the common past of the Habsburg Monarchy. These populations have sent generations of immigrants to both North and South America, and more recently to Western Europe.

There are also more than 2,000,000 Moslems with an affinity for their co-religionists in the Middle East. Given these competing cross-currents, the policy of nonalignment constituted a viable compromise giving partial satisfaction to all. Any departure from nonalignment in favor of the USSR would have had major repercussions in Slovenia and Croatia; any overly close affiliation with the West would have alienated significant party elites with southern constituences. Nonalignment enabled the Yugoslav government to keep a balanced approach toward all states externally and all nationalities domestically. Nonalignment enabled the leadership to maintain open lines to the Soviet bloc while concluding major economic agreements with the West. While this policy was functional in maintaining a national consensus, it also created serious strains, insofar as all the factions and the regime itself could never be sure that its conflicting commitments were not leading it to renewed isolation.

Yugoslavia's foreign policy of nonalignment is closely related to the entire issue of regional autonomy in the diverse ethnically conditioned preferences of its population. Any close affiliation with the Soviet bloc would demand the abandonment of workers' self-management as the leading state ideology. It is doubtful that the Soviet Union could tolerate in Yugoslavia that which they suppressed in Czechoslovakia. Since the abandonment of socialism by the League of Communists is unlikely, workers' self-management and nonalignment formed the core of Yugoslavia's nationality policy. The government, in theory, tends to intervene only in those republican areas which are of prime concern to the federation; it defends the powers which are traditionally reserved to the federal government in most contemporary constitutions, e.g., defense, central banking, and those issues which might threaten the stability of the state in the view of the federal leadership. It is not claimed here that this idea is fully realized in Yugoslavia, but merely that it constitutes the self-image which guides the federal leadership.

Particularistic Nationalism and the Yugoslav Model

Workers' self-management and the decentralization of power has changed the entire political framework in which the Yugolsav political game is played. Since the allocation of scarce resources is decided on the local levels, and economic decisions fall almost entirely within the scope of the republics, these became the central focus in the Yugoslav system. The Constitutions of 1963 and 1974 both were built on the principle of regional representation. In the period between 1963 and 1971 republican elections were almost always contested and the office holders represented a consensus of at least elite opinion within the republics. In the late 1960s, the League could not always insure the election of the candidate they favored for national and republican offices. Moreover, each republic and commune decided major investment issues without reference to federal or even republican authorities insofar as its disposition over independent investmest resources. Under those circumstances the monies which were taxed away by the federal enterprises became prominent and noticeable. This was particularly true of scarce foreign exchange, for which the republics compete fiercely. No major project of industrialization in Yugoslavia could be carried out without reliance on foreign imports which had to be paid for with foreign exchange. The losing republics, Slovenia and Croatia, particularly resented the sharing of what they felt were their hard-won resources with the less developed areas of the South. This partially stemmed from the accepted proposition in the North that these funds were wasted in the South and accentuated a general lack of identification between Yugoslavs of divergent national origins. These issues became bitterly contested and republican politicians tried quite logically to enlarge the base of their support by appealing to their ethnic constituency on the basis of economic and national interest on principles. Such appeals were far removed from the line of the League of Communists. In Croatia the economic issues then became organically linked with Croat nationalism. The system demanded that ever-widening publics be included in the political process, even those which stood outside the League of Communists. Both the Catholic Church and Matica Hrvatska wielded political power which had to be taken into account by all levels of government. The membership of the League and Matica Hrvatska overlapped and ethnic nationalism formed the common bond between the Croatian League political leadership and the non-League publics which supported them.

In Communist states, the Communist Party is charged with delineating policy for all executive bodies. By the mid-1960s, the League constituted somewhat of an anachronism because most of the power had migrated from the League to the organs of self-management and government. The meeting of League primary organizations became sporadic and, at times, resembled social clubs rather than a serious political organization. In a system in which most of the candidates on the commune level are non-League members, and in which the League did not have even the powers to exercise control over candidates for office in a relatively open system of nominations, the League became moribund. Its most energetic members exercised their influence through non-League bodies ranging from the Socialist Alliance to communal councils and executive committees of workers' councils. Until 1971, Yugoslavia was on a path toward a pluralistic system in which the single party system and not the government showed all signs of withering. The vacuum of enthusiasm for a national cause was filled by a revitalized ethnic nationalism which manifested itself openly in all parts of the country. The state itself denied there was such a thing as "a Yugoslav nationality" and the citizenry, particularly those who did not have a previous commitment to the Party, defined their participatory roles as members of their national community rather than the vague ideal of Yugoslav nationalism.[13]

Civil Rights and Nationalism in Yugoslavia

In Yugoslavia all political problems are intimately linked with the issue of nationalism. The less developed southern reaches of the state usually demand a more redistributive role from their government because they view it as the only method for the equalization of the vast economic discrepancies between the northern and southern republics. This redistributive role can be achieved only at the expense of curtailing civil rights on the northern republic where there is always active opposition against the siphoning of investment funds from the rich to the poor. The people who favor a centralistic or authoritarian approach to the state's political and economic role can easily find inspiration in Soviet practice. Most of the centralists, also called Cominformists or Stalinists if perjorative epithets are needed, have their main strength in the orthodox, undeveloped South, i.e. Bosnia-Hercegovina, Kosovo, Macedonia, Montenegro, and Southern Serbia; there centralism can be linked with traditional nationalist pro-Russian feelings which have their roots in the pre-revolutionary period. Russia was viewed as the main protector of Montenegrin nationalistic aspirations before World War I; via pan-Slavism and ties of sentiment, these feelings were translated into admiration for the Soviet model in modern times. The existence of such sentiment has been used by the centralists for a measure of agitation against the self-management policies of the federal government, and the federal security organs tended to use the same activities as evidence for Soviet subverison.

It is not surprising that Montenegro was the scene of arrests in 1974 when a group of neo-Cominformists were accused of holding an illegal Congress of the Communist Party of Yugoslavia in Bar. While the personalities involved were obscure, after the listing of the thirty-two names of the pariticipants, the locus of the meeting added special significance to the seriousness with which the Yugoslav authorities viewed this event. The confiscated documents were taken at their face value and the participants received long sentences for this effort to "overthrow Tito's personal dictatorship."[14] The centralist Communists probably constitute the largest component of political prisoners held under arrest within Yugoslavia. Vladimir Bakarič, long-time secretary of the Croatian League of Communists placed the total number at 502 during a press conference in Zagreb on April 16, 1977.[15] Marshal Tito blamed the high number of political prisoners on Stalinist agitation with a thinly veiled reference to their possible foreign sponsorship at a press conference in Novi Sad on April 17, 1977, when he stated that Yugoslavia would not "bow to foreign pressure on behalf of political dissidents."[16]

Until the mid-1960s, there was a standing joke in Yugoslavia to the effect that the country had only two political prisoners, Milovan Djilas and Mihailo Mihailov, and that neither was in jail. In the wake of the Croatian crisis in 1971 this situation changed quite drastically due to the arrest of hundreds of "activists" from the Matica Hravska and the ranks of the Croatian League of Communists. The increased activity of the centralist elements can be viewed as a Soviet reaction to an effort to test the waters in a situation which had become somewhat destabilized. While the populations of the much poorer South depended on the federal government playing a more centralist role, the political sentiments in Slovenia, Croatia, and the northern portions of Serbia tended to accentuate maximum local and republican autonomy. These are the areas whose surpluses would be "redistributed" away toward republics with whom they do not find easy common points of identification, and whose needs and efficiency they rate below their own. To these republics the continued practice of worker's self-management and economic partnership with the West appear as the best guarantee for their continued prosperity and superior affluence. The two world views are symbiotic and the government has attempted to apply prophylactic pressure on both groupings to keep them within the bounds of that which is considered politically permissible. Therefore, the patterns of arrests frequently seem a strange balancing act to an outside observer in a state where most major clusters of institutions are staffed on the basis of one Serb, one Croat, one Slovene, and so forth. Similar practices seem to have carried over into the field of political repression, since news of arrests of Cominformists are accompanied by stories of similar reprisals against nationalists so that no deviant view or nationality can claim neglect by the state organs. For example, in January 1975, four Yugoslavs of Albanian origin were sentenced to terms of from three to nine years for plotting against the state, while during the same time-frame fifteen Croats were accused of plotting to bring about the secession of the Republic of Croatia and they received terms of up to fifteen years in February 1975.[17] Moslems in Bosnia and Hercegovina were accused of "selfish nationalism" after an exchange of hostile words with Serbs followed the violent treatment of a Moslem allegedly at the hands of a Serb.[18] The Belgrade newspaper, *Politika,* reported the arrest of nine more persons in the Vojvodina accused of being pro-Soviet Communists "inspired and encouraged from abroad."[19] The Soviet union is not in a position to help its followers exercise any influence and they have few sympathetic champions in the West. As a result, the Yugoslav government can move against them with relative impunity causing only a minimal international reaction.

The state of civil rights in Yugoslavia is marked by a number of factors absent in the other states of the communist bloc. The seemingly quota-like offsetting arrests of various nationalities is not entirely the result of a predetermined policy. It results obviously from increased federal exhortation to the republic organs to maintain a state of vigilance and this is reflected in a number of arrests and increased police activity in all parts of the country, since all the security organs have to manifest the results of increased vigilance. In every republic there are tendencies both to the left and right of the official line and the security organs tend to hammer at what they consider the most extreme manifestations of these. In other words, in other communist states the tone is set by the central party organs which work through a national ministry of the interior. In Yugoslavia, the *Sekretarijat unutrasnjih poslova* (SUP) does a great deal of investigation, but the law is implemented through republican judicial organs, and therefore, the political atmosphere between republics varies widely; in the year 1972, when Croatia and Serbia were both in the midst of purging nationalists, Bosnia-Hercegovina hardly experienced a ripple. Nevertheless, the national government increased pressure against all forms of dissidence and sometimes utilized the technique of striking at their lawyers or at their relatives. Thus, Mr. Srdja M. Popović, a defense attorney for a number of people charged with political offenses, was accused of agreeing with the views of a client, Dragoljub S. Innjatović. Mr. Popović received a one-year sentence on March 10, 1974, but his sentence was suspended and he was barred from practice for one year.[20] The sentence and the charge caused a shock-wave of outrage in the legal community around the world since it was reminescent of similar occurences during the Soviet purges. Serbia, in 1976, proclaimed political tests as a factor of relevance for attorneys given the rights to practice.[21] The 1976 arrest of Judge Franc Miklavčić, while sitting in court, and his subsequent conviction for treason and other crimes on October 15, 1976 for advocating civil rights in an article published in a Trieste Slovene newspaper, *Primorski Dnevnik*, was merely illustrative of the decline of judicial independence.[22] Before 1971, such flagrant offenses against the decor of courtroom procedure would have been unthinkable and it demonstrates the broad grant of power which the secret police again possessed. In 1977, a cousin of Milovan Djilas, Vitomir Djilas, was convicted to two and a half years for "hostile propaganda" against the state.[25] The sentence was widely interpreted in the West as a response to Milovan Djilas' public accusation of the large number of political prisoners held in Yugoslavia, which coincided with the opeining of the session in Geneva of the UN Commission on Human Rights. The fact that Milovan Djilas was not imprisoned for an offense judged "hostile to the state" perhaps proved the sensitivity of authority to the pressures of international public opinion. Apparently the object is to utilize that degree of pressure necessary to dampen overt expressions of dissent and hostility. As in all other matters, the approach of the government seems to be governed by pragmatism rather than by an effort to maintain conformity with a rigidly interpreted ideology. The goal of the effort is to prevent dissenters from congealing into comprehensive oppositional groupings which carry out their work in semi-legality, as did the Matica Hrvatska between 1968 and 1971, and to prevent local alternatives to the political monopoly of the League of Communists. Apart from the Stalinists there is no national integrative opposition on the horizon. This cross-cultural potential of the centralists may be a reason why they are singled out for the most attention, totally apart from the larger issue of aid and comfort from the Soviet Union.

The present system is committed to maintain the leading role of the party, the League of Communists, and to fight down all deviations. The state of civil rights in Yugoslavia is a reflection of this concern and it is the product of a number of major factors:

1) The current situation is conditioned by events in the most liberal era of Yugoslav development between 1966 and 1971.

2) The liberal era, due to a substantive change in the rule of the political game, brought about major manifestations of particularistic nationalism, especially in Croatia and Kosovo.

3) The federal government administratively removed leaderships which the bulk of the Croats and Slovenes and Serbs considered legitimate. The individuals who did the purging derived their positions from Tito's authority rather than popular support.

4) The nationalist wave in Yugoslavia evoked a strong reaction in more orthodox party circles which demanded that the government crack down.

5) The crack-down and the installation of more orthodox leaders stimulated the hope among pro-Soviet elements that Yugoslavia might return to the Soviet bloc.

6) With domestic turmoil there was fear that outside influences may take advantage of the factionalization of Yugoslav politics. This suspicion was largely directed at the Soviet Union, whose agents had been active among the centralist faction. The concern intensified after the entry of Soviet troops in Afghanistan in 1979.

Given these circumstances the Yugoslav leadership felt itself obliged to intervene and dampen down nationalist agitation and pro-Soviet influences, in 1972, to ward off a perceived threat to the stability of the internal order, as it had been chartered in the preceding era. The proceedings of the Tenth Party Congress and the 1974 Constitution did not eliminate either workers' self-management or nonalignment, nor did it impose Soviet style censorship. It merely sought to control those expressions of nationalism which went beyond the politically permissible parameters of the Yugoslav system, i.e., a quest for republic autonomy or independence on one hand, and demands that Yugoslavia resume its association with other socialist states within some Soviet-approved framework on the other hand.

To achieve these ends the Yugoslav state had to be changed structurally to permit some arbitrary exercises of power. It meant the upgrading of the police powers of the Ministry of Interior, which had been severely curtailed after 1966. It does not take greater activity on the part of the secret policy to signal a new era. In the aftermath of the Croat crisis in 1972, many Croat intellectuals who had exposed themselves on behalf of the nationalist cause were interrogated and detained by the secret police for substantial periods. Hundreds were charged with various forms of anti-state activity and received multi-year sentences. This created an atmosphere which had been unknown in Yugoslavia since the early 1950s. These sentences compromised the integrity of the judicial process itself, insofar as judges were retired and shifted to obtain the desired judgments. There were frequent and loud complaints in 1972 when the prosecuting agencies could not obtain the indictments and sentences the federal government deemed desirable. There was talk in 1972 and 1973 of creating a federal police force not subject to republican authority, and a federal judiciary which would be subject to federal rather than republican authority to obtain the proper level of control. In Yugoslavia the authorities always strove to preserve balance in all matters and the nationalists were singled out for special attention, as were the centralists. The pro-Soviet plot, which was at best obscure, was a signal that the League intended to strike at both ends in the Yugoslav political spectrum.

Before 1971, private Yugoslav citizens could carry out individual and official contacts with foreigners on a person-to-person and institution-to-institution basis without seeking prior authorization. This is no longer possible; there have been internal directives which spell out the proceedings for any contacts. This has had the effect of tightening the supervision of all facets of contact with the outside world and rendered the Yugoslav press and universities far more cautious.[24] It was the intellectuals, the universities and Marxist dissidents who, in a period of great freedom of expression, opened the Pandora's box of nationalism, although this was far from their intentions, since most were not nationalists themselves.

From the point of view of civil rights the Tenth Party Congress and the Constitution of 1974 represent a serious regression. This can be summarized under a number of subheadings:

1) The Constitution of 1963 provided for direct contested elections for the National Assembly. The Constitution of 1974 abolished this concept and provided for a system of delegation from communal bodies to the whole hierarchy of assemblies, including republic and federal. Some commentators stated frankly that this system gave the League of Communists increased control over the political process. It was a curtailment of the process of democratization and a return to institutions which lent themselves more to manipulation by the League apparat. The principle of delegation can easily deteriorate into cooptation.

2) The Tenth Congress of the League of Communists of Yugoslavia called for a new confidence in the older and more experienced comrades who also, coincidently, favored a more authoritarian approach. Most of them had been in eclipse after the Ninth Party Congress, but the Tenth restored them to their positions.[25] This became necessary when the popular and elected leadership were administratively removed in the course of 1972.

3) The increased activity of the security organs and convictions in political cases led to a change in the political atmosphere. Individuals manifested caution in expressing themselves. At the Sixth Congress of the Yugoslav Sociological Association, held in Portoroz in February 1972, despite great openness of discussion, not one paper dealt with national conflicts directly.[26] These conflicts, while openly acknowledged, have been relegated to the darker recesses of the institutes which carry out important scholarly activity in Yugoslavia.

4) A shift in civil rights protection in the Constitution of 1974, is apparent in the revision from the earlier provision for detention by statute to the change that detention "shall be ordered by a court of law."[27] It also limited the earlier right of appeal by an individual and provided that no person could use the freedom and rights established

by the Constitution in order to disrupt the foundations of the socialist self-management democratic order.

With this level of tension, it cannot be said that national problems have been ignored completely. The Slovenes and the federal government chose to draw attention to the treatment of the Slovene minority in the neighboring province of Carinthia which had a tendency to disappear as an ethnically distinguishable entity in the post-World War II period. Officials of the Yugoslav government charged that this was due to the essentially Germanizing policies of the Austrian government. The Austrians replied vigorously that it was largely due to the voluntary choice of the resident Slovenes to send their children to German schools and their desire to amalgamate into Austrian life as many non-Germanic minorities had done since the days of the Habsburg Monarchy. In any instance, the Yugoslav government drew attention dramatically to the situation in Austria at least in part to point up the fate of minor nationalities, such as the Slovenes, outside of the framework of the Yugoslav state. It was to serve as a graphic warning as to what might happen to Slovenes in case Yugoslavia faltered. The government, sensing its vulnerability, made aggressive noises directed at the address of many neighbors and foreign powers. The United States and the USSR did not escape some hostile pronouncements. The object of the Yugoslav authorities was to achieve, perhaps, the irreconcilable, to continue the system of workers' self-management and affirm Yugoslavia as a federal, multinational state.

Yugoslavia cannot be divorced from ethnic representation as long as it insists on workers' self-management and delegation from communal assemblies. Such bodies will always form compact ethnic blocs and organize their activity along "tribal" lines regardless of the form of formal organization chosen. The government and the League are trying to find a formula whereby expression of nationalism would be kept within the bounds considered "decent." As a means of achieving a center of gravity for the system the League has chosen to punish those who would stray from the League-imposed permissible outer limits.

The Commune is now the focus of local politics and the republic is no longer as important as it had been in the Constitution of 1963. Many of the conflicts which formerly took place on the inter-republic level have become intra-republican.

The League of Communists has launched a legalistic attack on the practices of the liberal era. It took the form of constitutional changes which contravened the spirit of the document of 1963.[28] Yugoslav citizens participate directly only in the election to the Communal Assembly and to the basic organizations of "associated labour." Since League members manifest greater political efficacy and are again subject to Party discipline, the resolutions of the Ninth Party Congress of the League of Communists held in Belgrade from March 11-15, 1969, granted the League members the freedom of conscience in the event they dissented from League policy. The Tenth Congress of the League of Communists, which met in Belgrade, May 27-30, 1974, brought back Party discipline to its full bloom. "Liberalism," "spontaneity," "pluralism" and the "federalization of the Party" are categorically condemned.[29] The traditional Party discipline in which higher bodies direct lower Party bodies has been reestablished with "passivity as punishable as opposition."[30]

The Party is viewed again as the "state building" force despite constant commitment to the principles of workers' self-management and the equality of nationalities. It is evident that the League is again to act as the central political force in the formulation of policy, and that the orderly processes which evolved over a decade in various self-managerial bodies can be subordinated to League policies. In the overall distribution of power, despite the drum-fire verbiage about workers' self-management, the balance of power has shifted in the direction of the League. The League in its massive efforts to revitalize its ranks and goals significantly curtailed the scope of decisionmaking on the local level by both communes, republican chambers, and organs of self-management. It also rededicated itself to the achievement of equality among the nations and nationalities.[31]

The League continues to invoke its determination to safeguard the cultural autonomy of all "nations and nationalities" which make up Yugoslavia. The safeguarding of these rights is no longer entrusted to a plethora of republican and self-managerial organs but is to be placed under the overall orchestration of a recentralized Party. In June 1978, the Eleventh Congress of the League recommitted the system to maintain it in the leadership role and to fight against deviations.[32]

The 1974 Constitution of the Socialist Federal Republic of Yugoslavia curtails *de facto* political participation. The Constitution specifies that self-employed individuals may not be elected to delegations, this excludes substantial categories of the Yugoslav citizenry from independent agriculturists to housewives.[33] The rights to referendum are deleted from the 1974 Constitution.[34] Article 171 maintains the right of "nations and nationalities" to use their language and alphabets but departs from the concept of equality of the languages of the peoples of Yugoslavia expressed in the earlier constitution.[35] The present constitution strengthens the hand of the federal organs by declaring a wide variety of behavior patterns unconstitutional.[36] These can be used to punish many forms of conduct considered undesirable, ranging from the incitement of hatred among nationalities to immoral conduct. Such provisions are further fleshed out in the criminal codes under which many individuals have suffered prosecution at the present time. The most direct result of the restoration of party *dirigisme* is apparent in the field of human rights. Since 1974, no nationality has been spared the attention of the secret police.

In Serbia, the struggle has revolved principally about the heads of eight university professors of the philosophy faculty at Belgrade University who maintained their position in the face of strong League pressure to abandon it. They were branded "anarcho liberals" for their positions on Marxism which were at variance with official League doctrine. The autonomy of the University protected them from arbitrary dismissal until the Serbian Parliament, in December 1974, amended the self-management law of the University of Belgrade to enable fifty percent of the Faculty Council to be composed of outsiders; this was the first time that the self-management principle was changed to effect the dismissal of professors.[37] Earlier, the law faculty of Belgrade University moved against seven of its faculty members for having signed a petition requesting amnesty for an imprisoned former faculty member, Dr. Mihajlo Djuric, accused of Serbian nationalism. Three of the seven were dismissed from the League.

Quite predictably, the bulk of the cases originating in Croatia and Slovenia are based on the strong local nationalisms prevalent in both areas. Trials took place in all parts of the country to bring home the message that no particularistic movements would be tolerated. While the principal center of gravity for such trials lay in Croatia where secessionist sentiments are strong in some quarters, Slovenia was not exempt from its share of cases. Advocacy for civil rights earned Judge Franz

Miklavičić a six-year sentence, while another Slovene, Victor Blažić, a journalist, was sentenced to two years.[38] It takes very few cases to change materially the political atmosphere in a country.

Aside from domestic foes, the Yugoslav government also prosecuted a number of foreign citizens, both Soviet and American; the most famous of these wàs the case of Laszlo Toth, which seriously strained relations between United States Ambassador Silberman and the Yugoslav government. Such acts are usually balanced by the Yugoslav authorities to demonstrate their nonaligned status.[39] The Yugoslav government points out that foreign criticism of limitations placed on domestic freedom is exaggerated and deliberately misrepresented.[40]

The ultimate effect of the campaign of the last five years has been to confine nationalism within approved boundaries. Yet, judicial sanctions can be purchased only at a price. Local organs can be effective only so long as they arbitrate the perceived interests of their constituencies. The Yugoslavs had to sacrifice a system which went further than any other communist state in the institutionalization of local politics. By suppressing nationalists' excesses the government and Party produce a situation which was qualitatively different from that which existed during the previous era. Yet, after all is said and done, Yugoslavia still remains unique among the communist states because it permits the most untrammeled egress and entrance into the country to nationals and foreigners alike. As long as this situation prevails there is a ceiling on the means of compulsion which the regime can utilize. Any curtailment of free travel would have profound dislocating effects on the Yugoslav economy. Under the circumstances, the domestic and international balancing act which constitutes Yugoslav politics will continue.

Tito's Succession and the National Question

It is generally believed that Tito's long illness contributed to a smooth transition of power. Even before Tito fell ill and became disabled he had gradually withdrawn from the day to day management of the affairs of state and left them in the hands of the team which comprised the collective leadership. It is a tribute to the achievements of the Tito era that the state has so far suffered no major turbulence in the face of major economic problems and external pressures. While some of the internal response to these threats might be viewed as over-reactions from the vantage point of outside observers, they are, nevertheless, based on a variety of disconcerting realities.

Yugoslavia faces a constant threat from exiled nationalist Croat organizations which have proved their ruthlessness and determination during the past few decades. They never proved strong enough to cause a major disruption within the country by various acts of terrorism, yet, many responsible Yugoslavs fear that they might set off an incident with unforeseen and dire consequences. These organizations have remained quiescent in the aftermath of Tito's death. Another major fear of the Yugoslavs is that Bulgarian agitation of the Macedonian issue which might be used as a pretext by the Warsaw Pact forces for expanded political activities on the border with Bulgaria.[41] Above all, there is the fear that the present leadership might not handle a domestic incident which escalates into a major crisis as adroitly as the departed president, who possessed vast political acumen and experience as a truly national figure. No member of the succeeding collective leadership holds national stature.

They are all representatives of the major nationalities of Yugoslavia, but there is not a sense that any one of them belongs to the entire nation in Tito's manner. No doubt these leaders are highly aware of their individual weaknesses. This is a powerful impetus from them to cling together in such collective institutions as the State Presidency, Party Presidency, and other collective bodies of governance. Their problem is compounded by the typical dualism between party and state. Government consists of the various institutions which represent local, republican and federal. The League of Communists is the only supranational entity in Yugoslavia which in its top organs is intended to be the cement between the fissures left by purely ethnic representation in other institutions. So far the mechanism has proved its viability for the very reason because it continues through a period which would have tested any regime in a very volatile setting.

Such events as the Islamic revitalization, so much in evidence in Iran, Pakistan and Libya has its faint echoes in Yugoslavia as well. The leadership, therefore, maintains a policy of keeping all possibilities of nationalistic incidents under control. This is accomplished by publicizing the somewhat sporadic charges against all fringe edges of nationalistic dissent.

For example, eight Yugoslavs of Albanian origin were sentenced from three to eight years for "hostile activity" in June 1980.[42] The District Court in Zagreb found seven members of an illegal terrorist group guilty in June 1980 for bringing dynamite and pistols into Yugoslavia. The sentences ranged from five to fifteen years.[43] The Bosnia-Hercegovina Supreme Court sentenced Zarko Aleksic, a lawyer from Doboj, for a seven-year term and confiscation of property for "hostile propaganda activity." He was convicted of supporting greater Serbian positions since 1973 and negating the existence of individual "nations and nationalities."[49]

Attacks against Milovan Djilas, long-term Serbian critic of Tito's communism, increased after Tito's death. In frequent news articles during June and July 1980, Djilas was called an enemy,[45] a "warmonger" inviting people "to violence and hatred,"[46] and a "front for reactionary forces."[47]

Moreover, there is a determination not to permit strict interpretation of the Constitution to stand in the way of realities. There are two major evidences of this. The State Presidency was enlarged during Tito's fatal illness by adding seven *ex officio* members. This action doubled the number of Serbs from three to six and tripled the number of Croats from one to three; the number of Montenegrins doubled from one to two.[48] This gave the Serbs a membership of eight in a fifteen-member body, since the Montenegrins are culturally Serb and tend to side with them on most ethnically divisive issues. It is true that four of these positions are non-voting, but this many not carry much significance since the authors have it on good authority that votes in such bodies take place only on rare occasions and they operate mostly by consensus. It is immaterial whether the expansion took place with or without Tito's blessing. It obviously conformed more closely to the genuine power relationships in the country, rather than to the formal constitutional formula of national representation. The party also avoided to formalize the election of a League President to replace Tito, who was President for life, which might be a violation of Article 321 of the 1974 Constitution. The Chair of the Central Committee was instead appointed President of the Central Committee for a one-year term. The decision was postponed until the 1982 Twelfth Party Congress takes place. Obviously, no one dominant figure has emerged in the collective leadership which has postponed taking a position on this divisive issue.[49]

One example of the effort by the party leadership to effect decisions at the republic level is found in the resignation of Dr. Anton Vratuša. On June 23, 1980 the Presidium of the Slovenian Central Committee selected Janez Zemljaric, the Slovenian Minister of Interior, as the replacement for Prime Minister Vratusa. The statement made by the Central Committee President, Franc Popit, in announcing the resignation pointed out the need at the republican level to implement "in a more operative way things which we agreed upon."[50] The replacement may have been extra-constitutional insofar as it is not the function of the Central Committee to determine the Prime Minister of the republic but it should be left to the Slovene Assembly to which Vratusa tendered his resignation.

The most important aspect of the Yugoslav transition is that it took place in an atmosphere of tranquility and again documented that all Yugoslav nationalities have a stake in the maintenance of the system, particularly in view of the far less attractive alternatives.

Conclusions

The development of Yugoslav policy on nationality questions can be divided into two discrete eras. One, commencing in 1966 with the removal of Alexander Ranković as Vice President, marked the beginning of the abolition of threat as an institutionalized means of government policy. During this period, workers' self-management prospered but soon developed strong linkages to republican and communal political organizations which were ethnically bounded and defined. With increasing decentralization and institutionalization of the system the influence of the League of Communists underwent perceptible erosion due to disfunction. Most of the patronage and economic decisions were depoliticized through the medium of workers' self-management. Policies were undertaken largely on rationalistic criteria which left the Party little room to exert influence. Since the Party was no longer a dominant factor, regional politicians attempted to broaden their constituency to non-Party or anti-Party strata of the population. They used nationalism unabashedly to integrate their changing communities. This trend reached explosive force in Croatia and the federal authorities viewed it as a threat to the stability and continuity of the entire federation. In the winter of 1971, the movement was suppressed through federal intervention.

The year 1972 saw the initiation of new efforts to stabilize the political situation through an effort to revitalize the League of Communists. The League is once more playing a guiding ideological role. The leadership concluded that the absence of such guidance was an abdication to the forces of nationalism which will fill any vacuum conceded by Communist ideology. The Constitution of 1974, the Tenth Congress of the League of Communists, and the revised statutes endowed the League with its traditional Leninist mission.

It is an open question how workers' self-management will co-exist with a strengthened League. Workers' self-management can thrive only if it has elbow room for autonomous decisions. If a revitalized League will permit the decentralized institutions the autonomy they once enjoyed is a question which remains to be answered.

NOTES

1. See Branko Horvat, *An Essay on Yugoslav Society* (White Plains, NY: International and Sciences Press, 1969), pp. 74-76 and 97-99.

2. The *New York Times*, April 8, 1967, p. 4.

3. Matica Hrvatska is a Croatian organization that has its root in the nationalist era of the nineteenth century. Its membership was drawn from the general populace and from the League of Communists.

4. A strong attack on National Bank policy can be found in Šime Djodan, "Evolucije gospodarskog sustava SFRJ i ekonomski položaj Hrvatske," *Hrvatski knjizevni zbornik* 2 (Fall 1971), pp. 82-85.

5. Jože Goričar, "Žarista globalnik konfliktu o Jugoslovensko drustveni drustvu," *Drustveni konfliktii i socijalistički razvoj Jugoslavije*. Referati III Deo. Portoroz, February 10-13, 1972, p. 143.

6. *Ibid.*, p. 149.

7. Ihor Kamenetsky, *Secret Nazi Plans for Eastern Europe* (New York: Bookman Associates, 1961), p. 34 and pp. 150-52.

8. The number of works and memoirs devoted to this issue is too broad to be emunerated here. Among them are: Vladimer Dedijer, *The Battle Stalin Lost* (New York: Grosset and Dunlap, 1972); Milovan Djilas, *Conversations With Stalin* (New York: Harcourt, Brace and World, 1962); Fitzroy Maclean, *The Heretic* (New York: Harpers and Company, 1957);

Government of the Federal Peoples Republic of Yugoslavia, Ministry of Foreign Affairs, *White Book on Aggressive Activities by the Governments of the USSR, Poland, Czechoslovakia, Hungary, Rumania, Bulgaria, and Albania Towards Yugoslavia* (Beograd: Ministry of Foreign Affairs, 1951).

9.   R. Barry Farrell, *Jugoslavia and the Soviet Union, An Analysis with Documents* (Hamden, CT: Shoe String Press, 1956).

10.   All Party congresses since the Sixth acknowledge the potential troublesomeness of the nationality problem. The Tenth Congress of the League of Communists was no exception. See, *The Tenth Congress of the League of Communists of Yugoslavia* (Beograd: Komunist Socialist Thought and Practice), p. 59.

11.   Horvat, *Essays on Yugoslav Society*, pp. 97-100.

12.   In 1946 Boris Kidrić, the first chairman of the State Planning Commission, proposed a bold plan for the equalization of income between the republics by 1964. However, the needs of reconstructing a war-torn economy dictated more practical strategies, which led to increasing gaps between regions. Fredy Perlman, "Conditions for the Development of a Backward Region," (Ph.D. dissertation, University of Belgrade, 1966), p. 14.

13.   The number of inhabitants who declared themselves of Yugoslav nationality dropped from 317,124 in 1961 to 273,077 in 1971 in spite of a population growth of almost 2,000,000. *Statisticki godisnjak Jugoslavije* (1974), p. 104.

14.   President Tito referred to this attempt to form a new Stalinist-line party in a speech in Jesenice on September 12, 1974. The *New York Times*, September 12, 1974, p. 7.

15.   Zdenko Antic, "Bakaric's Zagreb Press Conference," RAD Background Report/83 (25 April 1977).

16.   The *New York Times*, January 16, 1975, p. 8.

17.   *Ibid.*, February 18, 1975, p. 6.

18.   *Politika*, Belgrade, June 12, 1975.

19.   The *New York Times*, November 23, 1975, p. 6. Stane Dolanc announced on November 24, 1975 that several hundred pro-Soviet Communists were arrested in Yugoslavia. *Ibid.*, November 25, 1975, p. 11.

20.   *Ibid.*, May 27, 1976, p. 5.

21.   *Ibid.*, June 2, 1976, p. 31.

22.   *Ibid.*, October 3, 1976, IV, p. 3, and October 16, 1976, p. 3.

23.   *Ibid.*, March 24, 1977, p. 2.

24. Dennison I. Rusinow, "Yugoslavia's Return to Leninism: Notes On the Tenth Party Congress of the Yugoslav League of Communists," *Southeast Europe Series,* Vol. XXI, No. 1 (June 1974), p. 8.

25. *Ibid.,* pp. 6-7.

26. See *Drustveni konflikti i socijalisticki razvoj Jugoslavije.* None of the collected papers appearing in the three volumes of the conference dealt with national conflicts.

27. The Constitution of 1963, Article 48, provided that persons under suspicion of criminal offense "may be detained and held in detention only when this is indispensable for the conduct of criminal proceeding. . . when this is provided by statute."

28. The Constitution of 1963, Article 35, provided that: "All citizens who reach the age of 18 years have voting rights." The new Constitution of 1974, Article 156, limits voting to: "All citizens who have reached the age of 18 years shall have the right to elect and be elected members of delegations in basic self-managing organizations and communities, and to elect and be elected delegates to the assemblies of the socio-political communities."

29. Rusinow, "Yugoslavia's Return," p. 1.

30. *Ibid.*

31. *Tenth Congress of the League of Communists of Yugoslavia,* p. 61.

32. The Eleventh Congress of the League of Communists of Yugoslavia was held in Belgrade from June 20-23, 1978. For Tito's speech see: *Socialist Thought and Practice,* Vol. XVIII, No. 6 (June 1978), pp. 3-96.

33. See the Constitution of 1974, Article 134.

34. The Constitution of 1963, Article 34, states "The right of citizens to social self-government" was restated in the Constitution of 1974, Article 155, to read: "The working people and citizens shall have the inalienable right to self-management." This wording substantially weakens the previous version.

35. The Constitution of 1974, Article 171.

36. The Constitution of 1974, Article 203, states:

"No one may use the freedom and rights established by the present Constitution in order to disrupt the foundations of the socialist self-management democratic order established by the present Constitution to endanger the independence of the country, violate freedom and rights of man and the citizen guaranteed by the Constitution, endanger peace and

278 THE POLITICS OF ETHNICITY

equality in international cooperation, stir up national racial or religious hatred or intolerance or abet the commission of criminal offences nor may these freedoms be used in a way which offends public morals."

Civil rights are further interpreted by the 1974 Constitution, Article 178 which states "A person...may be detained and held in detention only when this is indispensable for the conduct of criminal proceedings." The clause "when this is provided by statute" was present in the 1968 Constitution.

37. The *New York Times,* May 27, 1976, p. 5.

38. The Slovene Judge Franz Miklavčić was convicted of treason and other crimes on October 15, 1976, and received a six-year sentence. The *New York Times,* October 16, 1976, p. 3. Another Slovene, Viktor Blažić, a journalist, was sentenced to two years imprisonment. The *New York Times,* September 29, 1976, p. 12.

39. Following the release of Laszlo Toth, a US State Department spokesman confirmed that US Army Captain Sedmak and a total of five Americans were in Yugoslav prisons. The *New York Times,* July 27, 1976, p. 9. The arrest of a Soviet woman in Yugoslavia on a spy charge in April 1976 resulted in the conviction of Ingra Pozhega, for espionage; sentenced to five years in prison. The *New York Times,* May 27, 1976, p. 5.

40. A statement attributed to Tito that large numbers of persons were imprisoned in Yugoslavia was charged as falsified by the foreign press at a press conference held together with the Prime Minister of Sweden, Palme, and Tito. See Dragan Bartolovic, "On Freedom and Freedoms," *Socialist Thought and Practice,* Vol. XVII, No. 3 (March 1977), p. 67.

41. Bulgarian Declaration of July 24, 1978, from the Foreign Ministry. Text in *Borba* (Belgrade) August 5, 6, 1978. Also Stankovic, "New Escalation in Yugoslav-Bulgarian Polemics Over Macedonia," *Radio*/176 (August 1978).

42. *FBIS-EEU* (10 June 1980), Vol. II, No. 113, p. I 14.

43. *Ibid.,* (18 June 1980), Vol. II, No. 119, p. I 21.

44. *FBIS* (31 July 1980), Vol. II, No. 149, p. I 10.

45. *Politika* (2 June 1980).

46. *NIN* (13 July, 1980).

47. *Vjesnik* (23 July 1980).

48.   Stankovic, "Yugoslavia's Collective State Leadership Enlarged," *Radio*/148 (29 February 1980), p. 3.

49.   Stankovic, "Yugoslav Party Without a President-A Preliminary Solution," *Radio*/148 (18 June 1980).

50.   Quoted in *Borba* (Belgrade) 26 June 1980 and Stankovic, "Slovenia's Prime Minister," p. 2.

EAST EUROPEAN MONOGRAPHS

The *East European Monographs* comprise scholarly books on the history and civilization of Eastern Europe. They are published by the *East European Quarterly* in the belief that these studies contribute substantially to the knowledge of the area and serve to stimulate scholarship and research.

Political Ideas and the Enlightenment in the Romanian Principalities, 1750-1831. By Vlad Georgescu. 1971.

America, Italy and the Birth of Yugoslavia, 1917-1919. By Dragan R. Zivjinovic. 1972.

Jewish Nobles and Geniuses in Modern Hungary. By William O. McCagg,Jr. 1972.

Mixail Soloxov in Yugoslavia: Reception and Literary Impact. By Robert F. Price. 1973.

The Historical and National Thought of Nicolae Iorga. By William O. Oldson. 1973.

Guide to Polish Libraries and Archives. By Richard C. Lewanski. 1974.

Vienna Broadcasts to Slovakia, 1938-1939: A Case Study in Subversion. By Henry Delfiner. 1974.

The 1917 Revolution in Latvia. By Andrew Ezergailis. 1974.

The Ukraine in the United Nations Organization: A Study in Soviet Foreign Policy. 1944-1950. By Konstantin Sawczuk. 1975.

The Bosnian Church: A New Interpretation. By John V. A. Fine, Jr., 1975.

Intellectual and Social Developments in the Habsburg Empire from Maria Theresa to World War I. Edited by Stanley B. Winters and Joseph Held. 1975.

Ljudevit Gaj and the Illyrian Movement. By Elinor Murray Despalatovic. 1975.

Tolerance and Movements of Religious Dissent in Eastern Europe. Edited by Bela K. Kiraly. 1975.

The Parish Republic: Hlinka's Slovak People's Party, 1939-1945. By Yeshayahu Jelinek. 1976.

The Russian Annexation of Bessarabia, 1774-1828. By George F. Jewsbury. 1976.

Modern Hungarian Historiography. By Steven Bela Vardy. 1976.

Values and Community in Multi-National Yugoslavia. By Gary K. Bertsch. 1976.

The Greek Socialist Movement and the First World War: The Road to Unity. By George B. Leon. 1976.

The Radical Left in the Hungarian Revolution of 1848. By Laszlo Deme. 1976.

Hungary between Wilson and Lenin: The Hungarian Revolution of 1918-1919 and the Big Three. By Peter Pastor. 1976.

The Crises of France's East-Central European Diplomacy, 1933-1938. By Anthony J. Komjathy. 1976.

Polish Politics and National Reform, 1775-1788. By Daniel Stone. 1976.

The Habsburg Empire in World War I. Robert A. Kann, Bela K. Kiraly, and Paula S. Fichtner, eds. 1977.

The Slovenes and Yugoslavism, 1890-1914. By Carole Rogel. 1977.

German-Hungarian Relations and the Swabian Problem. By Thomas Spira. 1977.

The Metamorphosis of a Social Class in Hungary During the Reign of Young Franz Joseph. By Peter I. Hidas. 1977.

Tax Reform in Eighteenth Century Lombardy. By Daniel M. Klang. 1977.

Tradition versus Revolution: Russia and the Balkans in 1917. By Robert H. Johnston. 1977.

Winter into Spring: The Czechoslovak Press and the Reform Movement 1963-1968. By Frank L. Kaplan. 1977.
The Catholic Church and the Soviet Government, 1939-1949. By Dennis J. Dunn. 1977.
The Hungarian Labor Service System, 1939-1945. By Randolph L Braham. 1977.
Consciousness and History: Nationalist Critics of Greek Society 1897-1914. By Gerasimos Augustinos. 1977.
Emigration in Polish Social and Political Thought, 1870-1914. By Benjamin P. Murdzek. 1977.
Serbian Poetry and Milutin Bojic. By Mihailo Dordevic. 1977.
The Baranya Dispute: Diplomacy in the Vortex of Ideologies, 1918-1921. By Leslie C. Tihany. 1978.
The United States in Prague, 1945-1948. By Walter Ullmann. 1978.
Rush to the Alps: The Evolution of Vacationing in Switzerland. By Paul P. Bernard. 1978.
Transportation in Eastern Europe: Empirical Findings. By Bogdan Mieczkowski. 1978.
The Polish Underground State: A Guide to the Underground, 1939-1945. By Stefan Korbonski. 1978.
The Hungarian Revolution of 1956 in Retrospect. Edited by Bela K. Kiraly and Paul Jonas. 1978.
Boleslaw Limanowski (1835-1935): A Study in Socialism and Nationalism. By Kazimiera Janina Cottam. 1978.
The Lingering Shadow of Nazism: The Austrian Independent Party Movement Since 1945. By Max E. Riedlsperger. 1978.
The Catholic Church, Dissent and Nationality in Soviet Lithuania. By V. Stanley Vardys. 1978.
The Development of Parliamentary Government in Serbia. By Alex N. Dragnich. 1978.
Divide and Conquer: German Efforts to Conclude a Separate Peace, 1914-1918. By L. L. Farrar, Jr. 1978.
The Prague Slav Congress of 1848. By Lawrence D. Orton. 1978.
The Nobility and the Making of the Hussite Revolution. By John M. Klassen. 1978.
The Cultural Limits of Revolutionary Politics: Change and Continuity in Socialist Czechoslovakia. By David W. Paul. 1979.
On the Border of War and Peace: Polish Intelligence and Diplomacy in 1937-1939 and the Origins of the Ultra Secret. By Richard A. Woytak. 1979.
Bear and Foxes: The International Relations of the East European States 1965-1969. By Ronald Haly Linden. 1979.
Czechoslovakia: The Heritage of Ages Past. Edited by Ivan Volgyes and Hans Brisch. 1979.
Prima Minister Gyula Andrassy's Influence on Habsburg Foreign Policy. By Janos Decsy. 1979.
Citizens for the Fatherland: Education, Educators, and Pedagogical Ideals in Eighteenth Century Russia. By J. L. Black. 1979.
A History of the "Proletariat": The Emergence of Marxism in the Kingdom of Poland, 1870-1887. By Norman M. Naimark. 1979.
The Slovak Autonomy Movement, 1935-1939: A Study in Unrelenting Nationalism. By Dorothea H. El Mallakh. 1979.
Diplomat in Exile: Francis Pulszky's Political Activities in England, 1849-1860. By Thomas Kabdebo. 1979.

The German Struggle Against the Yugoslav Guerrillas in World War II: German Counter-Insurgency in Yugoslavia, 1941-1943. By Paul N. Hehn. 1979.

The Emergence of the Romanian National State. By Gerald J. Bobango. 1979.

Stewards of the Land: The American Farm School and Modern Greece. By Brenda L. Marder. 1979.

Roman Dmowski: Party, Tactics, Ideology, 1895-1907. By Alvin M. Fountain, II. 1980.

International and Domestic Politics in Greece During the Crimean War. By Jon V. Kofas. 1980.

Fires on the Mountain: The Macedonian Revolutionary Movement and the Kidnapping of Ellen Stone. By Laura Beth Sherman. 1980.

The Modernization of Agriculture: Rural Transformation in Hungary, 1848-1975. Edited by Joseph Held. 1980.

Britain and the War for Yugoslavia, 1940-1943. By Mark C. Wheeler. 1980.

The Turn to the Right: The Ideological Origins and Development of Ukrainian Nationalism, 1919-1929. By Alexander J. Motyl. 1980.

The Maple Leaf and the White Eagle: Canadian-Polish Relations, 1918-1978. By Aloysius Balawyder. 1980.

Antecedents of Revolution: Alexander I and the Polish Congress Kingdom, 1815-1825. By Frank W. Thackeray. 1980.

Blood Libel at Tiszaeszlar. By Andrew Handler. 1980.

Democratic Centralism in Romania: A Study of Local Communist Politics. By Daniel N. Nelson. 1980.

Prelude to Appeasement: East European Central Diplomacy in the Early 1930's. By Lisanne Radice. 1981.

The Soviet Regime in Czechoslovakia. By Zdenek Krystufek. 1981.

School Strikes in Prussian Poland, 1901-1907: The Struggle Over Bilingual Education. By John J. Kulczycki. 1981.

Romantic Nationalism and Liberalism: Joachim Lelewel and the Polish National Idea. By Joan S. Skurnowicz. 1981.

The "Thaw" In Bulgarian Literature. By Atanas Slavov. 1981.

The Political Thought of Thomas G. Masaryk. By roman Szporluk. 1981.

Prussian Poland in the German Empire, 1871-1900. By Richard Blanke. 1981.

The Mazepists: Ukrainian Separatism in the Early Eighteenth Century. By Orest Subtelny. 1981.

The Battle for the Marchlands: The Russo-Polish Campaign of 1920. By Adam Zamoyski. 1981.

Milovan Djilas: A Revolutionary as a Writer. By Dennis Reinhartz. 1981.

The Second Republic: The Disintegration of Post-Munich Czechoslovakia, October 1938-March 1939. By Theodore Prochazka, Sr.

From Trianon to the First Vienna Arbitral Award: The Hungarian Minority in the First Czechoslovak Republic, 1918-1938. By Charles Woyatsek.

Financial Relations of Greece and the Great Powers, 1832-1862. By Jon V. Kofas. 1981.